PLA Results Series

MANAGING FACILITIES for Results

OPTIMIZING SPACE FOR SERVICES

Cheryl Bryan *for the*
Public Library Association

AMERICAN LIBRARY ASSOCIATION

Chicago   2007

The paper used in this publication meets the minimum requirements of American National Standard for Information Sciences—Permanence of Paper for Printed Library Materials, ANSI Z39.48-1992. ∞

Library of Congress Cataloging-in-Publication Data

Bryan, Cheryl.
    Managing facilities for results : optimizing space for services / Cheryl Bryan for the Public Library Association.
        p.   cm. — (PLA results series)
    Includes bibliographical references and index.
    ISBN 0-8389-0934-5 (alk. paper)
        1. Libraries—Space utilization. 2. Library buildings—Remodeling. 3. Public libraries—Planning. 4. Public services (Libraries)—Planning. I. Public Library Association. II. Title.
Z679.55.B79 2007
022'.3—dc22   2006036896

ISBN-10: 0-8389-0934-5
ISBN-13: 978-0-8389-0934-8

Printed in the United States of America

11 10 09 08 07   5 4 3 2 1

*This book is dedicated
to Anna Parrott and
Patsy Patrick, who
first showed me the
great, fun adventure
of library work.*

Contents

Figures

Acknowledgments

I thank Ruth O'Donnell for the depth of experience and breadth of knowledge that went into her coauthorship of the first draft of this book. She was an excellent and valued partner, and I only regret that personal priorities prevented her from completing the book with me.

I also thank Sandra Nelson for her commitment to constant improvement in libraries—a commitment that is generously demonstrated through her writings and teachings, and through her commitment to the Results series. Thanks also to Joan Grygel, who edited the book to its current level of clarity.

The contributions of the PLA review group, particularly June Garcia, have made this book more comprehensive and useful than it would have been had I not had the benefit of their knowledge and experience. Other members of the review committee were Carolyn Anthony, Skokie (IL) Public Library; Lowell S. Berg, Clark Enersen Partners (NE); Lucinda Brown, Boone County (KY) Public Library; Linda Demmers, Libris Design Project Manager (CA); Jane Kolbe, Arizona State Library; Greg Pringle, Bulverde/Spring (TX) Branch Library; and Arthur Weeks, Ames (IA) Public Library. Thanks to you all.

Finally, I thank and acknowledge my husband David, whose patience, support, and talent are reflected throughout the book.

Introduction

Managing a public library has always been hard work, and it is becoming even more difficult under the twin pressures of restricted public funding and rapid change. The Public Library Association (PLA) plays a major role in providing the tools and training required to "enhance the development and effectiveness of public librarians and public library services."[1] During the past eight years, the PLA has provided support for the development of the Results series, a family of management publications that are being used by library managers, staff, and boards around the country to manage the libraries in their communities more effectively. The seven publications in the Results series that are available in 2007 are

The New Planning for Results: A Streamlined Approach[2]

Managing for Results: Effective Resource Allocation for Public Libraries[3]

Staffing for Results: A Guide to Working Smarter[4]

Creating Policies for Results: From Chaos to Clarity[5]

Technology for Results: Developing Service-Based Plans[6]

Demonstrating Results: Using Outcome Measurement in Your Library[7]

Managing Facilities for Results: Optimizing Space for Services

These publications provide a fully integrated approach to planning and resource allocation, an approach that is focused on creating change—on *results.* The underlying assumptions in all of the books in the Results series are the same:

Excellence must be defined locally. It is a result of providing library services that match community needs, interests, and priorities.

Excellence does not require unlimited resources. It occurs when available resources are allocated in ways that support library priorities.

Excellence is a moving target. The best decision-making model is "estimate, implement, check, and adjust"—and then "estimate, implement, check, and adjust again."

The Results Publications

All of the books in the Results series are intended to be used with *The New Planning for Results: A Streamlined Approach.*[8] *The New Planning for Results* describes a library planning process that is focused on creating an actual blueprint for change rather than a beautifully printed plan for your office shelf. As you can see in the diagram of the *Planning for Results* model shown in figure 1, the process starts by looking at the community the library serves in order to identify what needs to happen to improve the quality of life for all of the community's residents. Once the community's needs have been established, library planners look for ways the library can collaborate with other government services and nonprofit agencies to help meet those needs. This, in turn, provides the information required to establish the library's service priorities.

FIGURE 1
Planning for Results Model

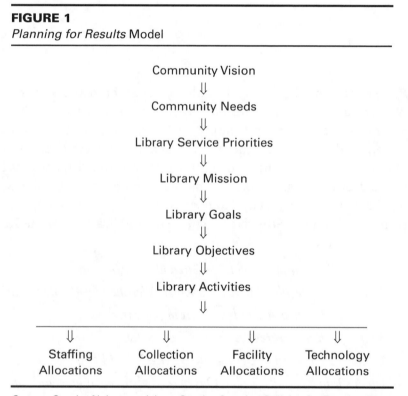

Source: Sandra Nelson and June Garcia, *Creating Policies for Results: From Chaos to Clarity* (Chicago: American Library Association, 2003), xii.

The planning process includes significant participation by community residents who represent all of the constituencies served by the library: parents and children; working adults and seniors; businesspeople and civic leaders; students and educators; the various racial, ethnic, and religious groups in your community; government and nonprofit leaders; and all of the other groups that together create your unique community. By involving all of these groups in your planning process, you ensure that the services you provide are really what community residents want—and not what you or your staff or board think (or wish) that they want.

Because *The New Planning for Results* is focused on identifying and implementing the activities that will help library managers and staff to accomplish community-based goals and objectives, the decisions that are made are sure to affect every part of the library's operations. Every library manager, every library staff member, and every library board member are going to have to become used to the idea of continually evaluating all of the services and programs the library currently provides and all of the policies that support those services in the context of the library's identified priorities—and then be willing to make any changes that are necessary. Changes don't happen because we want them to or hope they will. Changes only happen when we do things differently.

Managing for Results

Managing for Results: Effective Resource Allocation for Public Libraries was the first resource-allocation book in the Results series.[9] It presented an overview of resource-allocation issues in the areas of staffing, collection, technology, and facilities. *Managing for Results* included six workforms for collecting basic information about facilities and provided advice on thinking about facilities as resources that can and should change as community needs and service priorities change. In some cases, these basic resources may be sufficient to provide you with the information you need to reallocate your facilities resources. If a simple solution for implementing your project is identifiable, then a simple process can be used to implement changes. If your project is as straightforward as cabling a part of the meeting room to create a computer training area, then your library may be able to use the basic facilities-change approach described in *Managing for Results*. On the other hand, if your project is more complex, you will probably want to use the processes and tools in this book. For example, if you have decided to create a teen area in your library, you will be dealing with a project that will have a significant effect on the library's facilities resources. In that instance, this book provides the appropriate processes and tools.

There's Always a Plan

All of the books in the Results series assume that libraries have current strategic plans with clearly defined service priorities that were developed using *The New Planning for Results*. However, a strategic plan is not the only way that library staff and board members can determine service priorities. Some libraries participate in city or county strategic planning processes. Others choose to develop annual goals and objectives rather than a multiyear plan. Yet others develop goals and objectives for individual units, for branches, or for specific programs or services. A library's annual budget sets and reflects service priorities for the upcoming year whether a library has engaged in a formal planning process or not. Any process used to determine the library's service priorities, goals, or outcomes can serve as the starting point for the tools and techniques described in this book.

When Service Priorities Have Not Been Identified or Are Out of Date

If there are no clearly defined and generally understood service priorities in your library, you will need to develop service priorities before you begin to use the tools in this book. It is important to understand that this book is about allocating—and reallocating—your facilities resources to support the library's priorities and *not* about determining what those priorities should be. Before you can decide whether or not the way you are currently using your facilities resources is both effective and efficient, you must know what you want to accomplish. Any process used to determine the library's desired outcomes can serve as the starting point for the activities described in this book.

Basic Concepts

Managing Facilities for Results begins with the assumption that you have a library facility that is being used to deliver public library service. It also assumes that your building feels pretty full to both staff and library users and that you are looking for ways to initiate new services or expand existing services. The tools in this book will help you, your colleagues, and the members of your board to decide how to get the most out of your available space, which will lead to improved use of staff time and better access to resources for both the staff and the public.

This book is based on three key concepts. As noted earlier, the first key concept is that *the library has defined its public service goals or priorities* and that those goals are *based on identified community needs.* Whether you are working from a formal services plan, a grant proposal, or a list of ideas brainstormed in a meeting, decisions about the use of space should always be based on library service goals. Unfortunately, this is not always the case. Too often we allow our buildings to set our service priorities rather than adapting our spaces to support our priorities. Library space configurations are often the way they are because that is the way they have always been. Managers regularly struggle to add new services with workaround solutions to spatial problems, rather than reallocating space to meet new needs. This book will provide you with the tools you need to use your service goals and objectives as touchstones for making decisions on how to organize and utilize the space and furnishings in your library.

The second key concept is *effectiveness.* Effectiveness focuses on the relation of library activities to the library's service priorities. Effective activities align library resources in ways that support those service priorities. Efficiency, on the other hand, focuses on ways to streamline the ways that activities are accomplished in order to reduce the resources required. In other words:

Efficiency means "doing the thing right."

Effectiveness means "doing the right thing."

A service or activity may be provided very efficiently—staff are able to do it at a high level of skill, for example—but at the same time it may be unrelated to the service focus of the library or program of services of which it is a part. In other words, it is well done but not relevant to the library's effort to meet community needs. An effective service or activity, on the other hand, relates directly to the library's goals and objectives. Obviously, it should also be provided in an efficient manner.

The third key concept is *measurement.* In the past, most of our evaluative measurements looked at inputs of resources and outputs of service units. Input or resource measures include how much of a given resource is dedicated to a specific purpose—square feet, number of staff, collection dollars, computers, public programs, number of chairs, and so forth. Inputs are the "stuff" libraries offer to the public, including the materials and services provided. Outputs are measures of use of available resources, such as number of books circulated, reference questions answered, or programs sponsored by the library.

In the last several years there has been a growing emphasis on measuring success through the use of outcomes. Measurable outcomes are documented benefits to the end user that demonstrate the effectiveness of the service. They use qualitative evaluation to document what benefit the pubic is receiving from the library's services, or, to phrase it another way, the impact the library is having on the people who use its services. *Demonstrating Results,* a companion volume in the Results series, teaches how to measure and evaluate outcomes.[10]

Definitions

Before you begin to read this book and use it to make decisions about the way you are using your facilities resources, it will be helpful if you understand how some basic terms are used. Every public library is a little different. At some libraries people refer to "branches," in others the term is "agencies," and in still others the term for departments and branches is "units." Some libraries have "central" libraries; others have "main" libraries. There are libraries that report to authority boards and libraries that are units of the government entity that funds them. They may or may not have advisory boards. These differences can be confusing as the reader looks for his or her reality reflected in the terms and examples used in library literature. A list of terms and their meaning *in this book* follows. Definitions appear within each chapter as needed to introduce new terms.

> *Branch.* A separate facility.
>
> *Central library.* The largest library facility, usually in a downtown area; referred to as the main library in some places.
>
> *Department.* A unit within a single facility.
>
> *Library.* The entire organizational entity and its units.
>
> *Manager.* A generic term that refers to the staff member or members who are responsible for resource allocation in a particular area; in some libraries the "manager" is actually a team of staff members.
>
> *Team.* A group of staff members brought together to work on a specific project or program; often includes members from different departments and with different job classifications.
>
> *Unit.* A term used to refer to individual library departments and branches, if any.

In addition, terms used within the process described in this book include the following. These terms are listed in the order in which they occur within the process.

> *Goal.* The outcome your community (or a target population within your community) will receive because the library provides a specific service response.
>
> *Objective.* The way the library will measure its progress toward reaching a goal.
>
> *Activity.* A grouping of specific tasks that the library will carry out to achieve its goals and objectives, resulting in an output of things done or services delivered.

Project. A temporary endeavor requiring concerted effort by one or more people to initiate or implement an activity.

How to Use This Book

The *Managing Facilities for Results* process is made up of eight tasks, with the steps that must be accomplished to complete those tasks. *Tasks* are "the sequential processes that constitute a project." *Steps* are "the sequential actions taken in the performance of a task." See figure 2 for a list of the tasks and steps of the process.

As you progress through the book, you will see a chart of tasks repeated, with one task highlighted and the steps for that task listed. This basic chart will help you see how the highlighted task fits into the overall process and how each step moves you through the task. Because every library has unique facilities and different service priorities, it will be important for you to adapt the tasks and steps of the *Managing Facilities for Results* process as needed to apply to your own situation. You will find specific suggestions for modifying the tasks and steps throughout this book.

The Project Approach

Making decisions about a library's facilities should be an integral part of planning for change. The process described in this book for arriving at such decisions is referred to in various ways—as a model, a method, a process. Using the process can also be called a project. In all likelihood, it will be a piece of a larger project related to changing library services. For the purposes of this title in the Results series, the project approach and terminology are used to refer to the facilities component of any broader change efforts. Chapter 1 provides more information on the project approach to planning.

Case Study

Managing Facilities for Results follows one case study through its chapters to help you see how the process might work in a "real" library. The library in the case study, the Anytown Public Library, is a mythical library somewhere in the United States. This library serves a population of 100,000 people and has a governing board. It operates from a single facility and has no branches.

Workforms

This book includes twenty-three workforms to help you collect and organize information. It is unlikely that any library will use all of the workforms that are provided. Each chapter includes one or more figures that list the workforms that support the tasks and steps in the chapter. These figures provide information to help you decide when you need to use the workforms and when you don't. Samples of portions of the workforms show the results of action in the case study. All workforms are also available for download in Microsoft Word format at http://www.elearnlibraries.com. The electronic format allows

FIGURE 2

Tasks and Steps in the *Managing Facilities for Results* Process

Task 1: Define the Project

Step 1.1: Select the project

Step 1.2: Define the project's scope and intent

Step 1.3: Develop a task list and timeline

Step 1.4: Decide if a project committee is required

Task 2: Plan the Project

Step 2.1: Select the committee

Step 2.2: Determine the role of outside experts

Step 2.3: Plan how to keep the board and staff informed

Step 2.4: Develop an orientation packet

Task 3: Prepare the Committee

Step 3.1: Review the orientation packet

Step 3.2: Understand facility-related data elements

Step 3.3: Develop a detailed timeline

Task 4: Organize the Data Collection Process

Step 4.1: Define the project in detail

Step 4.2: Make committee assignments

Task 5: Collect Preliminary Data

Step 5.1: Identify the furniture and equipment needs and current allocations

Step 5.2: Identify the shelving needs and current allocations

Step 5.3: Describe the physical plant and technology support needs and current conditions

Step 5.4: Describe access, spatial relationships, and signage needs and current conditions

Step 5.5: Make preliminary recommendations for the amount and type of space

Task 6: Identify Gaps and Evaluate Options

Step 6.1: Identify gaps between needed and existing facility resources and space allocation

Step 6.2: Identify options for filling the gaps

Step 6.3: Identify placement options

Step 6.4: Evaluate options

Step 6.5: Develop committee recommendations

Task 7: Present Recommendations

Step 7.1: Prepare the preliminary report

Step 7.2: Present the preliminary report and seek approvals

Task 8: Prepare the Final Report and Get Approvals

Step 8.1: Prepare and assemble the final report

Step 8.2: Present the final report to funding authorities

you to expand space for entering data or to adapt the workforms for your needs. In addition to their important role in the *Managing Facilities for Results* process for reallocating space, the workforms will also help you and your staff avoid thinking up all kinds of data that "would be nice to have," a common statement in the world of librarianship and one that can get you stuck forever in the data collection phase of a project.

Tool Kits

Managing Facilities for Results includes three tool kits: Calculating Square Footage, Assessing Your Library's Physical Message, and Americans with Disabilities Act Requirements. These tool kits were included to provide you with easy access to detailed information about specific issues that have to be considered when planning for changes in your library facility.

Notes

1. Public Library Association Mission Statement, http://www.pla.org/factsheet.html.
2. Sandra Nelson, *The New Planning for Results: A Streamlined Approach* (Chicago: American Library Association, 2001).
3. Sandra Nelson, Ellen Altman, and Diane Mayo, *Managing for Results: Effective Resource Allocation for Public Libraries* (Chicago: American Library Association, 2000).
4. Diane Mayo and Jeanne Goodrich, *Staffing for Results: A Guide to Working Smarter* (Chicago: American Library Association, 2002).
5. Sandra Nelson and June Garcia, *Creating Policies for Results: From Chaos to Clarity* (Chicago: American Library Association, 2003).
6. Diane Mayo, *Technology for Results: Developing Service-Based Plans* (Chicago: American Library Association, 2005).
7. Rhea Rubin, *Demonstrating Results: Using Outcome Measures in Your Library* (Chicago: American Library Association, 2006).
8. Nelson, *The New Planning for Results*.
9. Nelson, Altman, and Mayo, *Managing for Results*.
10. Rubin, *Demonstrating Results*.

Chapter 1

Project Definition and Planning

MILESTONES

By the time you finish this chapter you will know how to

- identify the facility projects needed to implement a strategic plan, grant, or new service
- determine the priority of the facility projects you identify
- modify the *Managing Facilities for Results* process to meet local needs
- identify the staff members and others who will be involved in planning for the needed changes in your facility
- develop a preliminary task list and timeline for the planning of changes to your facility to support your selected activities
- develop a plan for communicating with staff and library stakeholders about the facility project

Every public library is housed in some sort of facility, and while every facility is different, there are many common elements among them. A public library's facilities are among its most expensive assets—expensive to build and furnish; to heat, cool, and humidify; and to maintain. The available facilities have an effect on the types of services the library can offer and on the public's perception of the library as a service provider. A library's facilities serve many functions, and not all of those functions are compatible. Some of the many demands on facilities are to

- offer comfortable, attractive, and well-lit public-use spaces
- present a safe, welcoming, clean, and attractive environment for users and employees
- effectively use space to support service priorities

- house and preserve collections of materials in a variety of media formats
- support access to electronic resources and the Internet
- house furnishings and equipment
- provide adequate work space for administrative, support, and direct public-service library staff members
- offer meeting and gathering space
- provide easy access to the interior, to movement within it, and to the resources located there
- serve as a cultural and community connection point
- serve as a community icon

The list of facility-related functions is constantly changing as customer needs evolve and new tools are developed to meet those needs. This creates challenges, particularly in older buildings not designed to support those new needs. The building program used to define the function and allocation of spaces when a library was first constructed gradually becomes less and less reflective of current needs. No community can afford to build a new library facility every time the library's service priorities change. Instead, the library facility has to be adapted to meet changing demands.

The organization and use of space to house collections, furnishings, equipment, and direct and indirect service areas should support a library's service goals, which in turn should be based on community needs. The principles of continual review and evaluation underlying good collection development can also be applied to library services and spaces. Services, like books, can become outdated. When that happens, library staff and board members have to be willing to let go of what has become irrelevant and reallocate the resulting resources to support new and needed services. Most library managers and board members understand that the services a library offers should not be dictated by the existing allocation of any resource—including space. The real issue is whether library planners choose to integrate these new or redefined services into current library operations or simply layer new services into an existing facility without giving consideration and planning to the effect of piling more and more services into the same space.

One example of this is the addition of public-access computers in libraries across the country in the late 1990s. Staff in virtually every library had to reallocate the use of existing space to provide for an ever-increasing number of public-access computers. The facility implications of this change were often quite significant, but the level of planning for the change varied from library to library. In some cases it was quite casual: "Let's weed, remove a range of shelving, and put them there," or "How about moving the copier closer to the tables and putting the PCs there?" This approach may have worked in a few libraries, but others found they had computers without adequate access to electrical power or network connectivity. In libraries where staff took a more organized approach to reallocating space, the result was both more effective and more efficient.

Turning Ideas into Action

The identification of service priorities, goals, objectives, and activities for a library can be time-consuming; when the process is complete, it is natural to think, "Thank goodness that is done; now we can get back to our real work." However, just describing the desired changes will not make those changes occur. If you want to create a change, you have to do things differently, and that always means reallocating resources. You have to review each new or modified service or activity to determine the staffing that will be required, the collection support that will be needed, and the technological issues that will need to be addressed. You also have to consider the facility requirement for each new or modified service or activity.

Managing Facilities for Results provides a clear and easily understood process to help you and your colleagues deal with facility reallocation needs in a structured and organized manner. The process is based on collecting and analyzing data about the current and potential use of your facility's resources. Using data for decision making eliminates the danger of relying on fleeting personal impressions that may or may not be accurate. Basing your facility resource decisions on data also makes it much easier to explain the reasons for your decisions to others. The data often provide convincing justification for your decisions, even to those who aren't happy with the result.

Public library boards and staff often use the term *project* to identify efforts that are distinct from their day-to-day work. In this book, a project is defined as "a temporary endeavor requiring concerted effort by one or more people to initiate or implement an activity." Projects have a beginning and an end; they are not ongoing. Most facility-related resource allocation projects share the same elements:

- determining the project's scope and intent
- making committee appointments
- gathering and analyzing data
- identifying options
- making recommendations and decisions

Figure 3 shows the flow of the tasks and steps between library management and a separate project committee for this process.

Making the Process Yours

Managing Facilities for Results has been described as a technical manual for an imaginary problem. The case studies presented in this book are by necessity artificial, and in some ways so is the process, which is based on the assumption that a library is completing a single facility-related resource allocation project. In reality, the staff in your library may be working on a number of facility-related resource allocation projects at the same time, which could mean that more than one person or committee would be involved in planning. If that is the situation in your library, it will be important for everyone who is working on a facility-related project to communicate regularly. Close and continuous cooperation and coordination between planners will be essential. Among other things, that will keep them from developing incompatible recommendations. It may be appropriate to encourage the committees working on facility resource-allocation issues to work together to develop a single final proposal so that all of their facility-related recommendations can be presented at one time.

This book also assumes that a person or project committee will only be charged with determining the facility-related resources needed to implement a new service or activity.

FIGURE 3
Process Flowchart

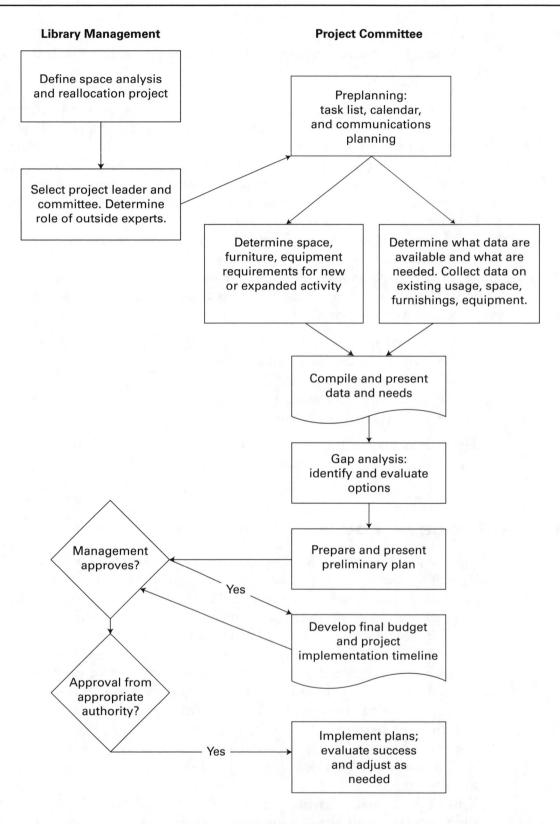

Library Management

Project Committee

Define space analysis and reallocation project

Preplanning:
task list, calendar, and communications planning

Select project leader and committee. Determine role of outside experts.

Determine space, furniture, equipment requirements for new or expanded activity

Determine what data are available and what are needed. Collect data on existing usage, space, furnishings, equipment.

Compile and present data and needs

Gap analysis: identify and evaluate options

Management approves?

Prepare and present preliminary plan

Yes

Develop final budget and project implementation timeline

Approval from appropriate authority?

Yes

Implement plans; evaluate success and adjust as needed

Implicit in this assumption is that other people or committees will be making recommendations about needed staffing, collections, and technology. This is not always the case. Sometimes a committee or a person is appointed to develop a comprehensive plan for reallocating all of the resources needed to implement a new or expanded activity or service. If that is your situation, the process and materials in this book can easily be modified to be used during the identification of the facility resources required to implement the activity.

Level of Effort

The most common way for you to modify the process will be to determine the level of effort that will be required to accomplish a specific outcome. You will be making decisions about which tasks are important in your library, which steps of the tasks you select need to be completed, and what data you will need to complete those steps. You may find that some facility-related decisions are so clear-cut that you don't need to go through a formal reallocation process at all. Other facility-related decisions may require significant study and data.

As you develop your project, remember that this book describes a comprehensive process that is intended to be used by libraries of all sizes to plan for projects of all sizes. No library will complete the entire process as described for every facility-related project. You are encouraged to read through all of the tasks and steps, review the workforms, and then think carefully about your project. Who should be involved in making recommendations? What data will you need? How will you collect it? As you consider those questions, go back and review the tasks and steps again. Which tasks and steps will help you to make the resource allocation decisions that are needed?

Chapter 1 presents Tasks 1 and 2, with three workforms supporting Task 1 and one workform supporting Task 2. See figure 4 to help you determine whether *you* will use all the workforms for the tasks in this chapter.

> **LEVEL OF EFFORT NOTE**
> **When to Use the *Managing Facilities*
> *for Results* Process**
>
> Staff members frequently identify the need for small changes in space use or additional equipment or furnishings. Typically these changes only affect one area of the library, cost little or nothing, and can be easily implemented by existing staff. Most of these changes can—and should—be addressed without going through the process described in this book.
>
> This process is intended to be used when you are initiating or expanding one or more new activities or services, normally as a result of a strategic planning process or a grant project. You may not need all of the data suggested in this book to determine the facility resources required to implement one new or expanded service or program. However, if you are dealing with multiple new services or significant changes that require facility resources, you will certainly want to carefully consider each task, step, and workform. You will find that by using the processes and tools in this book your planning will be more efficient and more effective.

FIGURE 4
When to Use the Workforms That Support Tasks 1 and 2

Workform	When to Use	When Not to Use
Workform 1: Facility Projects (Step 1.1)	Use this workform if you are evaluating activities that support multiple goals from a strategic plan or grant project to determine the priority of each.	Do not use this workform if you have already selected the facility project.
Workform 2: Project Priorities (Step 1.1)	If you completed Workform 1, use this workform to briefly describe the facility-related projects you have identified, the priority of each, and the projects you selected for the current year.	Do not use this workform if you didn't use Workform 1.
Workform 3: Preliminary Task List and Timeline (Step 1.3)	Use this workform to identify project benchmarks and deadlines.	Everyone will use this workform.
Workform 4: Need for Outside Experts (Step 2.2)	Use this workform if you know you will be using outside experts during the project or think you might need to use outside experts during your project.	Do not use this workform if you know you will not be using outside experts at any time during the project.

TASK 1: DEFINE THE PROJECT

Task 1: Define the Project
    Step 1.1: Select the project
    Step 1.2: Define the project's scope and intent
    Step 1.3: Develop a task list and timeline
    Step 1.4: Decide if a project committee is required
Task 2: Plan the Project
Task 3: Prepare the Committee
Task 4: Organize the Data Collection Process
Task 5: Collect Preliminary Data
Task 6: Identify Gaps and Evaluate Options
Task 7: Present Recommendations
Task 8: Prepare the Final Report and Get Approvals

Library staff become aware of the need to reallocate facility resources in a variety of ways. For example, increased public demand for a service can result in the need to increase the space allocated for that service. A new technology or material format can require new or modified furniture, equipment, or shelving, and those elements, in turn, can require that space be reallocated. In these two examples, there is no need to go through a process to select the project—the focus of the facility-related reallocation project is clear.

But what do you do if you have more than one facility-related project to consider? What if there has been a significant increase in public demand for a service *and* the library is purchasing materials in a new format that will require that space be reallocated? What if the library has just received a grant that may require a number of facility-related resources? What if the library has just completed a strategic plan and identified dozens of activities to support the plan's goals and objectives, and found that many of the activities will require facility resources? In these instances, you will have to identify which of the many facility-related projects that are needed will be addressed first and which will be addressed later. One or more members of the library's administrative team normally complete the four steps in Task 1.

Step 1.1
Select the Project

The work in Step 1.1 begins after you have selected the final activities to support your strategic plan, grant, or service. Remember, this process is about *implementing* activities, not identifying them. The process is based on the assumption that you have already evaluated a group of activities and decided that they are both effective and efficient. When you have done that, you are ready to determine the facility resources that will be required to accomplish each activity.

> **LEVEL OF EFFORT NOTE**
> **Select the Project**
>
> If you have already identified your facility-related project, you can skip Step 1.1 and start the process with Step 1.2: Define the Project's Scope and Intent.

Identifying Facility Projects

The process starts by developing a comprehensive list of the facility projects that will be required to implement the activities in the strategic plan, grant, or service under review. There are several ways to do this. If you have assigned one or more staff members to determine the resource requirements for each of the activities in your plan, you can ask those staff members to develop a list of the facility projects that will be required. You could also convene a small group to review the activities in the strategic plan or grant and go through a brainstorming process to identify needed facility projects. Regardless of the process used, the people involved should consider the following questions:

> Does the activity require new or modified public spaces?
>
> Will the activity require additional staff members? If so, will the new staff need desks, computers, filing cabinets, or other furniture or equipment?
>
> Will the activity require new furniture?
>
> Will the activity require new equipment? If new equipment is needed, will it sit on existing furniture that presently takes up floor space, will it require new furniture and require floor space, or will it be freestanding and require floor space?
>
> Will the activity require new materials and additional shelving?
>
> Will the activity require technology support, and if so, will that technology support have facility implications?

Use Workform 1, Facility Projects, to list the activities under review and make note of the facility resources required for each. The data can be found by studying activities described in grants or strategic plans.

When all of the activities under review have been evaluated, you will probably have multiple completed copies of Workform 1, all including lists of activities with the types of facility resources needed for each (if any). One or two people should be asked to review and consolidate the information on the workforms. They will begin by eliminating any activities from further study that do not require new or modified facility resources. Then they will write a brief project description of each of the activities requiring some type of facility resources and record those descriptions on Workform 2, Project Priorities. As they review the facility resources required for each activity, they should consider whether some of the facility projects that support related activities could be combined into a single project. For instance, they might combine an activity that will require additional shelving for adult fiction with an activity that will require reconfiguring space to better merchandise the adult fiction collection into a single project. The project descriptions should be brief and to the point. You will be expanding the descriptions of the higher-priority projects later in this chapter.

The following is the first part of a case study describing a facility resource allocation project completed by the Anytown Public Library. The case study illustrates specific parts of the process being developed through Workforms 1 and 2 and provides you with an example of how the process worked in one library.

CASE STUDY

Anytown Public Library Homework Center

PART 1: Identifying Facility Projects

The Anytown Public Library serves a population of 100,000 from a single library facility. The library just completed the first strategic plan in the library's history. In the past, new services were added with little modification of existing facility resources, and that has resulted in a very crowded and uncomfortable environment.

In preparation for the new fiscal year beginning soon, the Anytown Public Library management team reviewed the activities that had been selected to support the goals and objectives in their new plan. They used separate copies of Workform 1, Facility Projects, to list the activities that support each goal in the plan and to identify the facility resources required to support each activity. The following is part of the completed Workform 1 for their second goal.

When the members of the management team had identified the facility resources required for all of the activities in the plan, they reviewed their work and identified a variety of facility projects that needed to be addressed. The following is part of their completed Workform 2. Note that activities 2.1, 2.4, and 2.6 do not appear on Workform 2 because they do not require new or modified facility resources.

WORKFORM 1 Facility Projects

Goal 2: Students in Anytown will have the skills and tools they need to succeed in school.

A. Activity	B. No Facility Requirements	C. Current Facilities Adequate	D. Requires Additional or Modified Public Space	E. Requires Additional or Modified Staff or Storage Space	F. Requires Additional or Modified Furnishings, Equipment, or Shelving	G. Requires Support for New or Expanded Technology
2.1 Recruit and train volunteers to provide homework help		X				
2.2 Create a homework center			X	X	X	X
2.3 Provide expanded access to the Internet for students who need the resources for homework						X
2.4 Expand the homework help web page		X				
2.5 Identify and purchase print and electronic resources to support school assignments					X	
2.6 Plan and present twelve programs on study skills		X				

WORKFORM 2 Project Priorities

Projects for Fiscal Year 2XXX

A. Goal/Activity Number	B. Project Description	C. Priority	D. Why	E. Selected Yes	E. Selected No
1.3	Purchase new display furniture and rearrange the New Book area.				
2.2, 2.3, 2.5	Create a homework center that includes additional or modified spaces for the public and staff, additional shelving, and support for new public-access PCs.				

Determining Priorities

Once the needed facility projects have been identified, you have to determine the priority of each project. You will determine priority based on a three-point scale:

> 1 = Critical
>
> 2 = Important
>
> 3 = Desirable but not necessarily now

There are several factors to think about when determining the relative priority of the facility project. If the project supports one or more activities that are a part of the library's strategic plan, the first thing to do is look at the priority of the goal or goals that are supported by that activity and project. Generally, projects that support activities related to Goal 1 in your plan will have a higher priority than projects that support activities related to goals that are less important. Some projects will support activities related to more than one goal, and they will often have a higher priority than projects that support activities related to a single goal.

Another factor to consider when determining priority is how essential the facility project is to implementing the activity or providing the service. This applies both to activities that are part of a library strategic plan and to activities that are designed to support a new service or grant project. Let's say that you have decided to expand your services to teens and you don't currently have any specific area in the library that is designated as a teen space. A facility project to develop a teen space will be essential to providing the service and would, therefore, rank as a *critical* priority. On the other hand, if you already have a designated teen space and the project under review is to add more display shelving, you might easily rank that as *desirable but not necessarily now.*

A third factor to consider is the relationship among the projects. If you find that you have several projects that will affect the same space, it makes sense to work with them at the same time. You don't want to plan for changes in the young adult area to support a homework help center now, and then in six months start planning to add a new young adult librarian and a library assistant to the young adult department, and then come back in a year to start planning to house an expanded collection of young adult DVDs. It may be that the homework help center is a key element in implementing an activity that supports the library's first goal, that the new staff will provide activities that support the library's third most important goal, and that the young adult DVDs support the goal with the lowest priority. In this instance, the homework help center project would receive a *critical* priority ranking, and the other projects that affect the young adult area would receive the same priority. This will ensure that the projects are all addressed at the same time, even if by different individuals or committees. Record the priority of each project on Workform 2, and add a brief note that explains the priority ranking.

Anytown Public Library Homework Center

PART 2: Determining Priority

The members of the management team determined the priority of each of the projects on Workform 2. The following is part of their completed Workform 2.

WORKFORM 2 **Project Priorities**

Projects for Fiscal Year 2XXX

A. Goal/Activity Number	B. Project Description	C. Priority	D. Why	E. Selected	
				Yes	**No**
1.3	Purchase new display furniture and rearrange the New Book area.	2	This is not the most critical resource for this goal. The focus of this goal is on materials selection.		
2.2, 2.3, 2.5	Create a homework center that includes additional or modified spaces for the public and staff, additional shelving, and support for new public-access PCs.	1	This goal cannot be achieved unless a homework center is established.		

Prioritizing Projects

When you have determined the priority of all of the facility projects under review, you can decide which projects you will implement during the current year and which you will address next year and the year after. Start by reviewing the projects that you have determined to be critical or high-priority projects. These are the first projects to initiate. If you have designated too many projects as "critical" and you can't start them all at the same time, you will have to go back and reevaluate your priority ratings. Are some "critical" projects more critical than others? Look again at the factors to be considered when determining the priority of activities.

You may also want to consider two additional factors. First, your selections should provide a reasonable balance of services to all target audiences. Second, it is a good idea to include a combination of projects that support activities that can be implemented relatively easily so that you see some quick successes, along with projects that support activities that will require more time to complete. Indicate your final selections for the current year using the "Selected" column on Workform 2.

Review the final list of projects one last time. Are the most important ones scheduled to be addressed first? Have interrelated projects been combined to ensure that there is no duplication of effort? Do you have the staff resources to actually manage all of the projects you have identified for the first year? When you have completed this review, you are ready to move forward with planning the first project.

Step 1.2
Define the Project's Scope and Intent

The next step in this task is to expand the brief project description you wrote when completing Workform 2 by identifying the scope and intent of the project. The statement of project *intent* should describe the reason for initiating the project and the intended outcome. The statement of project *scope* defines the boundaries of the project. A project to develop a comprehensive plan to implement all facility-related changes required as a result of a new strategic plan of services has a very broad scope. A project to define the facility-related changes required to implement a single activity in a strategic plan or grant project has a much narrower scope.

The intent and scope of any project must be clearly articulated before the project begins. In part 2 of the case study, Anytown Library managers indicated that developing a homework center was their highest priority. The statement of intent and scope for the Anytown Public Library's homework center project might say:

> The intent of this project is to identify the facility-related changes needed to develop the homework center identified in the library strategic plan and present the recommended changes to the library administrative council by June 30, 2XXX.

This makes it clear that the intent of the project is to identify the facility resources required to establish a homework center, that the scope of project is limited to planning rather than implementing, and that the project will result in recommendations that will be acted on by others. Keep a record of your project's scope and intent to refer to during upcoming tasks and steps in the *Managing Facilities for Results* process.

Step 1.3
Develop a Task List and Timeline

Start by looking again at figure 2, Tasks and Steps in the *Managing Facilities for Results* Process, shown in the introduction. Decide which of the steps in Tasks 4 through 8 will be required to develop a plan to implement the project you have selected. Record your selections in the first column of Workform 3, Preliminary Task List and Timeline. Then estimate how long each step will take to complete. Keep in mind that these initial dates are just estimates. Dates may change as the project goes on, but setting a preliminary timeline now helps everyone be aware of expectations. When you are through, you should have identified the significant benchmarks for the project and established a general timeline for each.

Step 1.4
Decide If a Project Committee Is Required

Now that you have a clear idea of the intent and scope of the facility project you are planning, and of the tasks and steps that need to be completed, you will have to decide if you need to appoint a committee to manage the project. This will depend on the complexity of the project and the staffing levels and structures in your library, among other things. Answers to the following questions may help you decide if you need a project committee.

> Will the facility reallocation required to implement the activity affect multiple departments or units of the library?

Will the facility reallocation required to implement the activity affect staff work-flow?

Will you need outside expertise (architects, contractors, lighting specialists, etc.) to advise the committee on planning facility changes and space reallocation needed to implement the activity?

Will implementation have a temporary negative impact on current user services?

Will the facility-related changes required to implement this activity make a signifi-cant impact on your budget?

If you answer "yes" to two or more of these questions, you probably need a project com-mittee. You might also want to record your reasons for having a committee and share them with committee members at your first meeting.

> **LEVEL OF EFFORT NOTE**
> **No Project Committee**
>
> You may not need to appoint a project committee. If you decide that planning to provide the facility-related resources needed for the project under review can be done by one or two people, you can skip Step 2.1: Select the Committee.
>
> Most facility-related resource allocation projects are managed by committees, and much of the narrative in this book is based on the assumption that a committee has been appointed. Even if you don't appoint a full project committee, the people who are responsible for the project will need to review and complete the appropriate tasks and steps of this process. The decision about whether or not a task or step is necessary will be based on the nature of the project and not on the composition of the group doing the planning.

TASK 2: PLAN THE PROJECT

Task 1: Define the Project
Task 2: Plan the Project
> **Step 2.1: Select the committee**
> **Step 2.2: Determine the role of outside experts**
> **Step 2.3: Plan how to keep the board and staff informed**
> **Step 2.4: Develop an orientation packet**

Task 3: Prepare the Committee
Task 4: Organize the Data Collection Process
Task 5: Collect Preliminary Data
Task 6: Identify Gaps and Evaluate Options
Task 7: Present Recommendations
Task 8: Prepare the Final Report and Get Approvals

When you completed the steps in Task 1, you made a number of important decisions about your facility project. However, there are still issues to be resolved by library administrators before the project can be initiated. If you decided to use a project committee, you obviously have to appoint that committee. If you plan to ask one or two staff members to manage the project, they will need to be identified and notified. Once you have selected the staff members who will be working on the project, you will be able to assess their skills and make a preliminary decision about whether or not you will need to involve outside experts in the project. When you know who will be involved, you will be able to develop a plan to keep all of the *stakeholders* (people or groups who can affect or will be affected by your actions) informed about the project.

The last thing you will do in this task is create an orientation packet for whoever will be given responsibility for managing the project. This brief description of the project includes the scope and intent of the project from Step 1.2. It will help ensure that everyone involved in the project understands his or her responsibilities and authority. The packet will include a summary of all the decisions you made during Tasks 1 and 2, copies of completed workforms, and other information that might be of use to the project managers. The project manager should also receive a copy of this book. The steps in Task 2, like the steps in Task 1, are normally completed by one or more members of the library's management team.

Step 2.1
Select the Committee

Appointing the project committee is one of the most important tasks in any project. If the committee leader is skilled and committee members are competent and involved, your project is likely to be a success. A committee that is made up of members who have a history of failing to reach agreement, have personal conflicts, have an inability to meet deadlines, or who simply lack the skills needed to find and evaluate information will almost always result in a failed project.

LEVEL OF EFFORT NOTE
Select the Committee

If you decided not to appoint a project committee in Step 1.4, you can skip this step and go on to Step 2.2: Determine the Role of Outside Experts.

The project committee should consist of people with appropriate knowledge to make recommendations about facility and space use. It should also include staff who work in the area being studied, as well as staff who work in areas that may be affected by changes. Leadership of the committee should rest with a single person, the committee chair. If the project will affect only one area or department of the library, the manager of that area or department may be an appropriate leader. If the project affects more than one department, you may want to appoint a library administrator to chair the committee.

The committee chair's skills and abilities may be more important than his or her position. The chair must be experienced and skilled in leading groups. The chair should also have a proven track record in project management, including setting and meeting deadlines, collecting and analyzing data, keeping all stakeholders informed, and keeping a project committee on task. It is critical that the chair believe in and support the project being considered.

The committee chair's responsibility and authority should be clearly defined in writing. This is particularly important if the committee chair is not a library manager, but it is also important if the chair is a manager and the committee includes members who are the chair's peers or one or more members who are above the chair in the organization chart.

The project committee can include library staff members, people who work for your parent agency if you have one—county or city government, for example—and regular contractors, such as the people who provide your technology support. As noted previously, the committee should include staff from all units that will be affected by the project, as well as staff who have specialized skills or unique information about the project. A representative from the maintenance or facilities staff is often a helpful addition to a facility project. This employee (or contractor) may be aware of important considerations unknown to others. Be sure to find out if the library's governing or funding agency has a facilities management or capital projects committee or department that must be consulted and should be represented on the committee.

While differing roles and expertise may require a variety of personality types, try to appoint people who are productive, high-energy, and can-do types. It will also be important to have a mix of data- or information-directed people and creative or new-idea people.

Consider how the staff members who will be involved in the planning project can create time for this assignment in their workday. To do this, you will need to have some idea of the amount of time you expect staff to devote to the project. Obviously, the chair will spend more time on the project than committee members, but everyone involved will be using time currently allocated to other tasks to do project-related work. If the project timeline is three months and the chair plans to hold two two-hour meetings per month, the base time requirement is probably a minimum of fifteen hours, and that assumes little or no travel time. In addition to their time spent in meetings, committee members will have data collection and analysis assignments, which may be very time-consuming. Ask the supervisors of the people on the project committee to work with them to ensure that any needed job adjustments are made.

Once the committee list is established, review the list to decide the level of involvement of each person in the project. Is there a benefit from an individual's participation throughout the project? Or is this someone who should be consulted at a specific point, but who will not attend all meetings? Will some people be brought in during data collection but not be expected to attend all meetings? It is a good idea to keep the group that meets regularly fairly small in order to make meeting scheduling easier and create a more efficient working environment.

Step 2.2
Determine the Role of Outside Experts

The issues that need to be addressed when planning for facility-related projects often require specialized knowledge and experience. When you have appointed the people responsible for the project, you will be able to make an initial assessment about the additional expertise that might be required. This is a preliminary assessment. As the committee works through the process, it is possible that members will find that they lack the expertise needed in one or more areas. The decision to involve outside experts can be revisited at any time.

Outside experts that might be helpful for your project may include any one or a combination of the following:

Building and other types of library consultants can be a great resource for the project committee. In addition to bringing in a level of expertise that may not be available in your library, consultants can add a fresh perspective, new ideas, and an awareness of trends in public library service. Perhaps most important of all, they often do a lot of the work. The major factors to consider when deciding to hire a building consultant are how complex your project will be, whether you will need a formal document describing the building changes for an architect or consultant, whether you or a project committee will have the time and expertise to create the needed planning products or documents, whether you just feel more comfortable having an expert to guide the effort and process, and whether you can afford it. Sometimes it is politically useful to have someone from the outside make recommendations or bring up desired and mandated changes.

Architects are educated and licensed to design buildings; librarians are not. Architects may be required by law for public projects above a certain size. Check your state and local requirements to determine local trigger points such as access, facade, or stability changes. Adding a wall may not require an architect, but even small projects can raise questions about required fire exits and other types of regulations. In many jurisdictions, even a limited renovation can trigger regulations to bring the whole building into total compliance with current codes related to the Americans with Disabilities Act (ADA), fire and life safety, and seismic regulations (depending on your part of the country). The architect's role in writing specifications and overseeing the construction project can be important for the success of your project. Also, if you will need a building permit for any part of your project, you may need drawings produced by a licensed architect.[1]

Interior designers design interior layout and color schemes, assist with furniture selection and purchasing, and coordinate with the architect and project manager. Architectural firms often include interior designers as part of their bid, but these services can also be procured separately. A good designer can help blend changes into your existing environment and create a cohesive look and feel. Factors to consider include how extensive the project is, the visual impact the project will have on other areas of the library, whether or not you will have an architect or library building consultant who can help with this project, and how confident you and your staff feel about making interior design decisions yourselves.

Technology consultants assess technology needs, make recommendations, and assist with purchasing equipment and other technology-related items. If your project involves blending or integrating new technologies into your overall systems, then you may need advice on how to do it. The level of expertise available on staff or by contract is the major deciding factor for whether to bring in an outside consultant.

Signage consultants assist in the design of signage systems and develop bid documents to purchase those systems. Unless you are doing a full review and reorganization of library signage, you will most likely continue with the vendor and system that you have in place. If you want decorative signs to label a new area, you can work with a local sign company or seek expert help if local services are limited.

Structural engineers assess issues related to the structure of the building and its systems and coordinate with the architect. Architects often include engineering services as part of their bid, but, like interior designers, engineers can be hired on a separate contract to help with specific decisions, such as floor load capacity and air handling. If you are using an architect, that expert can tell you if you need engineering services. If you have questions relating to structural strength, ADA requirements, historic preservation regulations, hazardous materials, mechanical systems, lighting, or energy efficiency that no one available to you can answer, you definitely need an engineer.

Building contractors follow plans and carry out construction work. Building contractors arrange for and coordinate the work of subcontractors and may do some of the work themselves. If you are making changes that require construction, use a professional and licensed contractor. You may, however, have a department within the library governance structure that does some construction. The county facilities department, for example, may take out or build non-load-bearing walls.

Workform 4, Need for Outside Experts, is a tool to help you consider the various factors that affect decisions about using outside experts. Collecting all the information about your use of outside experts in one place will be useful in deciding which experts you will consult in the context of both final schedule preparations and final budget considerations. Keep Workform 4 handy to use in both your preliminary report and the final report once you have the project's budget and time parameters more firmly set. Remember, not all of these experts will cost you money. For example, a facility consultant may be available through your state library or library system. In addition, city and county governments normally have employees with facility expertise. Another source may be people on your board or in your Friends group who may have expertise and may be willing to volunteer their help. You might even find a staff member from another library who has facility-reallocation experience and could help.

If you decide to use outside experts, review the preliminary timeline created in Step 1.3 with the data collected on Workform 3. Be sure that your time estimates include the extra time that will be required to select and make arrangements for outside experts to participate in the process.

Step 2.3
Plan How to Keep the Board and Staff Informed

It is very important to keep your board or governing authority informed on the progress of the project committee. The members of your governing authority will probably be asked to approve the final recommendations. The more they know about how those recommendations were developed, the more likely it is that they will support them.

Building Consensus

Libraries by their nature are bureaucracies, not democracies. The majority does not rule, and final decisions on how a project can best meet the needs of the community rest with the library director and the library's governing authority. That said, it is still important to involve staff in planning for facility-related activities and to keep them informed about the progress of implementing those activities.

It is always wise to build consensus among staff members when considering changes in their work spaces. Consensus building means that the group seeks to develop solutions that all can live with. It does not necessarily mean that each person thinks the solution is the best possible way to proceed. A group has reached consensus when everyone can and will support the decision. It's generally accepted that people are more likely to support decisions they helped make. The opposite is also true; people may resist any changes they think are arbitrary, or ones that they are directed to implement with no discussion at all. Therefore, consensus building will be an important part of any facility project's success.

Library staff members in all positions have valuable information about how people use the library facility and about services that will be useful to the project committee. The people who perform the tasks that accomplish an activity know best how it is being done now, and they may have ideas about how processes and services could be improved. Staff members can provide information about how current furnishings, shelving, and equipment and their configuration are affecting user services; how workflows are affected by space configurations; and how traffic flows through the building. All of this information will be needed by the members of the project committee.

Bringing library staff into the process early will keep current and accurate information about the implementation of new service priorities flowing to all parts of the staff. Acknowledging the staff's expertise about their work space and how it is used and encouraging participation in planning the placement and development of new activities will lead to more cooperation and increased support for the new activities.

Communicating Effectively

Effective communication about the facility project involves both disseminating information and checking to be sure that the message was received and understood. The best way to be sure that all staff members are receiving information is to use multiple forms of communication. Project committee members can be assigned responsibility for informing their respective work areas, but there is no guarantee that information will reach everyone. Library intranets, blogs, or wikis can host a page on the project's progress with notices and results of meetings, notations of issues being discussed, and a list of frequently asked questions. However, if your intranet is not regularly used by everyone, a parallel staff communication system will be necessary. If a staff intranet is underutilized or not available, develop memos or special publications about the project on a regular basis, send them out to everyone, and post them on a bulletin board in a heavily used staff area. However, the best transfer of information about your facility project will be at face-to-face meetings. Oral communication in staff meetings should be supported by written handouts, which should be distributed to all staff at the meeting and to any staff members who could not attend. The following are some basic rules for clear communication:

Keep project communication direct and free of jargon.

Communicate with the whole staff; you may not see how the facility project's changes affect other departments, but the staff might.

Acknowledge staff concerns. Explain why facility changes are being made, and who will benefit. Include the definition of the project's scope and intent (Step 1.2).

Provide examples and models of how the activity or service has been implemented in other libraries. If possible, arrange field trips so staff members can see firsthand how facilities have been configured to support the activity or service.

Always provide an official spokesperson for questions and concerns so staff can get consistent answers from a single member of the project committee. Mention the name of the project contact every time you update staff.

Step 2.4
Develop an Orientation Packet

The library management team now has all of the information needed to develop a comprehensive orientation package for the members of the committee. If you have decided not to appoint a committee, the person who will be responsible for managing the project will also need most of this information. The packet should include the following information:

- a list of committee members and their contact information
- the goal, objectives, and activity in the strategic plan or grant proposal that the project supports (if the project is supported by such a document)

- a copy of the statement of project intent and scope you created in Step 1.2
- the name of the person or group that will receive and act on the committee's recommendations
- copies of completed Workforms 1–4
- a list of other working groups, library departments, and individuals to be kept informed as the project proceeds
- several copies of this book to be shared among committee members
- other information or issues pertinent to the project

Send a copy of the orientation packet to each committee member before the first meeting of the committee, and encourage the chair to review the materials in the packet during that first meeting. (See chapter 2 for additional information about the first meeting.) It is important that each committee member clearly understand the intent, scope, responsibilities, and authority of the committee.

Key Points to Remember

Library space is a valuable asset and should be reviewed regularly to be sure that space allocations reflect service priorities.

Library services should be dictated by user needs, not by how the space is currently being used.

Projects that will require complex or expensive facility-related resources and those that may elicit strong staff reactions are usually best managed by a project committee.

The process described in *Managing Facilities for Results* is flexible and should be modified to meet local conditions.

Your space-reallocation project may require or benefit from the services of library consultants, building professionals, and other outside experts.

The project committee needs to know the project's intent and scope and the committee's responsibilities and authority before the project begins.

Regularly communicate information about the project to the staff and the library's governing and funding bodies.

Note

1. Richard C. McCarthy, *Designing Better Libraries: Selecting and Working with Building Professionals* (Fort Atkinson, WI: Highsmith, 1995), 91.

Chapter 2

Committee Orientation and Data Collection Organization

MILESTONES

By the time you finish this chapter you will know how to

- provide an orientation for the project committee
- explain the gap analysis process
- identify the four facility resources that may be included in the project
- define and give examples of the six facility-related data elements that may be collected during the project
- describe in detail the activity or service that will be supported by the facility project
- organize the data collection process

Planning is often an iterative process. First you develop a general outline of what you want to accomplish, then you go back and fill in the details. Although this can seem repetitious, it is necessary to have a clear picture of your destination before you can make informed decisions about the best ways to reach that destination. A family of four planning a vacation will start by making some very global decisions. Will the whole family vacation together, or will the parents take a vacation while the kids are at summer camp? What do they want to do on their vacation: swim, ski, shop, camp, hike, explore? How long do they have for their vacation? Are there financial limitations that have to be taken into consideration when planning the vacation? Once these decisions have been made, the family members can move on to planning the actual vacation: dates, destination, transportation, and so on.

The same iterative process applies to the facility project that is being designed. In chapter 1 the library's management team made a number of global decisions about the facility project. Now the members of the project committee are ready to begin their work. The orientation packet developed in Step 2.4 includes a lot of general information about the project. However, it provides little or no guidance on how to actually complete the work that has been assigned.

Determining the facility-related resource requirements for a project can seem intimidating at first glance. Few library staff members are experts on facility-related resources. As a matter of fact, most staffers take the spaces in which they work for granted and tend to think of them as immutable. When faced with a facility problem, staff are more likely to develop work-arounds than to suggest substantive changes. After all, it is easier to change the way one performs a task than it is to rearrange books, shelves, and desks. Before the members of the committee can move forward, they will have to develop a new way of looking at the library facility and its various components.

Using Gap Analysis

The *Managing Facilities for Results* process is based on the gap analysis process, which was first introduced in *Planning for Results* in 1998.[1] The gap analysis process asks four basic questions:

1. What resources (in this case, facility resources) will be required to support an activity at the desired levels?
2. What resources do we have that are currently allocated to support the activity?
3. What is the gap between the two?
4. How can we fill that gap (or, more rarely, reallocate the surplus)?

To answer the four questions posed in the gap analysis process, the members of the committee will collect and analyze facility-related data for the specific project selected in Task 1. Committee members will need to spend some time discussing the library's facility resources and the data elements that will help them to understand the current and potential uses of those resources. The members of the committee will then develop a plan to collect needed data. The tasks in this chapter will prepare them for this work. Chapter 2 presents Tasks 3 and 4, with one workform supporting Task 3 and two workforms supporting Task 4. See figure 5 to help determine whether *you* will use all of the workforms in this chapter.

FIGURE 5
When to Use the Workforms That Support Tasks 3 and 4

Workform	When to Use	When Not to Use
Workform 5: Facility Resources—Data Elements (Step 3.2)	This workform should be used if a committee will be responsible for the project. Use this workform as a part of the orientation for the committee. The workform can be used to introduce the facility resources and the six facility data elements.	Do not use this workform if an individual has been given the responsibility for completing the project.
Workform 6: Project Description—General (Step 4.1)	This workform should be used along with Workform 7 to help project committee members develop a clear understanding of the activity or service under review, the facility resources that will be included in the project, and the types of data that need to be collected. It will be particularly useful if other groups or individuals are identifying the staffing, collections, or technology needed to implement the activity. This workform will be reviewed and approved by the library administrative team.	Everyone will use this workform.
Workform 7: Project Description—Physical Plant, Space, and Spatial Relationships (Step 4.1)	This workform is used with Workform 6 to help project committee members develop a clear understanding of the physical plant, space, and spatial relationships that will be required to support the activity. This workform will be reviewed and approved by the library administrative team.	Everyone will use this workform.

TASK 3: PREPARE THE COMMITTEE

The first meeting of any committee is important because it sets the tone for future meetings. Even if all of the committee members know one another, they may not have all served together on a committee before or worked with the chair in that capacity before. The expectations and behavior of the chair and the behavior of the committee members during the first meeting will establish their working relationships for the remainder of the project. If the chair is directive, presents the members with decisions to ratify, and doesn't encourage discussion, the members will either resist or passively accept the decisions—and in most cases the response will be passivity. If the chair is inclusive and presents the members with options to review and discuss, most members will actively participate in the problem solving. All three of the steps in Task 3 will be addressed during the first meeting of the project committee. A suggested agenda for the meeting can be found in figure 6.

The suggested agenda for the meeting is based on the assumption that the chair intends for the project to be managed in a collaborative manner. The agenda describes a participative process in which all committee members are engaged in learning about facility resources and data elements and are involved in developing a detailed plan of action for the project.

Step 3.1
Review the Orientation Packet

The first meeting of the project committee starts by reviewing the orientation packet that was prepared during Step 2.4 and distributed to the members before the meeting. The chair should start the meeting by reviewing the project's scope and intent to be sure that everyone understands them. Once everyone is clear about the charge, they will be ready to look at the activity or activities that are the focus of the project. It will be important for all the members of the committee to have the same understanding of the activity before the project begins. Review the goal and objectives in the strategic plan or grant proposal that are supported by the activity (if the activity is supported by such a document) as a part of this discussion. The committee will be discussing the activity in considerably more detail later in the process, so you don't need to spend too much time on this now. Just be sure that everyone knows how the activity was identified, why it was selected as the focus of the committee's project, and what, in general, it includes. Remember, the activity itself is *not* debatable. The decision to implement the activity was made before the committee was appointed. The committee is only responsible for identifying the facility resources required to implement the activity.

The next thing to discuss is the completed copy of Workform 3, Preliminary Task List and Timeline, that is in the orientation packet. The list of tasks and steps on the workform will help committee members have a better idea of their responsibilities. The important thing to note about Workform 3 is that it only includes a *general* list of tasks and steps and *preliminary* deadlines. The members of the committee will be developing a more detailed project plan and timeline in Step 3.3.

FIGURE 6
Meeting 1: Sample Agenda

First Committee Meeting

Purpose: Introduce the facility planning project, process, and timeline

Develop a shared understanding of our facility resources and the data elements that the committee will be collecting and analyzing

Who: All members of the facility project committee

Where: Small conference room

When: Date, start time, end time (meeting should be scheduled for two hours)

Materials: Orientation packet, a list of possible outside experts from Step 2.2, and figures 7, 8, and 9

Preparation: Please read the attached materials and be ready to discuss them and ask questions

AGENDA

[Start time] Introductions, if needed (5 minutes)

Review/discuss the materials in the orientation packet (35 minutes)

Committee charge, responsibility, and authority

The activity as written in the strategic plan, grant, etc.

The goal and/or objectives the activity supports

Groups or individuals that are working on projects that will affect this project (identifying other types of resources required for this activity or planning other facility-related projects)

Task list and timeline (Workform 3, Preliminary Task List and Timeline)

Outside experts, if any (Workform 4, Need for Outside Experts) and a list of possible outside experts (Step 2.2)

Discuss potential issues (25 minutes)

Issues included in the orientation packet

Other issues identified by committee members

Possible solutions

Review/discuss facility resources and facility-related data elements (20 minutes)

Figure 7, Facility Resources—Common Elements

Figure 8, Facility Resources—Data Elements

Figure 9, Suggested Standards to Measure Age and Condition

Distribute and complete Workform 5, Facility-Related Data Elements (25 minutes)

Develop Detailed Timeline (15 minutes)

Schedule future meetings

Schedule other due dates

Questions (5 minutes)

[End time]   Adjourn

This would also be a good time to talk to other groups or individuals who are working on projects that might affect the committee's work, including any committees looking at the staffing, technology, or collections that will be required to implement the activity under review. It will be important for the members of the committee to understand the relationships between and among these various individuals and groups.

If the committee will use outside experts, the members of the committee may want to review the completed Workform 4, Need for Outside Experts, in the orientation packet to see why those experts were selected. It might also be helpful to distribute photocopies of the list of possible outside experts from Step 2.2 in chapter 1. There is a good chance that one or more of those outside experts will be needed at some point during the project. All the members of the committee will need to know that the possibility of using outside experts exists, and be able to identify appropriate outside experts for specific problems or issues.

Conclude the review of the orientation materials with a discussion of any issues in the library or the community that might affect the project. A list of such issues may have been included in the packet; if so, it could provide a starting point for the discussion. It is likely that the members of the committee will be able to identify additional issues as well. The point of this process is not to develop a laundry list of all of the roadblocks (real and imagined) that will make it impossible to complete the project. Instead, it is intended to provide a framework for anticipating potential problems and for developing plans to address those problems before they occur. This proactive problem solving will make the rest of the project much easier to manage.

Step 3.2
Understand Facility-Related Data Elements

The next part of the first committee meeting focuses on identifying, defining, collecting, and analyzing data. The typical library staff member thinks of "data" as the statistics that get reported to the board every month: X number of people used the library; Y number of children's books circulated; fines and fees generated Z number of dollars. When staff members talk about the use of the services they provide, they often think in descriptive terms: "We know the materials in the small business collection are valuable because Mr. Smith used them to start his successful dry cleaning business," or "The parents who bring their children to the lap-sit story program love it." Although these two examples seem quite different, in reality they reflect the two types of facility-related data that will be collected during the project: objective and subjective. It will be important for the members of the committee to understand the differences between these two types of data.

Understanding Objective and Subjective Data

Objective data are based in fact, not opinion, and can be expressed as numbers or words. Examples of objective data expressed as numbers include the statistics that come from your automated circulation system, the actual length and width of a room, and the number of tables and chairs in the children's department. The statement "the chair seat is torn" is an example of objective data expressed as words.

Subjective data are based on opinion and can be expressed as words or numbers, although they are most often expressed as words. For example, "the display table is messy," "the staff room smells funny," or "access to the circulation desk is adequate." Subjective data that are expressed as numbers are usually based on a numerical scale. For example, the cleanliness of an area might be rated on a scale of 1 to 5, with 1 meaning "filthy," 3 meaning "acceptable," and 5 meaning "spotless."

Both types of data are useful, and they are often used together. For instance, you might say that the 20 × 20-foot children's room (objective data) is too crowded to be user-friendly (subjective data). You could go on to say that 15,000 items in the children's collection (objective data) are not easy to access because of the way the shelving has been arranged (subjective data). Then you might say that there are three tables and twelve chairs in the children's room (objective data) and that their average condition is 3 based on a scale of 1 to 5, with 1 meaning "unusable," 3 meaning "showing wear but usable," and 5 meaning "perfect condition" (subjective data).

Identifying Facility Resources

As noted previously, *Managing Facilities for Results* is a data-driven process. An important part of the process will be to identify the facility resources about which data will be collected, and this is not as straightforward as it might seem at first glance. The problem is that librarians don't use a common vocabulary to describe facility resources.

Over the past century, librarians have created a common vocabulary to use when discussing collection resources. Everyone understands the distinction between volumes and titles and knows what the term *format* means. In fact, librarians are considered the experts in collections, and our terms are used by nonlibrarians to describe materials. Staffing resources are also clearly defined: FTE, full-time, part-time, and so on. These definitions were developed by human resource professionals, but library managers have had to learn to understand and use them because so much of their time is spent on personnel issues. Defining the terms used to describe ever-mutating technology resources can be a challenge, but most librarians recognize that problem and defer to the experts.

Architects and contractors have their own terms for facility resources, but those terms often seem overly technical to library staff. Furthermore, most staff aren't in positions where they have to use precise terms for the library's facility resources very often. A staff member could work in a library for his or her entire career and never be involved in a building project or major renovation.

The project committee will be considering four facility resources: physical plant; space; furniture, equipment, shelving; and signage. The definitions of these terms follow.

> *Physical plant* includes the walls, floor, heating and air-conditioning, electrical grid, and so on.
>
> *Space* describes an area of the library building that has a common usage or purpose.[2]
>
> *Furniture, equipment, and shelving* are the physical items within the structure; they can be freestanding or attached.
>
> *Signage* includes the publicly displayed notices that help people find their way around a library and get information about the library's contents and use.

See figure 7 for examples of each of these types of facility resources.

FIGURE 7
Facility Resources—Common Elements

PHYSICAL PLANT
- Entrances and exits
- Walls
- Floors
- Ceilings
- Window treatment
- Lighting
- Temperature/humidity
- Plumbing
- Electrical
- Telecommunication (voice/data)
- Stairwells
- Elevators
- Lifts
- Security equipment
- Storage

SPACE
- Age-level departments (e.g., children, teen, adult)
- Service-specific departments or units (e.g., reference)
- Computer lab
- Story room
- Meeting rooms
- Public areas
- Administrative/staff areas
- Kitchens
- Storage areas

FURNITURE, EQUIPMENT, AND SHELVING
Furniture
- Seating—Public
    At juvenile study table
    At teen study table
    At adult study table
    At adult/teen carrel
    Adult/teen lounge
    Juvenile lounge
    Rocking chair
    Bench for two
    Sofa for two or three
- Seating—Staff
    Executive chair
    Task chair
    Guest chair
    Lounge chair

- Tables
    Juvenile study table
    Teen study table
    Adult/teen study table
    Preschool table
    Lounge or end table
    Folding table
- Staff desks or service counters
    Counter, multiple staff workstations
    Counter, single person
    Desk, single person
- Meeting/conference/study room
    Auditorium/meeting, fixed chairs
    Auditorium/meeting, stacking chairs with table
    Conference room with table
    Study room with table
    Floor seating for children
- Technology workstations
    Technology workstation for one
    Technology workstation for two
    Stand-up OPAC station
    Self-checkout
- Other
    Stacking chair dolly
    Stacking table dolly
    Flip chart stand
    Lectern with computer space
    AV cart
    Coat/hat rack
    Atlas/dictionary stand
    File cabinet
    Microform cabinet
    Map file cabinet
    Change machine
    Book truck
    Book return
    Display case
    Copier preparation counter
    Recycling bin
- Fixed furnishings
    Kitchen unit
    Stage
    Cabinetry
    Food preparation area

Equipment
- Freestanding
    Photocopier
    Change machine
    Print or smart card dispenser
    Print station
    Computer use sign-up
    Self-checkout station
    Security system gates
    Locker
    Trash/garbage container
    Work table
- Equipment that does not occupy floor space
    Sound/PA system
    Computers/printers
    LCD projector
    Wall- or ceiling-mounted projection screen
    Wall-mounted flat screen monitor/TV

Shelving
- Cantilevered or case shelving
    Books
    Media—CD, DVD, etc.
    Magazine
- Display
    Books
    Media—CD, DVD, etc.
    Magazine
    Newspapers
- Bin
- Spinner
- Compact
- Specialty

SIGNAGE
Fixed
- Directory
- Directional
- Identification
- Informational/instructional

Movable
- Directory
- Directional
- Identification
- Informational/instructional

Understanding the Facility Resource Data Elements

When the members of the committee have a clear understanding of the four facility resources illustrated in figure 7, they will be ready to consider the data elements they will collect about each resource. Five of those data elements were first defined in *Managing for Results:* capacity, use, age or condition, access, and the impact of technology.[3] *Managing Facilities for Results* adds one more element to this list: spatial relationships. These six data elements are listed and briefly described in figure 8 and are described in greater detail in the following discussion.

There is no question that this part of the meeting will be content-dense. Committee members will be introduced to a new vocabulary and a new way of looking at the library's facility resources. The terms and concepts that will be discussed will form the foundation for the committee's work on the project, and *all* members of the committee must understand them. Distribute copies of figures 7 and 8 prior to the meeting to give the committee members a chance to think a little, in advance, about the four types of common elements and the six types of data elements.

During the discussion of figures 7 and 8, committee members can use Workform 5, Facility Resources—Data Elements, to record the definition of each element and to list examples and possible sources of data for each element. By using Workform 5 as the basis for your review and discussion of the facility resources data elements, you will ensure that each data element is covered and that all committee members have similar information and understanding of the terms and their applications.

FIGURE 8
Facility Resources—Data Elements

Data Element	Definition	Example
Capacity	The maximum that can be contained	The shelf can hold a maximum of three linear feet of items
Use	The number of times an item is employed for its intended purpose; the way that something is employed	An average of 15 children attend each program in the story room; 30 percent of the library's space is used for juvenile services
Condition/Age	The physical characteristics of something; the length of time something has existed	The building is 15 years old; the building is in good condition
Access	A means of entering, approaching, or making use of something	The meeting room has a separate entrance that allows access after hours; the children's room is upstairs, and since there is no elevator, it is hard to reach
Impact of Technology	The infrastructure needed to support computer hardware, networks, etc.	The computers in the teen room have video games that require expanded bandwidth
Spatial Relationships	The ways in which areas or items relate to one another	The circulation desk is near the front door

Although the primary purpose of this discussion is to be sure that all committee members have the same general understanding of the facility resources data elements, it is likely that some of the examples will relate to the committee's project. Just remember that this is *not* the time to develop an exhaustive list of examples and sources of the data that will be needed for the project. The committee has more work to do before that can happen. The six data elements are described in detail in the following sections.

At the end of the meeting, ask one or two committee members to collect all of the completed copies of Workform 5 and merge them into a single document that includes the committee's definition of each data element, plus actual examples and sources from the library. Such a summary will be helpful when committee members begin to collect data in Task 5 in chapter 3.

CAPACITY

Capacity is "the maximum that can be contained in a space or area." The capacity of an item is finite and static. You cannot exceed the capacity of a space or area. You cannot put 10 ounces of water in an 8-ounce cup, nor can you put a 5-foot-wide copy machine in an alcove that is only 4 feet wide.

The most important facility-related capacity measure is *square footage.* Square footage data about existing and needed space, and about the space that various furnishings and equipment require, is critical for space planning. Calculations of square footages for furnishings, equipment, and shelving include the footprint of the item on the floor—how much space it requires—plus the space needed around it for aisles and people movement. Tool Kit A, Calculating Square Footage, provides measurement data and methods of calculation. It will be discussed further in chapter 3.

Capacity data also depend on exactly *what* is being measured. While one measure of meeting room capacity is the square footage of the room, another capacity measure is the maximum number of people allowed in the room at one time by fire codes. Yet another measure of meeting room capacity is how many people seated at tables the meeting room can hold, and that measure will vary based on the kinds of tables used.

Shelving capacity is "a count of the number of items the available shelving can hold." The count may be subdivided by type of material and size of shelving, and may be affected by the regular nonuse of bottom or top shelves.

Seating counts are "data on available chairs and tables within categories." For example, seating counts may be categorized by adult and juvenile or table seating and lounge or reading seating.

Public-access computer workstation capacity might be counted by the total number of workstations available and perhaps by type—Internet only, Internet and informational databases, library catalog access only, thirty-minute access, all-in-one workstations, and so on.

USE

Use is "the number of times an item is employed for its intended purpose or the way that something is employed." Use data measure the utilization of spaces, furniture, equipment, and shelving. While capacity is a static and finite measure, use is a variable measure. The percentage of available table seating that is in use will vary by time of day, by day, and by time of year. Meeting room use will vary not only by the time of day, and so on, but will be based on the library's meeting room policy. *Use* is also the term used to describe data on the relative allocation of spaces in the building. Examples include the percentage of the building or a floor of the building that is allocated for children's services, and the percentage of the public area used for shelving nonfiction materials.

Use data can help you determine the effectiveness of current facility-related resources. You could compare the allocation of shelf space by Dewey class (facility-use data) with the circulation of the nonfiction collection by Dewey class (material-use data). You might find that the materials in the 800 and 900 classifications take up 30 percent of your nonfiction shelving and result in 10 percent of your nonfiction circulation. This would indicate that some of the shelving being used for materials in the 800s and 900s could be reallocated to house materials that are in higher demand. Of course, this also means that someone is going to have to decide which of the items in the 800s and 900s should be removed from the collection, which underscores an issue you will face throughout the facility review process: most library functions are interrelated. It will be hard to reallocate facility spaces without also having to reallocate collection resources and technology resources. In addition, every reallocation of any kind requires some staff resources.

CONDITION AND AGE

Condition is "a description of the physical characteristics of an item." *Age* is "the length of time something has existed." Condition and age are combined as a single data category in this book. Collecting data about age and condition can be particularly challenging. It is often difficult to determine the precise age of a piece of furniture or equipment. Data about the condition of the facility or its contents tend to be subjective in nature. It is important that terms used to describe condition be clearly defined and understood by all data collectors. Your definition of "poor condition" may not be someone else's definition of it, and if you don't reach some agreement about how to define the term before you begin to collect data, the data will be worthless. Figure 9 can provide a starting point for a discussion of the meaning of the descriptive terms that will be used during your process.

> **LEVEL OF EFFORT NOTE**
> **Definitions of Indicators to Measure Age and Condition**
>
> If you decide to make changes or additions to definitions given in the figure, you will want to have figure 9 retyped with the new definitions before it is distributed to all committee members.

The condition of the facility interior—its floors, walls, lighting, ceilings, and built-in fixtures—helps planners determine if repairs will be needed to implement the project under review. The condition of the items housed in the area—including furniture and equipment—guides decisions about whether new items must be purchased to replace existing items. Information on the age of an item can be compared to the average life cycle of the item to determine when an item will probably need to be replaced. The length of time since the last painting of walls is data that is as pertinent as the age of a copier. In both cases, the age data can be used to inform decisions about continued use.

Tool Kit B, Assessing Your Library's Physical Message, discusses library condition in general. Collecting data on building condition is a matter of observing the amount of wear and tear the building components show. You will want to look at both *cosmetic* concerns and *functional* concerns—how it looks and how it works. In some instances you will need an expert opinion as well as staff observation. For example, staff can observe that the heating, ventilation, and air-conditioning system is not working well because it is impossible to maintain a comfortable temperature. It takes an expert to give you information on why that is so.

FIGURE 9

Suggested Indicators to Measure Age and Condition

Rating	Standards
Excellent	Looks like new Hard surfaces not scarred or worn No tears, breaks, or stains on soft surfaces Exact match to others of its type, or match is not important Operates at maximum efficiency
Good	Clean Minimal scars/wear on hard surfaces No tears, breaks, or stains on soft surfaces that can be seen Close match to others of its type, or match is not important Operates as it should
Acceptable	Can be made clean Scars/wear on hard surfaces can be repaired Tears, breaks, or stains on soft surfaces can be repaired Similar in color/design to others of its type, or match is not important Operates as it should but is approaching or has passed its anticipated life span
Unacceptable	Stained/dirty beyond cleaning Hard surfaces scarred/worn beyond affordable repair Soft surfaces torn or stained beyond repair Does not match others of its type at all (if match desired) Does not operate reliably
Inappropriate for its current use	Not designed for the use it now has

ACCESS

Access is "a means of entering, approaching, or making use of something." Access data define how easy it is to use the space, furnishings, equipment, and shelving. The most common use for access data in public libraries has been to determine if the building and equipment meet the requirements of the Americans with Disabilities Act and the Architectural Barriers Act (ABA). Tool Kit C provides detailed information about selected requirements of the *ADA and ABA Accessibility Guidelines for Buildings and Facilities,* the document that is the basis for federal regulations regarding accessibility of buildings and that supports the

Americans with Disabilities Act.[4] You will want to be familiar with that information and local codes as you collect data on access.

Access data can also be used to evaluate the *traffic flow* in the library. Traffic flow data describe the patterns people use to move through an area. You can collect traffic flow data about public movements through the library and about staff workflow and use of space. The public spaces of the library should be convenient for users, and the traffic flow should maximize their ability to take advantage of the library's many resources. Examining the traffic flow of the public in a specific area of the library, and between that area and other areas, will help determine if the current arrangement needs to be changed. Identifying the best traffic flow for an activity is an important part of planning furniture layout. When collecting public traffic flow data, consider the following questions:

> Is access to service desks easy?
>
> Are quiet areas free of walk-through traffic patterns?
>
> Is anything blocking the view of, or access to, important paths of travel such as main hallways, elevators or escalators, and stairwells?
>
> Do bottlenecks occur in public spaces?
>
> Is it easy to reach shelving without navigating around other objects?
>
> Are amenities such as water fountains and restrooms easy to get to?
>
> Do traffic patterns contribute to the marketing of services and materials?

You may also collect traffic and workflow data about staff areas of the library. The most important traffic flow consideration for the staff areas of the library is efficiency. When collecting staff traffic flow data, consider the following questions:

> Can tasks be done as quickly as possible because staff movement within the area is minimized?
>
> Is an unnecessary amount of time spent moving materials between places and tasks?
>
> Can staff members move around without running into or interrupting others?
>
> Are staff spaces restricted from library users?

TECHNOLOGY IMPACT

Technology-impact data in a facilities project define the infrastructure needed to support new technology. *Infrastructure items* include electrical wiring and data cabling, adequate air handling and ventilation, security of space, wired and wireless access, power availability, enough and the right kind of spacing between electrical outlets to handle transformers or other plugs larger than standard, and lighting. Refer to *Technology for Results: Developing Service-Based Plans* for more information about technology infrastructure items.[5]

Technology-impact data are particularly important in library facilities that were built before the Internet became an integral part of library services. Older buildings have had to be retrofitted with the infrastructure needed to support multiple computers and their supporting printers, servers, and networks. This often means that making any changes that affect the placement of technology can be challenging—and expensive. In newer facilities, the technology infrastructure is usually more flexible and easily adapted.

You will be collecting data about technology impact for the physical plant and for furnishings, equipment, and shelving.

SPATIAL RELATIONSHIPS

Spatial relationships are "the ways in which areas or items relate to one another." Data about spatial relationships describe how the locations of service areas relate to one another within the library. The terms used in this book to describe spatial relationships are as follows:

> *Adjacent.* The areas are contiguous.
>
> *Close.* The areas are near one another but not contiguous.
>
> *In line of sight.* Each area can be seen from the other.
>
> *Away from.* The areas are separated by other areas of the library.

For example, in most public libraries the circulation and card registration activities are adjacent to the entrance. Shelving for new books is often close to the entrance. The teen area is often away from the children's area but within line of sight of a service desk.

The spatial relationships among the various spaces of a library and between the components of a single space are easily seen using Venn or other types of bubble diagrams or computerized mind mapping programs. Figure 10 is an example of a Venn diagram of some of the spatial relationships in a library. Library areas and subareas are shown in the diagram as either adjacent (overlapping circles), close to each other (connected with a solid arrow), in line of sight (connected with a dashed arrow), or away from each other (connected with an arrow that has both dashes and dots). Notice that the library entrance has two adjacent areas: the customer service desk and a multipurpose room. The public-access computers need only be close to the customer service desk, however, not adjacent to it. The public-access computers have been placed in line of sight of the front door, as have the new books. These are the two areas that many library users go to first when they come to the library. The children's room and teen area are placed away from each other, and both are away from the quiet reading area at the back of the library.

Step 3.3
Develop a Detailed Timeline

The final part of the first meeting of the project committee will be to develop a more detailed project task list and timeline. The task list and timeline in Workform 3, Preliminary Task List and Timeline, that was completed by library managers during Step 1.3 was, by necessity, general. It probably included the dates by which preliminary and final reports were due, but it couldn't have included the specific dates the committee would meet or the dates by which internal committee processes would be completed. Those decisions have to be made by the committee, and some of them should be made during the first meeting of the committee. This is the time to determine how long regularly scheduled meetings will last, how often and on what dates they will be held, and where they will be held.

This is also the time for the members of the project committee to review figure 2, Tasks and Steps in the *Managing Facilities for Results* Process, and to refine the task list that

FIGURE 10
Venn Diagram of Spatial Relationships in a Library

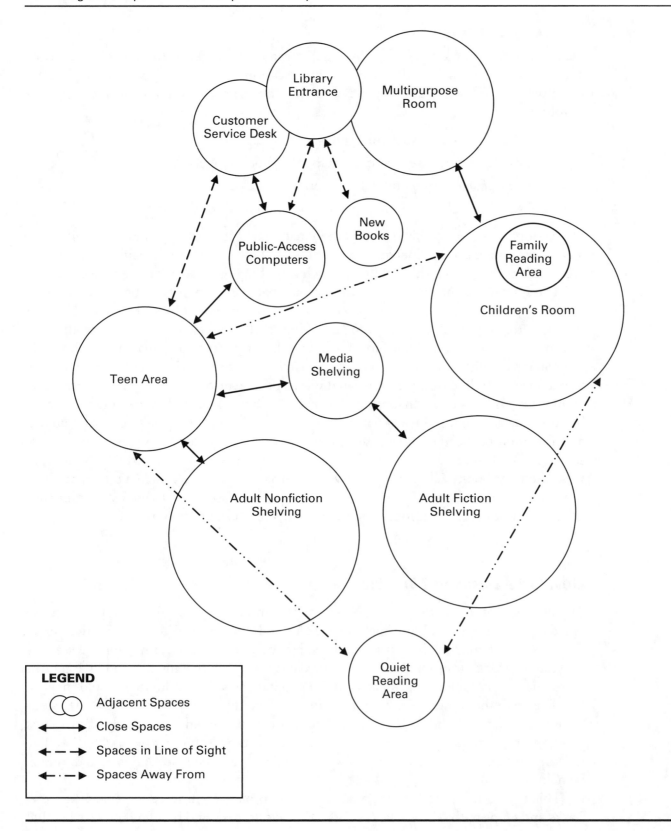

was developed and recorded by managers. If you know the date by which the final report from the committee is due and you have some idea of the tasks and steps that will be required to complete the report, you should have enough information to prepare a version of a detailed task list and timeline. The timeline will be modified as you move through the process and your planning becomes more detailed, but even in a preliminary form it provides an important road map for all committee members. They will know when to schedule time to attend meetings, the kinds of things that will have to be done during the project, and when the project is likely to be completed.

The chair should record the revised and expanded task list and timeline on a new copy of Workform 3, Preliminary Task List and Timeline, and clearly mark it "Revised on [date]." It will be a good idea for the chair to send a copy of the revised workform to the library management team for review and approval. As noted earlier, it will be important to keep everyone informed throughout the process.

TASK 4: ORGANIZE THE DATA COLLECTION PROCESS

Task 1: Define the Project
Task 2: Plan the Project
Task 3: Prepare the Committee
Task 4: Organize the Data Collection Process
    Step 4.1: Define the project in detail
    Step 4.2: Make committee assignments
Task 5: Collect Preliminary Data
Task 6: Identify Gaps and Evaluate Options
Task 7: Present Recommendations
Task 8: Prepare the Final Report and Get Approvals

The first meeting of the committee focused on laying the groundwork for the facility project. Committee members spent a lot of time reviewing and discussing facility-related terms and concepts and refining the project timeline. During the second meeting of the committee, members will begin the actual work of the project. They will start by expanding the description of the project, and then they will decide who will be involved in specific aspects of the data collection processes. A suggested agenda for the meeting can be found in figure 11.

Step 4.1
Define the Project in Detail

Library planners often see a picture in their minds when a new activity is proposed. They see people moving around, using the service, being assisted by staff members, and leaving happy. The surroundings in which all this takes place are often fuzzy, hidden by the rosy glow of imagining an engaged staff and satisfied customers. In this step, you and your colleagues will fill in the rest of the picture and begin to describe the ideal setting for the activity under review.

Deciding Who Should Participate

If your committee is only responsible for defining the facility-related needs for the activity, other staff members or committees may have been assigned the responsibility of defining the staffing, technology, and materials needed to support the activity. In that case, their work needs to be completed before your facility project can begin. Your facility-related recommendations will have to be based on the proposed staff size, technology support, materials formats, collection size, anticipated number of users, and so on.

FIGURE 11
Meeting 2: Sample Agenda

Second Committee Meeting

Purpose:	Discuss the activity or service under review and reach agreement on the types of facility-related resources that will be needed
	Assign committee members to collect data about the facility resources that will be needed and are currently allocated (if any), or that could be reallocated to implement the activity
Who:	All members of the facility project committee and staff who are currently providing the service or activity under review or who are providing some component of the service
Where:	Small conference room
When:	Date, start time, end time (meeting should be scheduled for two hours)
Materials:	The activity as written in the strategic plan, grant, etc. (from orientation packet)
	The goal and/or objectives the activity supports (from orientation packet)
Preparation:	Talk to other staff members about the activity or service under review to get their opinions about the resources that will be required to support it

AGENDA

[Start time]	Complete Workform 6, Project Description—General, and Workform 7, Project Description—Physical Plant, Space, and Spatial Relationships (45–60 minutes)
	Review the task and steps in chapter 3 (20–30 minutes)
	Figure 12, When to Use the Workforms That Support Task 5 (distribute during meeting)
	Make committee assignments for Task 5 (15 minutes)
	Questions (10–15 minutes)
[End time]	Adjourn

If these requirements have not been developed, the facility project committee will start by working with subject experts to develop them. In Step 2.2 of this process you considered whether or not you would need to use outside experts to help plan for the implementation of your project. This is one of the times when experts, whether they are staff who are trained to provide the service or outside experts such as library consultants, or both, may be used. As you will see in the case study later in this chapter, the members of the Anytown Public Library project committee asked the youth services consultant from the state library to participate in their discussions. You may want to do the same if a consultant is available to you from your library system or state library.

Whether or not you decide to use outside experts, it will be important to include the staff members with programmatic expertise who will be responsible for implementing the activity in this part of your discussions. As mentioned previously, at least one of those staff members should be a member of the project committee. You may want to ask others to participate in the committee meetings during which you define the facility-related needs of the activity. Those needs will be defined generally during this second meeting of the committee, and in more detail by the teams that will be appointed to collect data about facility resources required to support the project at the desired level.

This is also a good time to reaffirm roles. Everyone on the project committee should already be aware of the group's responsibilities and authority, but it's only human nature to offer opinions and suggestions about someone else's plans and work. If your project committee was not assigned the responsibility of recommending staffing levels, technology support, or needed collections, you will be working from the recommendations of others. When you meet with those people to get their recommendations, remember that this is still early in terms of planning—nothing is final yet. You will be working with them again to refine the list and then again, perhaps, after initial presentation of plans to decision makers.

Describing Intended Outcomes

This part of the committee's work begins by studying the intended results for the activity or service that the project will support. The initial question to ask is, "What is it that we hope to accomplish by doing this activity or providing this service?" If this activity was identified as a part of a strategic planning process, review the goal and objectives supported by the activity. If this activity or service is part of a grant project, review the goals and objectives of the grant. These goals and objectives should have been included in the orientation packet. If the activity stands alone and you have not identified specific results and measures of progress, you will have to do so now. The *Planning for Results* process suggests three types of measures: number of people to be served; whether or not the service meets the needs of the users; and number of units of library service provided (circulation, programs presented, reference questions answered, etc.).[6]

Objectives or other specific measures of progress provide information about service expectations and potential use. These are two important issues when considering facility resources. Objectives often indicate how many people are projected to use a service or activity in a fiscal year or during the life of the plan. Objectives may also indicate that the circulation of certain materials is expected to increase or that attendance at programs is expected to grow by a certain percentage. This information suggests that you will need to consider shelving and programming spaces in your planning.

Not all objectives provide such specific resource-allocation guidance. An objective that includes participant satisfaction as a measure of success for a series of adult programs doesn't address the way you want programming spaces to look, the level of comfort you want to offer in seating, the size of tables, and many other questions. It does, however, remind you to plan with user reactions in mind.

Defining the Target Audience

Start by identifying the target audience. The age of the intended audience has obvious implications for the allocation of facility resources. An activity intended to serve preschool children would require different furniture, shelving, and decor than an activity designed for adults. The spatial relationships would be different as well. The preschool activity would probably be within or adjacent to the children's area of the library. The adult activity would be away from the children's area.

It is important to be as precise as possible when defining the age of the target audience. In the previous example, the facility requirements for activities serving preschool children and adults were compared. It would have been just as true to say that the facility resources required for preschool children and school-age children are different. Even within the general group *school-age children,* there are significant differences between the facility resources required to support activities for grade school students and those that support activities for high school students.

These distinctions may also apply when working with activities for adults. There are differences in the facility resources required to support activities for adults in their 20s and 30s and the resources needed to serve seniors, particularly seniors in their 70s and older. Older seniors are more likely to need spaces that are flat and easy to traverse, brightly lit, and furnished with firm chairs that are easy to get into and out of.

Determining the Number of Potential Users

After you have identified *who* the activity is intended to serve, you next determine *how many* of those people will be served. This number is critical for planning. It will be used when you are deciding how much furniture and equipment will be needed and how much space will be required to house them. Clearly, you will need far fewer facility resources to support an activity that is expected to serve 5 literacy students per week than you will to support an activity intended to serve 20 to 30 teenagers every day.

Establishing the number of potential customers is not always easy when you are projecting the use of a future service. If there are specific measures of success for the service or activity under review, one of those measures may be the number of customers who are expected to use the service within a one-, two-, or three-year period.

If a specific measure of anticipated use isn't available, you will have to establish such a measure. This can be done in several ways. If you don't currently offer a version of the activity or service, the easiest way to project possible use is to talk to staff from libraries similar to yours that offer the service. If you talk to staff from several libraries, you should be able to establish a realistic target number of potential users. Be sure to ask for hourly and daily average-use figures as well as weekly or monthly totals. You will be developing your recommendations based on estimated use at any given time.

If your library is currently offering a limited version of the activity or service, you can start with the number of current users and then estimate future use. For example, if you currently offer two story programs a month to a total of 375 children each year, you may decide that you want to increase the number of participants by 20 percent, or an additional 75 children per year. Another way to look at the same data is to decide that you want to increase the number of story hours offered from two per month to four per month, increasing the total annual number of participants from 375 to 750.

Once you know approximately how many people will be accessing the service in a year, you can divide that figure by 52 to determine average weekly use. This figure, in turn, can be divided by the number of days per week the library is open to determine average daily use. Finally, you can divide the average daily use by the average number of hours the library is open each day to determine the average hourly use. This will give you one indication of possible use. However, you may need to modify this process to fit the type of activity under review because some activities or services are not used evenly throughout the year or even throughout the library's service hours. The summer reading program only occurs during the summer months, homework help services are normally provided only during the school year, and events celebrating Black History Month occur in February. Part 3 of the Anytown Public Library case study illustrates how the members of the long-range planning committee anticipated the use of the homework center.

CASE STUDY

Anytown Public Library Homework Center

PART 3: Anticipated Use

During the second meeting of the project committee, the members discussed the homework center in greater detail. The chair had invited the youth services consultant from the state library to participate in the meeting because she was familiar with a number of homework centers around the state.

The committee started by looking at the goal and objectives the center would be designed to support:

GOAL: Students in Anytown will have the skills and tools they need to succeed in school.

Objective 1: Each year, at least 4,000 students will use the resources of the homework center.

Objective 2: Each year, library staff and volunteers will answer at least 6,000 homework-related reference questions.

Objective 3: By 2XXX, the number of hits on the library's homework help web page will increase by 20 percent.

Objective 4: Each year, at least 200 students will attend programs designed to improve their study skills, and 80 percent of those students will say the programs were "effective" or "very effective."

The members of the committee used the information in the objectives to identify the target audience and number of potential users. They started by identifying the target audience. Objective 1 states that 4,000 *students* will use the resources of the homework center. The committee refined this to focus on *students in junior and senior high school.* They discussed the special characteristics of that audience and decided that the most important thing to keep in mind was that students normally want to work in small groups or teams when doing their homework.

Next the committee projected the average daily use of the homework center. They started by agreeing on several assumptions:

The homework center is going to get little or no use during the summer.

The homework help center is probably not going to be used much on Friday, nor is it likely to be used on Saturday.

The library is open on Sunday from 1:00 to 4:00, and the center will be used then.

Based on those assumptions, they excluded the 10 weeks of summer vacation from their calculations.

52 – 10 = 42 weeks

4,000 users ÷ 42 weeks = about 95 students weekly

To project average daily use, they divided the weekly average number of students by 5 days (Monday–Thursday and Sunday).

95 students ÷ 5 days = 19 students per day

These students will not be using the homework center during all of the hours the library is open—they are in school during some of those hours. Most of the use will come in the two to three hours after school and in the early evening, and many of the students will stay in the library longer than an hour. Because they anticipate concentrated usage in the time period directly after school, the committee decided there should be seating for nineteen students at any one time. They recorded their answers on Workform 6. You can see their answers below.

WORKFORM 6   **Project Description—General**

Project Name: Homework Center

A. Age (grade level) of the people to be served: Students in junior and senior high school

B. Special conditions to be considered about the people to be served: Prefer to work in small groups or teams

C. Number of people to be served: Annual projection = 4,000; Daily estimate = 19; Seating: 19

Asking the Right Questions

When you have identified the target audience and the approximate number of people who are expected to use the activity, you are ready to discuss the facility resources that will be required to support the activity. You will be building on the project definition from Workform 2, Project Priorities, but you now have more information with which to work. This part of the process will involve answering the following series of questions.

Will new or reassigned staff be needed? You will need to know the number of anticipated new staff that will be assigned to the activity to be sure that each staff member will have the furniture and equipment needed and that sufficient space is available to house that furniture and equipment. It will be helpful to know the job classification of each new employee and to have a general idea of each person's duties. That will make it easier for you to estimate the required facility resources.

Will furnishings be required to support the activity? Review the activity and its intended results again and then refer again to figure 7, Facility Resources—Common Elements, earlier in this chapter. Describe the furniture that will be needed and estimate the number of items of furniture that will be required to serve the expected number of users. Remember, the estimate is just that—an estimate. These initial figures will be refined in Task 5: Collect Preliminary Data.

Will equipment be required to support the activity? Repeat the process you used to answer the preceding question about furnishings, focusing instead on specific equipment that will be needed to provide the activity.

Will materials be added to the collection? If the intended outcomes for the activity include an increase in circulation, additional materials will probably be purchased. It would be helpful to know the format, age level, and classification of the materials and approximately how much money has been allocated in the materials budget to purchase the materials. You will also want to know if the materials allocation is a one-time or a recurring allotment.

Will materials be removed from the collection? Some activities include an implicit or explicit assumption that part of the library collection will be weeded to remove outdated or damaged materials. If that is the case, it would be helpful to have an estimate of approximately what proportion of the collection is expected to be discarded.

Will public access to technology be required? Many new or enhanced services offered by libraries require public access to technology. If that is the case with the activity under review, briefly describe what is needed. Don't worry about the infrastructure requirements right now. You will address those in Task 5: Collect Preliminary Data.

Will staff access to technology be required? Repeat the process you used to answer the preceding question about public access to technology, focusing instead on staff access to technology.

Remember, other individuals or committees may already have answered some of these questions. If that is the case, review their recommendations and use them as the basis for your facility-related planning. Workform 6, Project Description—General, provides a form for recording answers to the previous list of questions. You can see how the Anytown Public Library project committee finished completing Workform 6 in part 4 of the case study.

CASE STUDY

Anytown Public Library Homework Center

PART 4: Project Description

After the members of the committee had completed items A–C on Workform 6, they used the information in the objectives to answer questions 1–7 on it. You can see their complete answers below. Note that although the answer to question 1 was No, it was explained in column F.

WORKFORM 6 **Project Description—General**

Project Name: Homework Center

A. Age (grade level) of the people to be served: Students in junior and senior high school

B. Special conditions to be considered about the people to be served: Prefer to work in small groups or teams

C. Number of people to be served: Annual projection = 4,000; Daily estimate = 19; Seating = 19

(Cont.)

	D. Yes	E. No	F. If Yes, Describe Here
1. Will new or reassigned staff be needed?		X	The assumption is that volunteers will staff the homework center under the direction of a current staff member. The hope is to have 10–15 regular volunteers.
2. Will furnishings be required to support the activity?	X		Study tables and chairs, furniture for added computers and printers, casual seating. This furniture should be teen-friendly.
3. Will equipment be required to support the activity?	X		New photocopier.
4. Will materials be added to the collections?	X		$8,000 added to the adult nonfiction budget for new materials for the homework center; this is a recurring increase, and the collection is expected to grow.
5. Will materials be deleted from the collections?		X	
6. Will public access to technology be required?	X		Four new public-access computer terminals and one new networked color printer will be added. Additional wiring and cabling may be needed. The space should support wireless access to the Internet.
7. Will staff access to technology be required?	X		There will be two new staff terminals that will share the public-access networked printer.

As you can see by the Anytown committee's answers, right now the answers to the questions on Workform 6 can be fairly general. For example, you know that you will need study tables and chairs, but you don't know exactly how many. You intend to add computers, but you don't have any real idea of the technology infrastructure required; you just assume that some infrastructure changes will be needed. The purpose of considering these questions now is to ensure that all of the members start the data collection process in chapter 3 with a common understanding of the scope of the project.

Considering Physical Plant and Space Needs

The last thing you need to do before you are ready to present your project description to the administrative team for approval is to complete an initial assessment of the physical plant and space required to support the activity. There are three broad issues to consider. First, should the activity be presented in a walled space? Second, should the activity be presented in a single-purpose space, or can it be presented in a multipurpose space? Finally, are there spatial relationships that need to be considered when determining where to house the activity? Each of these issues is discussed in more detail as follows.

Walled space. Some activities need to be presented in an area that allows for restricted access or sound control. For example, a meeting room that is used when the library is closed must be in a separate walled area with a door that can be locked to restrict access to the library during the hours it is closed. A literacy center that houses three computers loaded with specialized software might be placed in a small room to provide privacy for the students and restrict the number of students who try to use the computers at one time. Some libraries have created quiet rooms for people who want to read with no distractions from the noisier open spaces in the library.

Single-purpose space. Some spaces are fully utilized for a specific purpose the entire time the library is open. For instance, the children's area of the library is used for children's services all day. It is an example of one type of single-purpose space. However, that single purpose is broad—to serve children. An activity that focused on increasing the number of children's programs could probably be supported by facility resources in the current children's area of the library. Other activities require such specialized furniture, equipment, or shelving or such a unique layout that an area can only be used for that specific activity. Think about the circulation area in your library. If your library is like most libraries, the area holds a specially designed circulation desk that can only be used for circulation functions. This area is a single-purpose area. Other examples of single-purpose areas include the space housing preschool book bins, a teen center with specialized furniture and decor, and a space that houses periodical shelving.

Multipurpose space. Some activities can share an existing space or be offered alongside other activities or services. For example, a series of computer training programs for seniors could be offered in the library's computer lab on weekday mornings. The same lab could be made available to students doing homework on weekday afternoons. Another example would be library meeting rooms that often serve as community art galleries.

Spatial relationships. As noted earlier in this chapter, some activities will need to be in line of sight of, adjacent to, close to, or away from other parts of the library. For example, the Anytown Public Library's homework center will need to be close to the adult nonfiction collection, which will provide many of the resources needed for the students doing their homework.

Workform 7, Project Description—Physical Plant, Space, and Spatial Relationships, provides a form for recording your preliminary recommendations. You can see how the Anytown Public Library project committee completed Workform 7 in part 5 of the case study.

CASE STUDY

Anytown Public Library Homework Center

PART 5: Physical Plant, Space Projections, and Spatial Relationships

When the members of the committee had completed Workform 6, they moved on to Workform 7. They used their answers to the questions on Workform 6 and their understanding of the intended purpose of the homework center to complete the workform.

Project Description—Physical Plant, Space, and Spatial Relationships

Project Name: Homework Center

	A. Yes	B. No	C. Why
D. Walled Space			
1. Do you need to restrict access to the space?		X	We will want to make sure the area is available for use by students from 3:30 to closing during the school year. Access does not need to be restricted at other times.
2. Do you need to control how many people can be in the space at the same time?		X	Unlikely.
3. Does the space need to be soundproof, either to keep sound in or to keep sound out?	X		The students will be working together and making noise. Two or three small, walled study rooms designed for group use would help sound control. If the activity is presented in an open space, spatial relationships are going to be very important.
4. Is the space needed when the library is not open?		X	The space will be used primarily from 3:30 to closing during the school year.
5. Will the activity need to be presented in a walled space?	X	X	Although the entire activity does not have to be presented in a walled space, the staff who will be providing the activity strongly recommend that the space include two or three small, walled study rooms.
E. Single-Purpose or Multipurpose Space			
1. Will the furniture, equipment, or shelving needed to support the activity make it hard to use the space for other purposes?	X	X	This depends on how teen-friendly we want to make the space. If the center is housed in a single-purpose space, the furniture could be very teen-friendly. If the center is in a multipurpose space of the library, the furniture could be more traditional. The staff who will be providing the activity want the furniture to be teen-friendly.
2. Is the anticipated layout of the space so specialized that it will be hard to use the space for other purposes?		X	The space will be designed to support group work and shared use of resources. However, it will also support individual use of the resources.
3. Will the activity be available during the entire time the library is open?		X	The space will be used primarily from 3:30 to closing during the school year.
4. Will the activity need to be presented in a single-purpose space?	X	X	It is not absolutely necessary to have the center in a single-purpose space, but staff hope that the space's decor can be teen-friendly.
F. Spatial Relationships			
1. Does the activity need to be in the line of sight of a service desk?	X		The center will need careful supervision.
2. Does the activity need to be presented in space that is adjacent to other parts of the library?	X		The center needs to be adjacent to the adult reference collection.
3. Does the activity need to be presented in space that is close to other parts of the library?		X	
4. Does the activity need to be presented in space that is away from other parts of the library?	X		The center needs to be away from the children's area and the quiet areas of the library.

Notice that the committee members answered questions D5, E1, and E4 both *Yes* and *No*. They explained their answers in column C. These answers leave these questions open for further discussion as the process moves forward, which is perfectly appropriate. The people collecting data in the next chapter will explore the alternatives and provide the committee with more information before a final recommendation is made.

Obtaining Administrative Approval

Now that the committee has defined the project more completely, the chair will want to meet with the members of the library management team to be sure that the committee's assumptions are valid. If the members of the management team have questions or concerns, the project committee may need to meet again to resolve those issues. Before moving on to the tasks in chapter 3, everyone involved in the project should have read and endorsed the completed Workforms 6 and 7.

Step 4.2
Make Committee Assignments

Once the administrative team has endorsed the completed Workforms 6 and 7, it is time to begin the data collection process. Remember, this process is intended to answer the four questions in the gap analysis process:

1. What facility resources will be required to support the activity at the desired levels?
2. What facility resources do we have that are currently allocated to support the activity?
3. What is the gap between the two?
4. How can we fill that gap (or, more rarely, reallocate the surplus)?

In the next chapter you will begin by answering questions 1 and 2 in the list above. Figure 12, When to Use the Workforms That Support Task 5 (in chapter 3), provides an overview of the types of data that will be collected as you answer those questions. When you review the workforms listed in figure 12, you will notice that there are a pair of workforms addressing each of the resources and their data elements being considered. One of the workforms in each pair will be used to collect data about the resources *needed* to support the activity at the desired level, and the companion workform will be used to collect data about the *current* resources, if any, that are being used to support the activity. Each pair of workforms is formatted in a similar way and includes appropriate data elements. This will make the data on the paired workforms easy to compare when the committee members are answering question 3 to identify the gap between the resources that are needed and the resources that are currently allocated.

While there are a variety of ways to organize the data collection for the next task, the most logical way is to assign teams of committee members to collect data about each of the resources under review. The workforms address issues as varied as furniture and access, and it is probable that each member of the committee is more interested in some of the data elements to be collected than others. When possible, it is a good idea to let committee members volunteer for the assignments they prefer. For example, if you are completing all the workforms (use figure 12 in chapter 3), you might assign two committee members to collect data about both the furniture and equipment that will be needed and the furniture and equipment that are currently allocated to support the activity, if any (Workforms 8 and 9). Another team might look at needed and current shelving (Workforms 10 and 11). A third team could collect data pertaining to the physical plant, space, and technology support (Workforms 12 and 13), and another team could collect the data on needed and current access, spatial relationships, and signage (Workforms 14 and 15). You won't assign a team to complete Workform 16, which deals with square footage; that workform aggregates data from the other workforms and must be completed last.

If you organize the data collection in this manner, each team of data collectors will become familiar with the type of resources it is examining. That expertise will be valuable in Task 6, when the members of the committee are determining the gap between what is needed and what is currently allocated to support the activity. It will be helpful to review the workforms and accompanying instructions with the members of the whole project committee before making assignments, so that everyone has a general understanding of the responsibilities of each team.

Key Points to Remember

Know what you are trying to accomplish before trying to reallocate any resources effectively. Objectives from your strategic plan or grant project plans can provide this information.

Review all of the materials in the orientation packet during the first committee meeting to be sure that everyone has the same understanding of the committee's responsibilities, authority, and timeline.

Think carefully about issues or challenges that may arise during the process, and develop plans to address problems before they occur.

Spend the time necessary to be sure that everyone involved in the project understands the four facility resources under review and the six facility-related data elements.

Coordinate the work of the project committee with other committees or people working on related projects.

Use the gap analysis process as the framework for collecting data.

Assign teams of committee members to collect data about each of the resources under review.

Notes

1. Ethel Himmel and William James Wilson, *Planning for Results: A Public Library Transformation Process: The How-to Manual* (Chicago: American Library Association, 1998), 81–83.
2. *Libris DESIGN Glossary,* http://www.librisdesign.org/help/glossary.html.
3. Sandra Nelson, Ellen Altman, and Diane Mayo, *Managing for Results: Effective Resource Allocation for Public Libraries* (Chicago: American Library Association, 2000).
4. U.S. Access Board, *ADA and ABA Accessibility Guidelines for Buildings and Facilities* (*Federal Register,* July 23, 2004). Available at http://www.access-board.gov.
5. Diane Mayo, *Technology for Results: Developing Service-Based Plans* (Chicago: American Library Association, 2005).
6. Sandra Nelson, *The New Planning for Results: A Streamlined Approach* (Chicago: American Library Association, 2001), 84.

Chapter 3

Resources Required and Allocated to Support the Activity

MILESTONES

By the time you finish this chapter you will know how to

- differentiate between the resources that you need and the resources that you want to support the activity
- use the measures of success for an activity or service as the basis for identifying needed facility resources
- determine the furniture, equipment, and shelving that will be needed to support the activity
- identify the physical plant and technology that will be needed to support the activity
- identify access, spatial relationship, and signage issues to be addressed
- calculate the approximate square footage that will be required to support the activity at the desired levels
- identify the facility resources that are currently allocated to support the activity, if any
- determine whether the activity will be offered in multipurpose, single-purpose, or walled space

In this chapter you will collect the data needed to fully answer the first two questions in the gap analysis process:

What facility resources will be required to support the activity at the desired levels?

What facility resources do we have that are currently allocated to support the activity?

The key part of the first question is the last phrase, "at the desired levels." As was stated earlier, you have to know what you are trying to accomplish and how you will track your progress *before* you can allocate any resources effectively.

As you and your colleagues gather and review data to further define the facility-related resources required to provide the service or activity "at the desired levels," there will be a lot of discussion about exactly what the term *desired* means. For example, a staff member may want a new preschoolers' story area to be separated from the rest of the children's area with walls so the noise of these lively patrons will not disturb others. That's an understandable *want* that may be thwarted by a number of considerations: perhaps there isn't enough space in the existing children's room to carve out a story room large enough to hold the intended audience, or maybe other staff members do not want the children's area chopped up into separate rooms. The best way to separate the required from the desired is to ask whether or not it is possible to implement the activity without the resource in question. Are the walls really essential to provide the activity, or are they just something that would be nice to have?

As another example, consider the new activity of providing information assistance with reference librarians circulating throughout the library rather than remaining stationary behind a service desk. Some who will be doing this work may suggest that a staff station near the adult computer area is needed because they expect to use it heavily and the station will be a place to keep paper, pens, and so on. However, the real motivation for the suggestion may be fear of change. The station would offer them a sense of security during the transition from traditional reference work to this different approach. Again, the real question is whether or not the resource is essential to offering the service. Is it a need or a want? Who gets to decide? These questions can only be answered through group discussion, and the answers may vary from library to library—and from person to person.

This is often the point at which resource allocation and reallocation projects break down. Committee members with divergent points of view are unable to reach consensus on the most basic questions of need and want, and the project grinds to a halt. This does not have to happen. The purpose of this part of the process is not to reach consensus on need versus want, nor is this the time to think too much about feasibility. Rather, the members of the committee should be exploring all of the ways that facility-related resources might be used to support the activity under review. Members should be encouraged to be as creative and imaginative as possible. The committee may end up with several different scenarios. There will be more than enough time to consider cost, available space, and other competing needs later in the process. Balancing these considerations to identify the most effective allocation of facility-related resources will be easier if the committee has several options from which to select.

Collecting and Recording Data

Task 5 of *Managing Facilities for Results* is the heart of the process, and it is data-intensive. There are a total of nine workforms associated with this step, and at first glance they may seem quite daunting. However, now more than ever, the members of the committee must remember to collect only the data that are needed to make decisions about the project.

In *Staffing for Results: A Guide to Working Smarter,* authors Diane Mayo and Jeanne Goodrich provided project planners with this excellent advice:

The first rule of data collection is to collect only that data you plan to use for a specific end. Collecting data can be time-consuming and expensive. If you cannot or will not make changes based on the information you develop, don't spend time and money developing it. The corollary to this is to collect only data you will use soon. Conditions in the library are changing too rapidly to act on old data.[1]

Mayo and Goodrich were referring to data about staffing levels, but the rules apply to collecting facility data as well. This is a process that can easily become complicated and difficult to manage, particularly if the project committee includes people who have never met a statistic they didn't like. The library field attracts people who are detail-oriented and truly enjoy any kind of fact-finding process. These people make wonderful reference librarians, but their enthusiasm for data can easily overwhelm the project committee with irrelevant information.

The members of the committee defined the data that will need to be collected when they completed Workform 6, Project Description—General, and Workform 7, Project Description—Physical Plant, Space, and Spatial Relationships. The information on these two workforms should guide the data-collection processes in Task 5 when you are deciding what is needed to support the activity under review and describing what you have that is currently supporting the activity. See figure 12 to help you determine whether you will use all the workforms for the tasks in this chapter. Also remember that you can collect additional data if you need it, but you can never regain the time you wasted collecting data that you didn't need.

TASK 5: COLLECT PRELIMINARY DATA

Task 1: Define the Project
Task 2: Plan the Project
Task 3: Prepare the Committee
Task 4: Organize the Data Collection Process
Task 5: Collect Preliminary Data
    Step 5.1: Identify the furniture and equipment needs and current allocations
    Step 5.2: Identify the shelving needs and current allocations
    Step 5.3: Describe the physical plant and technology support needs and current conditions
    Step 5.4: Describe access, spatial relationships, and signage needs and current conditions
    Step 5.5: Make preliminary recommendations for the amount and type of space
Task 6: Identify Gaps and Evaluate Options
Task 7: Present Recommendations
Task 8: Prepare the Final Report and Get Approvals

All of the committee members should be familiar with the types of facility resources that might be used to support an activity (see figure 7 in chapter 2) and the data elements that can be collected about each of them from the orientation meetings that were held earlier (see figure 8 in chapter 2). In Step 4.2, it was recommended that a team of committee members be assigned to complete each applicable pair of workforms in Task 5. When those assignments have been made, it is time to begin the data collection process. The information in the five steps in this task will guide that process.

Step 5.1
Identify the Furniture and Equipment Needs and Current Allocations

During this step, you will first collect data about the furniture and equipment that will be needed to support the activity at the desired levels, and then collect data about the furniture and equipment that are currently allocated to support the activity, if any. Figure 7, Facility Resources—

FIGURE 12
When to Use the Workforms That Support Task 5

Workform	When to Use	When Not to Use
Workform 8: Need—Furniture and Equipment (Step 5.1)	Complete this workform if the activity will require furniture or equipment (see Workform 6, Project Description—General).	If the activity will not require furniture or equipment, you will not complete this workform.
Workform 9: Have—Furniture and Equipment (Step 5.1)	Complete this workform if you currently provide this activity and there is furniture or equipment that has been allocated to support the activity.	If the activity is not currently offered in your library, you will not complete this workform.
Workform 10: Need—Shelving (Step 5.2)	Complete this workform if the activity will require that additional items be added to the collection (see Workform 6, Project Description—General).	If the activity does not have a materials component, do not complete this workform.
Workform 11: Have—Shelving (Step 5.2)	Complete this workform if the library currently provides this activity and there are materials that support the activity.	If the library owns no materials that support this activity, you will not complete this workform.
Workform 12: Need—Physical Plant and Technology Support (Step 5.3.)	Everyone will complete this workform.	
Workform 13: Have—Physical Plant and Technology Support (Step 5.3)	Complete this workform if the library currently provides this activity.	If the library does not currently provide this activity, you will not complete this workform.
Workform 14: Need—Access, Spatial Relationships, and Signage (Step 5.4)	Everyone will complete this workform.	
Workform 15: Have—Access, Spatial Relationships, and Signage (Step 5.4)	Complete this workform if the library currently provides this activity.	If the library does not currently provide this activity, you will not complete this workform.
Workform 16: Square Footage—Needed and Current (Step 5.5)	Everyone will complete this workform.	

Common Elements (in chapter 2), includes a partial list of furniture and equipment that can serve as the starting point for your discussion. You might want to make photocopies of this figure for the team members involved in this process.

This step will require creative thinking. The library world is changing rapidly, and the furniture and equipment needed to support library services are changing just as rapidly. Spend some time talking to other librarians and to vendor representatives to get ideas about future products. Try to identify a limited number of furniture and equipment items that can serve multiple functions, rather than a large number of single-purpose items. For example, if you decide you will need an AV cart for a data projector, select a cart that is large enough to hold any of the pieces of audiovisual equipment the library currently owns or might own in the future.

Identifying Needed Furniture and Equipment

Workform 6, Project Description—General, includes a brief listing of the types of furniture and equipment (if any) that will be required to support the activity. You will build upon that list to develop a comprehensive list of the furniture and equipment that will be needed, and will record your recommendations on Workform 8, Need—Furniture and Equipment.

Look first at any furniture that the public will need to use the activity (chairs, tables, workstations, etc.). Will the furniture need to be sized for children? Will it need to be attractive to teens? Will the furniture be impacted by ADA accessibility requirements? (See Tool Kit C, Americans with Disabilities Act Requirements.) List and briefly describe the furniture that will be required in the "Furniture for Public Use" section of Workform 8, Need—Furniture and Equipment. Next list and briefly describe the types of furniture that the staff will need in order to provide the activity in the "Furniture for Staff Use" section of the workform. Refer back to Workform 6, Project Description—General, for information on any new or reassigned staff who may be working with the activity. Will the staff members need desks and chairs in a public space in the library? Will they need work tables in a staff section of the library?

When you have completed listing and briefly describing all of the furniture that will be needed, go on to do the same thing for the equipment that will be needed by both the public and the staff. You will be considering both freestanding equipment and equipment that doesn't occupy floor space. The two kinds of equipment that don't occupy floor space include equipment that is installed in or on the walls, such as a sound system or a wall-mounted projection screen, and equipment that sits on furniture that occupies floor space, such as a computer terminal, which sits on a computer workstation. If you list equipment that sits on furniture, be sure that the furniture is listed in the earlier part of the workform.

FURNITURE AND EQUIPMENT CAPACITY

In chapter 2, capacity was defined as "the maximum amount that can be contained in a space or area." To determine the capacity of the furniture that will be required by the public, start by referring back to Workform 6, Project Description—General, to review the anticipated use of the activity or service. You must plan for enough furniture to serve the anticipated number of users at any given time. The challenge for the committee members will be to decide how many of each of the types of furniture items are needed.

Obviously, if you expect to have twenty users at a time, you will need the furniture capacity to serve twenty users. However, the types of furniture required to meet the needs of those twenty users will vary depending on the project. For example, if you are working on a project to redesign the library's entrance to better merchandise new books and media, you won't need tables and chairs for twenty people because most of the users will be standing and browsing through the materials. At most, you may decide you need to provide seating capacity for one or two people who want to read a little of a book before making a decision. On the other hand, if the project is a homework center, like the one being designed in Anytown, you will need seats for all nineteen anticipated users because students rarely stand to study. Although some of the seats will be at study tables, some may be at computer workstations, and some may be in more comfortable armchairs, the total number of seats must at least equal the anticipated capacity of the project. The Anytown committee members may decide that they want to have the capacity to seat all nineteen anticipated users at study tables at the same time. They would still have to provide seating for any computer workstations and study rooms that will be part of the project, but this would mean that they would be providing more seating than required to simply meet capacity. (There is more discussion of determining the number of items needed in the next section.)

The process used to determine the furniture capacity needed for staff use is the same as that used to determine the capacity of furniture needed for the public. Look at the "Furniture for Staff Use" that you identified on Workform 8 and then consider how the staff will use that furniture. You may believe it is important that each staff member have a chair, but you probably won't think it is essential to provide each staff member with the capacity to file enough documents to fill a three-drawer vertical file.

When you consider the capacity of the equipment you listed on Workform 8, you may be looking at more than the total number of anticipated users. You might also be concerned with the capacity of the equipment to produce whatever it produces, as in the number of pages per minute produced by a photocopier. You might also need to consider the issue of competing capacities. Many library staff members would say that library users would be delighted if the library provided one computer for each anticipated user during all of the hours the library is open. However, few libraries have the capacity in their budget or the square footage to do that. Therefore, the discussion of the capacity for some types of equipment will have to include the maximum acceptable wait time. As you can see, determining capacity, particularly for equipment, is not always straightforward. The staff in two different libraries might be working on very similar facility projects yet reach two different conclusions about the capacity needed for some furniture or equipment, depending on funding or space availability. Record your recommendations about the capacity of the furniture and equipment that will be required to support the activity in column A of Workform 8.

NUMBER OF ITEMS NEEDED

After you have determined the capacity for each type of furniture item that the public and the staff will need (for example, workstations, copiers, two-seat tables, four-seat tables), you will be ready to decide how many of each item will be required. On one level, this is often easy. If you decided that you need seating for twenty, you will need to allocate at least twenty chairs. However, knowing that you need twenty chairs does not tell you what kind of chairs you need or how many of each type of chair that you have identified is appropriate. Base your projection of the needed number of items of a particular type on the anticipated use of that item.

You will also want to consider the configuration and use patterns for each item. In the example from the Anytown Public Library in the preceding chapter, committee members decided that they wanted to have the capacity to seat all nineteen anticipated users at study tables at the same time. However, if they plan to include workstations in the project, they will have to provide additional chairs. The number of additional chairs will be determined by the configuration of the workstations—how many people can sit at one workstation at the same time. Other examples include study carrels, which can be configured to allow groups of people to work together. Tables can seat anywhere from one to eight people or more. Service desks may be set up to assist one person at a time or two or three or more.

Another factor to consider when determining the number of items needed is how the items are used. Use patterns vary widely for different types of furniture and equipment. Observation of table seating areas in many public libraries tells us that people prefer to sit at a table where no one else is sitting. Does the use in your library of this item of furniture reflect that observation? If so, should you recommend purchasing more two-person tables than four-person tables? The same observation applies to couches—people don't seem to want to sit on a couch with a stranger, so maybe you should consider three lounge chairs instead of a single couch. Record your recommendations for each item in column B of Workform 8, Need—Furniture and Equipment.

SQUARE FOOTAGE PER ITEM

The square footage of an item of furniture or equipment is calculated by determining the amount of space that item occupies plus the space needed for movement around the item. You can't just use the actual square footage of the item (its footprint) because virtually every item requires additional space to be usable. For example, an adult lounge chair that is 20×20 inches takes up a little less than 3 square feet of space (20×20 inches = 400 inches $\div$ 144 = 2.75 square feet). However, when you add in the space required to sit in and move around the chair, the total square footage required for the chair is increased to around 5 square feet. A photocopier that is 20×26 inches takes up 3.6 square feet, but when you add the space required to use the machine and walk around it, the total square footage needed increases to perhaps 6 square feet.

Tool Kit A, Calculating Square Footage, lists types of furniture and equipment commonly found in libraries and the average square footage each item occupies, including circulation space around it. Use the information in Tool Kit A to estimate the square footage of each of the items of furniture and equipment listed on Workform 8. Although the actual square footage needed for each type of item cannot be precisely identified at this point in your work because you have not selected the specific items and don't know exactly how big they will be, you can be sure that the estimates you use from Tool Kit A will be relatively close to the actual requirements for the items. Record the square footage of individual items in column C of Workform 8, Need—Furniture and Equipment.

TOTAL SQUARE FOOTAGE FOR FURNITURE AND EQUIPMENT NEEDED

When you have identified the number of items of a type of furniture or equipment and the average square footage required for each piece of that type of furniture, you will be ready to complete the last column on Workform 8. To determine the total square footage for all the items of a type of furniture or equipment, simply multiply the number of items (recorded in column B) by the square footage for each (column C). For example, if you planned to buy three of the adult lounge chairs in the earlier example, you would multiply 3 (the number of chairs) times 5 (the average square footage for each) and determine that the 3 chairs will require 15 square feet. Record your computations in column D of Workform 8.

The square footage for each item of furniture and equipment is just part of the overall square footage needed, of course, so all the item square footage calculations will be added together to establish a grand total of square footage needed for all furniture and equipment. That figure will later be used in determining the overall square footage needed for the activity.

Describing the Furniture and Equipment Currently Allocated to Support the Activity

If the activity is not currently being offered in your library, you will skip this part of the process. However, if the activity is currently being offered *in some form* in the library, there may be furniture or equipment that has been allocated to support the activity. Start by talking to the staff who provide the activity and visiting the space in which the activity is being provided. Working with the staff, list all of the furniture and equipment used by the public and by the staff on Workform 9, Have—Furniture and Equipment. Briefly describe the furniture and equipment and then indicate the capacity and number of each item. You should also record the condition of each individual item listed on the workform. For example, if your project is to identify the facility resources needed to provide a quiet reading area, you would include any chairs or tables that are currently being used by people who read magazines or newspapers in the library. You might find that there are currently three lounge chairs, two side tables, and a wooden table with four wooden chairs being used for this purpose, and that they are all in fair condition. Use the information in Tool Kit A, Calculating Square Footage, to estimate the square footage of each of the items, and then calculate the total square footage for all of the items of each type by multiplying the square footage per item by the number of items.

The brief description in the preceding example identifies the specific items that are currently being used to support the activity, but it provides no information about the condition of those items, nor does it indicate whether these items are used solely for reading within the library. As you may remember, during the second meeting of the project committee, members reviewed and discussed figure 9, Suggested Indicators to Measure Age and Condition, and were given an opportunity to modify the indicators in the figure if they thought modifications were needed. You will use either figure 9 or the modified version of the figure to assess the condition of each of the items listed on Workform 9. It is very important that everyone use the same criteria to assess the condition of the items.

Finally, you will indicate if each of the items you have listed on Workform 9 is used *solely* to support the activity under review or if the item is used for other purposes as well.

This information will be needed when committee members compare what is currently available with what is needed. (See chapter 4.)

Step 5.2
Identify the Shelving Needs and Current Allocations

During this step you will be looking at the capacity of, and square footage required for, various types of library shelving. Tool Kit A, Calculating Square Footage, contains data from a variety of sources that can be used as the basis for your calculations. The only reason *not* to use the data in Tool Kit A is if your library has custom-made shelving units that are significantly different in size than standard shelving units. All of the members of the team working on gathering data about needed and current shelving should have copies of Tool Kit A.

Identifying Shelving Needed

In some instances, achieving one or more of the desired outcomes of an activity will require that materials be added to an existing collection, that new collections of materials be developed, or that materials be weeded from a current collection. If your project will include shelving for materials, the members of the project committee will have provided a brief description of the materials to be added or deleted on Workform 6, Project Description—General. The description should have included the type and format of the materials, the approximate number of items to be added or deleted or the amount of money allocated for the new materials, and whether the allocation is for a one-time purchase of materials for a collection that is not expected to grow substantively larger or is for recurring funds intended to increase the size of the collection annually.

Now you will need to estimate how much shelving will be needed to house the additional materials and how much floor space that shelving will occupy. Determining the number of items to be shelved is the key to making calculations about how much shelving space is needed. You will also need to identify the specific types of shelving that will be used. You will use Workform 10, Need—Shelving, to record your recommendations.

This is an area of data collection that would benefit from the use of a little common sense. If you determine that 100 new items will be added to the collection during the first year of the activity and that there are no plans to add a significant number of new items thereafter, you will have a very different data-collection environment than if you determine that 1,000 new items will be added to the collection during the first year of the activity and the intent is to continue adding items annually until the collection reaches 5,000 items. In the first instance, you will begin by collecting the minimal data needed to determine if the new items can be housed in existing shelving. In the second instance, you already know that the existing shelving is likely to be inadequate.

When you review Workform 10, you will see that it has two parts. Use "Part I: Minimal Collection" if you will be adding a relatively small number of items to the collection. Use "Part II: Significant Collection" if a large number of materials will be purchased to support the activity or if the collection is expected to grow over a period of time. Clearly, the number of items that would be considered *relatively small* or *large* will vary depending on the size of the library and the size of the current collection. This is just one of many judgment calls the members of the project committee will have to make as they work through this process.

NUMBER OF NEW ITEMS TO BE SHELVED

Start by determining approximately how many new items will be purchased to support the activity. This can be easily calculated by dividing the amount of money allocated for new materials for the activity by the average cost of the type of material being purchased. You won't have to provide shelving for every new item you add to the collection (unless the items are noncirculating); you will only need to provide shelving for the portion of those items that are not checked out at any one time. For example, in many public libraries a larger percentage of the fiction collection is checked out at any one time than is checked out from the nonfiction collection. If that is the case in your library and you are adding nonfiction items for the new activity, those items will require more new shelving space than if they were fiction. You should be able to get information about the average circulation of various parts of the library's collection from the people who manage the library's automated circulation system. Use this data to determine approximately what proportion of the new items that you intend to purchase will be on the shelf at any one time. For example, if you will be adding 1,000 adult fiction books to the collection and, on average, 20 percent of the adult fiction collection is checked out, then you can assume that you will need shelving for approximately 800 items (1,000 total books × .20 = 200 books checked out at any one time; 1,000 – 200 = 800 books to be shelved).

MINIMAL COLLECTION

Remember, if you determine that a *relatively small* number of the new items will be on the shelf at one time, you will be completing part I of Workform 10. First you will determine how many items similar to the new items are in the collection now. Then you will calculate the percentage of the collection of similar items that will be represented by the new items. For instance, if you are adding 200 preschool storybooks to an existing collection of 4,800 preschool storybooks, for a total of 5,000 storybooks, the new books would represent 4 percent of the total collection of new *and* existing storybooks (200 ÷ 5,000 = .04 or 4%). Circulation records indicate that, on average, at any one time 40 percent of the storybook collection is checked out. Therefore, to calculate the number of books you would plan to have on the shelf at any one time, you might want to be conservative and plan on 35 percent of your enhanced collection being in circulation. This would mean that 65 percent would be on the shelves at any one time (100% – 35% = 65%). To calculate your shelving needs, you would then multiply your total collection number by the amount expected to be on the shelf at any one time (5,000 total storybooks × .65 anticipated being in = 3,250 books that need shelving). When you know approximately what your new book count will be, you are ready to look at the shelves holding the current collection. How much empty space is there on an average shelf? Does it look like the shelves can accommodate the increase in the collection without undue crowding? Has the collection been weeded recently? Does it need to be weeded? If so, what percentage of the collection do you anticipate will be withdrawn? While these questions are somewhat subjective, most experienced library staff members will have little trouble answering them and deciding whether the existing shelving will be adequate. If the number of items to be shelved is large enough to require new shelving, you will complete part II of Workform 10 as described in the following sections.

NUMBER OF ITEMS PER LINEAR FOOT OF SHELVING

When you have determined the approximate number of items to be shelved, you will be ready to calculate how many items of each type will fit in one linear foot. Printed books and bound magazine issues are customarily shelved side by side with the spine out for maximum storage efficiency or stored face out for display. Obviously, face-out shelving occupies more space per item. Materials of different types can vary markedly in size, so they require more or less shelf space per item. Tool Kit A, Calculating Square Footage, provides a thorough description of the different kinds of shelving that are used for different materials and the variations in their space requirements. These variations can also require differing depths of shelving. For instance, the shelves for reference and easy books are often wider than those for adult fiction, so they usually require 14-inch-deep shelving, while adult fiction uses 10-inch-deep shelving. Easy books are very thin; reference books are often quite thick; and audiovisual materials that are housed on flat shelves vary in the amount of shelf space occupied. You will need an estimate of how many items of each type of material to be shelved will fit within a linear foot (one foot of flat shelving) before you can determine how much shelving is needed. Please note that you don't need to record on Workform 10 items per linear foot for specialty shelving such as spinners, bins, and drawers. Such shelving is designed to hold a specified number of items, and the manufacturer can provide that information.

As noted earlier, the easiest way to determine items per linear foot is to use published lists. Tool Kit A, Calculating Square Footage, offers an average number of items per linear foot for a variety of material types and can be used to determine shelving needs. For instance, the data in the tool kit indicates that you can fit an average of eight adult fiction books on a linear foot of shelving. That figure is based on the assumption that you will leave approximately 25 percent of each shelf empty. The extra space makes the collection easier for the public to use and for staff to maintain. It also allows for growth of the collection over time.

In a preceding example, you were planning to purchase 1,000 new adult fiction books to support the activity, and you determined that 800 would be on the shelf at any given time. Now you would divide 8 books per linear foot into the 800 new books and find that you needed 100 linear feet of shelving to fill each shelf to 75 percent of capacity.

If you don't find the information you need in Tool Kit A, Calculating Square Footage, you can make your own estimates. One way to do this is to count the number of items on four shelves that are as full as you like the shelving to be for the type of material you plan to purchase. Divide the total number of items by the number of shelves to determine the average number of items per shelf. Then divide the number of items you plan to shelve at one time by the average number of items per shelf to determine the number of shelves that will be required to house the collection. As you see in this instance, you are not concerned with linear feet of shelving, just the total number of shelves required.

For example, if you count 128 adult fiction books on four shelves of three-foot width that are as full as you would like your shelves to be, you would determine that there are 32 books per three feet of shelving. This is calculated as

$$128 \div 4 = 32 \text{ books per shelf}$$

If the entire fiction collection is 100,000 books, but 25 percent are out at any one time, leaving 75 percent on the shelf, this would be calculated as

$$100,000 \times .75 = 75,000 \text{ books shelved}$$

If you then divide the 75,000 books to be shelved by 32 books per three-foot shelf, you need 2,344 three-foot shelves to hold that collection. This is calculated as

$$75,000 \text{ books} \div 32 \text{ books per shelf} = 2,344 \text{ shelves}$$

WIDTH AND NUMBER OF SHELVES PER UNIT

Most manufactured shelving has shelves just short of three feet wide because, with the frame that supports the shelves, it is three feet wide. The number of shelves per unit varies greatly, however, because shelving comes in so many heights. Took Kit 1, Calculating Square Footage, includes a table that provides information about the typical number of shelves in units of standard height. Use that data unless your library has unique shelving. You will also need to remember that most libraries purchase double-sided shelving more often than single-sided shelving. If that is the case in your library, you will have to double the number of shelves per unit.

NUMBER OF ITEMS PER UNIT AND NUMBER OF UNITS NEEDED

When you know how many linear feet of shelving you will need and the width and number of shelves in the units of shelving you will be using, you have the information needed to determine the number of new units of shelving that will be required. In a preceding example, you determined you needed 100 linear feet of new shelving. If your library uses single-faced, 90-inch-tall shelving units with seven 3-foot-wide shelves and does not shelve items on the bottom shelf, each unit has a total of 18 linear feet of shelving available per unit (6 shelves at 3 linear feet = 18 linear feet). This would mean that you require 5.5 units of shelving (100 ÷ 18 = 5.5). You will not be able to purchase 5.5 units, so you will have to decide whether to round down to 5 units, which would mean the shelves would be more crowded than you planned, or round up to 6 units, which would mean that the shelves would have more empty space than you planned. If you use double-sided shelving, the decision is made for you: you will use 3 double-sided units, which will provide 6 units of shelving.

SQUARE FOOTAGE FOR SHELVING

When you know how many units of shelving will be needed, you are ready to determine how much square footage will be required to house the shelving units. Two factors to consider are aisle width and shelf depth. Tool Kit A, Calculating Square Footage, includes tables that provide the average square footage for various types of shelves and various widths of aisles. Refer to those tables and use the square footage that is closest to the conditions in your library. In part 6 of the case study, which follows, the members of the Anytown Public Library project committee complete Workform 10, Need—Shelving.

Anytown Public Library Homework Center

PART 6: Shelving Needed

Two members of the project committee were assigned to determine the shelving that would be required to support the homework center. They referred to the completed Workform 6, Project Description—General (part 4 of the case study), and noted that $8,000 in recurring funds had been allocated to purchase new adult nonfiction materials.

They started by estimating the number of new items that would be added to the collection during the current year. The objectives for the homework center include an increase in circulation of adult nonfiction, so they assumed that most of the new materials would be in that category. They did some research and found that the average cost for an adult nonfiction item was $32 and that the average library discount for those items was 45 percent. Therefore, the average per-item cost was $17.60, and approximately 454 items could be added to the collection this year ($8,000 budget ÷ $17.60 per item = 454 items). Because the allocation is recurring, a similar number of items would be added to the collection over the next several years.

They asked library technical services to determine the average circulation of adult nonfiction items from the library's online catalog statistics and found on average that each item was checked out about 15 percent of the year. That meant they would need shelving for about 386 new items during the first year (454 items × .15 = 68.1; 454 − 68 = 386 items to be shelved). They discussed the collection with the librarians who would be supporting the homework center and found that the staff expected to replace about 25 percent of the items in the homework support collection each year to ensure that the information is current and accurate. Based on this, they decided that new shelving would be needed to house the new materials. Therefore, they completed part II of Workform 10, Need—Shelving.

The library's nonfiction collection is housed on double-sided cantilevered shelving, and that was entered in column 1 of part II of the workform. Then the committee members referred to Tool Kit A, Calculating Square Footage, and found that an average of 10 nonfiction items can be shelved per linear foot allowing for 75 percent capacity. They divided the number of items expected to be on the shelf at one time (386) by the average number of nonfiction items that can be shelved per linear foot (10) and found that they would need 38.6 linear feet of shelving if the shelving were filled to 75 percent of capacity. They rounded that figure up to 39 linear feet.

The shelving units in the Anytown Public Library nonfiction section are 3 feet wide, and that number was entered in column C. Then the staff divided the number of linear feet of shelving needed by the width of shelves and found that they would need 13 shelves, and that number was entered in column D. Each of the shelving units in the nonfiction section of the library has 7 shelves, but the library only uses 6 of those shelves for materials; that number is entered into column E. They divided the number of shelves needed (column D) by the number of shelves per unit (column E) and found that they needed 2 new units of shelving (13 ÷ 6 = 2.1). Because nonfiction is shelved on double-sided cantilevered shelves, they would recommend the purchase of 1 double-sided unit.

They referred again to Tool Kit A, Calculating Square Footage, and found that the *Libris DESIGN Glossary* recommends that they allocate 18 square feet for each unit of 24-inch-deep double-faced shelving with three-foot shelves and a 36-inch aisle. The units in their library are 22 inches deep, but their aisles are 40 inches wide, so they decided the estimated square footage was close enough and entered the data into column G. Because they are purchasing a single unit, they entered the same number in column H.

When they had finished completing Workform 10, the two staff members agreed that although the process required a number of different data elements, it was easier to do than it first appeared it would be. The copy of Workform 10 that they completed follows.

Project Name: **Homework Center**   *Library or Unit:* **Anytown**

Part II: Significant Collection

	Needed Number of Shelving Units						Needed Square Footage for Shelving	
1. Regular Shelving	A. Number of New Items to Be Shelved	B. Linear Feet of Shelves Needed	C. Width of Shelves	D. Number of Shelves Needed	E. Number of Shelves per Unit	F. Number of Units Needed	G. Square Footage per Unit	H. Total Square Footage
Double-sided cantilevered shelving	386	39	3	13	6	1	18	18

Describing the Shelving Currently Allocated to Support the Activity

If the library collection currently contains materials that support this activity, you will complete Workform 11, Have—Shelving. Although at first glance the workform looks a lot like part II of Workform 10, the data needed for the workform is considerably easier to collect because it deals with actual conditions. Most of the data on the workform can be gathered by going to the shelves that currently hold materials that support the activity, and counting—first the number of shelves, then the number of shelves per unit, and finally the number of units used.

You will complete the last part of this workform by answering the same questions asked in part I of Workform 10: what percentage of the shelves are empty, and does the collection need weeding? As noted in the discussion of Workform 10, most experienced librarians should have no difficulty answering these questions, although the answers will be based on a combination of observation and judgment. It is important to involve in these decisions the staff who work with the materials under review.

Step 5.3
Describe the Physical Plant and Technology Support Needs and Current Conditions

The questions pertaining to the physical plant and technology support required to support the activity are interrelated. For instance, if the activity under review requires a separate walled space, you will also have to consider physical plant issues such heating, ventilation, and air-conditioning (HVAC), as well as lighting levels, doors, windows, flooring, and so on. Electrical issues are a part of the physical plant and play a role in providing the infrastructure needed to support the technology. If on Workform 4, Need for Outside Experts, you decided to use a general contractor, architect, engineer, or electrician, those experts will be able to help you determine the needs for the new space. All of these issues are addressed on Workform 12, Need—Physical Plant and Technology Support, and Workform 13, Have—Physical Plant and Technology Support, and are discussed in greater detail in the following sections.

Identifying the Physical Plant and Technology Support Needed

You will begin this part of the process by referring to the approved copies of Workform 6, Project Description—General, and Workform 7, Project Description—Physical Plant, Space, and Spatial Relationships, which were completed by the entire project committee during their second meeting (Step 4.1). These workforms will provide information to help the team make decisions about building components that will be required for the activity.

Issues to consider when describing the needed physical conditions in which to house the activity under review range from structural considerations to the infrastructure needed to support technology to the appropriate decor. Some of the questions to consider include the following:

Flooring. Will special flooring be needed? Do the floors need to be load-bearing? Will the flooring in part or all of the space need to be elevated? Will the space need special floor covering (carpet, tile, etc.)?

Walls. Will the activity need to be presented in an area with full walls, or will partial walls be adequate?

Doors. Should the space have a door? Does the door need to lock?

Windows. Does the activity require natural light? Should the activity be presented in an area in which light can be completely blocked? Are windows needed for visual supervision of the activity?

Electrical. What are the electrical needs for lighting, computers, and other equipment? Do outlets need to be in specific places?

Heating, Ventilating, and Air-Conditioning (HVAC). Will the activity require new or altered heating, ventilation, and air-conditioning? Will the area need a separate zone? If you wall off an area, will you need new ducts and air returns?

Lighting. Are there special lighting requirements? Will the activity require task-specific lighting, or will ambient lighting be sufficient? Is it important to have natural daylight in the area (see *Windows*)?

Plumbing. Will sinks, restrooms, or other plumbing be required to support the activity?

Security. Will the activity require special security measures? Will the activity include the use of portable equipment or materials that might be easily stolen?

Technical Support. Will the activity require special technical support? Will the activity require staff Internet connectivity? Does the activity depend on connectivity to a particular network? Will additional electrical outlets be needed? The committee will want to talk to the library's technical support people to be sure they know these requirements.

Decor. Are there special requirements for ceilings, walls and wall coverings, and window treatments? Will the members of the target audience be more comfortable in a special decor?

Other Issues to Consider. Have you considered security for outside exits? If you will be adding elevators or lifts to meet the requirements of the Americans with Disabilities Act or local codes, you will need to hire an outside expert to help you make the needed decisions.

You may want to look again at the "Physical Plant" section of figure 7, Facility Resources—Common Elements (in chapter 2), to be sure that you have considered all of the issues that are pertinent to your project. Note that size was not included in this list of issues to consider. This is because the size of the space that is needed will be determined by the type, number, and size of the items that have to be housed in the space. The space needed will be calculated in Step 5.5 later in this chapter.

Describing the Current Physical Plant and Technology Support

If the activity is currently being offered in your library, you will complete Workform 13, Have—Physical Plant and Technology Support. The data elements are similar to the data elements on Workform 12. You will be recording descriptions of the items, information about their current condition, whether they are currently being used for a single purpose or are multipurpose in use, and the approximate square footage of the space. Square footage information is best gathered from floor plans of the library. If your current space has been wired for special access, like the wired stations for a computer training lab, you will make a note of the outlets and cable access points that are in the room. Whether you use floor plans or not, it is best to use a tape measure to double-check the length and width of the space. Then multiply those measurements to determine the square footage. You will also measure the square footage of the space that is currently being used to support the activity.

Step 5.4
Describe Access, Spatial Relationships, and Signage Needs and Current Conditions

Access issues, spatial relationships, and signage are interrelated and need to be considered together. Access describes the means of entering, approaching, or making use of an area or item. Spatial relationships describes how areas or items relate to one another. Signs are publicly displayed notices that help people in various ways in the library. Taken together, descriptions of desired access, spatial relationships, and signage provide an overview of what is required for people to move easily through the library to find and use furnishings, equipment, and materials and fully participate in the activity under review. If you are currently providing the activity or service in your library, you will be able to observe how easy it is for people to find and use the spaces allocated for the activity. The questions to ask and issues to consider are described in the following sections. You will record your recommendations for future needs on Workform 14, Need—Access, Spatial Relationships, and Signage, and your observations about current conditions on Workform 15, Have—Access, Spatial Relationships, and Signage.

Identifying Needed Access, Spatial Relationships, and Signage

Begin by reviewing Workform 6, Project Description—General, and Workform 7, Project Description—Physical Plant, Space, and Spatial Relationships. Workform 6 describes the target audience and identifies any special characteristics that need to be considered. Workform 7 provides an initial assessment of the spatial relationships that will be needed and serves as a starting point for your discussions about both access and spatial relationships.

ACCESS

When librarians think about access, often the first thing that comes to mind is the Americans with Disabilities Act. This is understandable, given the emphasis that has been placed on making all public spaces fully accessible since the act passed in 1990. You will, of course, be required to meet the requirements of the ADA for any project you are planning. The earlier discussions of needed furniture, equipment, and shelving all addressed ADA issues, and you will need to keep ADA concerns in mind during this part of the process as well. (See Tool Kit C, Americans with Disabilities Act Requirements, for more information.) However, access is not simply a question of making sure that people with disabilities can fully participate in an activity. Other access issues can affect participation in an activity by all potential customers. The flow of traffic into the library and the paths people follow as they circulate through the library are both access issues that will need to be addressed. Part I of Workform 14 includes the following four questions.

Will the activity be offered when the library is closed? If the activity will be offered when the library is closed, it should probably be housed in an area that can be closed off from other parts of the library and has an exterior door. Otherwise, it will be difficult to keep users from wandering into parts of the library that are closed and not staffed. Remember that even after-hours users will need to be able to get to restrooms. Some activities that are offered at times when the library is closed may include providing food and drink. If that is the case, users will need kitchen facilities. There may be security issues to consider as well.

Will the activity be offered to groups of people at the same time? If the activity includes programs or services to be presented to groups, you will need to consider how the members of the group get to the area housing the activity. You probably don't want twenty-five children from a day-care center to have to take an elevator to get to the place where the story program will be held—nor do you want them to walk from the front door through the quiet reading areas of the library to the back corner to get to their destination.

Is the activity or service one that will be used if people can see it but not one that people are likely to search for? Some users come to the library to participate in a specific activity and will ask for directions if they need them. For instance, literacy students who are referred to a library's literacy center will probably ask for help finding the center if they need it. They may even be more comfortable knowing that the literacy center is not easily visible to everyone who comes in the front door. Genealogists and local history buffs will assume you provide services to support their interests, and are likely to ask for directions. On the other hand, if the activity is to merchandise the collection, your target audience will include the people who come to the library "to find something good to read, view, or listen to." You are more likely to reach them if you put your new high-demand materials near the front door, so they are the first things that users see when they enter the library. This is the same principle that grocery stores use when they put sale and display items at the ends of aisles.

Is the activity one for which users will need significant staff assistance? If you expect the users to need a lot of help from staff, you will need to be sure that there are clear and easily followed paths to service points.

As you can see, there is a certain amount of overlap between the issues pertaining to access and those pertaining to spatial relationships. Generally, access issues are concerned with the flow of people from the outside to the inside of the building and between and among the various spaces in the building. Spatial issues, discussed in the following section, are more concerned with the relationship of various areas, subareas, or items of furniture and equipment within the building.

SPATIAL RELATIONSHIPS

The terms *adjacent to, close to, in sight of,* and *away from* are used to describe relationships among various areas or subareas, or among the furnishings and equipment within an area of the library. Start by thinking about the area that will house the activity and how that area should relate to the rest of the library. You may want to draw a Venn diagram to illustrate the spatial relationships that will be needed for the activity. Venn diagrams use shapes, usually circles, to represent something, in this case an area of the library or a subarea within an area. The relationships of the circles echo the relationships of what are being represented. See figure 10 in chapter 2 for a sample Venn diagram. Use part II of Workform 14 to describe the ideal relationships.

Next think about the subareas that are likely to be developed within the area housing the services. For example, the children's area has distinct subareas: staff desk, shelving, story area, table and chair area, and so on. The homework center that the staff of the Anytown Public Library is planning will also have distinct subareas: tables and chairs, carrels, computer workstations, shelving, staff desks, and perhaps small study rooms. On the other hand, the new book area in a library tends to be a single entity with few if any subareas. List the probable subareas that will be needed to support the activity under review in part III of Workform 14, and describe their relationships to one another.

You will also want to think about the furniture and equipment that are needed for the activity and the most effective relationships for those items within the activity area. For example, if an activity requires computer workstations for the public, do those stations need to be adjacent to a service desk so staff can assist people using them? Should they be away from quiet study areas because the computer area can get noisy? Do they all need to be together? Review the completed Workform 8, Need—Furniture and Equipment, then list in part III of Workform 14 the furniture and equipment that will be needed and describe their relationships to one another. Remember, some items on the workform may not have spatial relationship requirements.

SIGNAGE

Signage is the final issue to consider when talking about how people get to and use the area housing the activity under review. In some cases, the activity or service you are considering will have special signage needs. For example, if the activity you are planning is designed for new Hispanic residents in your community, you may need to consider having Spanish-language signs. As you may remember from figure 7, the four types of signage are directory, directional, identification, and informational/instructional. Which of these types of signs will be needed to support the activity under review? What language or languages should be used on the signs? Where should the needed signs be placed? How many signs are needed? What colors, shapes, and sizes should they be? Keep in mind the following general guidelines. Signs should

- serve their intended purpose (for instance, directional signs should name the place they point to and include an arrow but no other information)
- be located where they are needed and only where needed
- be easily seen—draw attention to themselves
- meet ADA requirements if they are permanent labels for doors or provide other non-changing information
- reflect a carefully planned signage system that establishes the types and look of signs in a building

Record your signage needs on part IV of Workform 14.

Describing Current Access, Spatial Relationships, and Signage

The workform you used to record the information about the access, spatial relationships, and signage needed to support the activity is very similar to the workform you will use to describe current conditions. However, the difference lies in the way in which you find the data to complete the workforms. In the preceding section you described an ideal. Now you are going to be looking at reality, and the data you collect will be based on observation.

If the activity is currently being offered in your library, go to the area in which the activity takes place and walk around. Talk to the staff who provide the activity and the people who participate in the activity. Stand in one place and watch how people actually move into and within the space. Does the current location work well? Can people find it easily? Can people get to and from the location without disrupting others? Are the members of the target audience compatible with users in adjoining spaces? Are all of the materials needed to support the activity readily accessible? Is the signage adequate and in good condition? You will consider these and other questions as you complete Workform 15, Have—Access, Spatial Relationships, and Signage.

You might think that it would be easier to collect current data than it is to project the resources that will be needed to support an activity at desired levels. That is not always the case. Some librarians have an easier time with the hypothetical "what if" world—where all things are possible—than the more limited and pragmatic environment they cope with on a daily basis. It can be surprisingly difficult to assess current conditions realistically. People become so used to their physical environments that they no longer actually look at their surroundings. Tool Kit B, Assessing Your Library's Physical Message, provides a checklist of questions to help you evaluate the condition of various aspects of your building. Figure 9, Suggested Indicators to Measure Age and Condition (in chapter 2), provides standards that can be used to assess whether the resources currently in use are excellent, good, acceptable, or unacceptable. When creating such subjective evaluation data, it helps for everyone to agree on the standards they will be using as they assess the various resources now in place in the library.

When you walk into a strange library for the first time, you notice everything—atmosphere, cleanliness, decor, spatial relationships, signage, and so on. By the time you walk into your own library for the hundredth day (your third month on the job), you have already become acclimated to the environment. By your thousandth day (nearing your third year on the job) or your ten-thousandth day (your twenty-seventh year on the job), you rarely think about issues of access, spatial relationships, or signage. Those issues are important to people who are not familiar with the building, not to people who know every nook and cranny of it. You might want to ask a colleague from a nearby library (perhaps the school media specialist) to help you evaluate current access, spatial relationships, and signage as these relate to the activity under review. Fresh eyes will undoubtedly see things that you might miss.

Step 5.5
Make Preliminary Recommendations for the Amount and Type of Space

The last step in Task 5 is to compare the total square footage needed for the project with the square footage, if any, that is currently allocated to support the project, and to decide whether the activity will be offered in multipurpose, single-purpose, or walled space. The furniture and equipment team has already estimated the square footage needed and allocated on Workforms 8 and 9, and the shelving team has square footage figures for shelving on Workforms 10 and 11. The physical plant and technology support team has recorded the approximate square footage currently being used for the activity on Workform 13, Have—Physical Plant and Technology Support. Now that team will use Workform 16, Square Footage—Needed and Current, to compile square footage information.

To complete Workform 16, Square Footage—Needed and Current, the physical plant and technology support team will get the needed and current square footage figures from the furniture and equipment and shelving teams and transfer the total square footage information to parts I and II of Workform 16. Part III of Workform 16 is also completed by the physical plant and technology support team. They transfer the approximate square footage of the area in which the activity is currently being offered to the appropriate row or rows. Part IV will be completed at the third meeting of the project committee.

Deciding on the Amount and Type of Space

The committee chair will call the third meeting so the committee can review all the information from Workforms 6 through 16 and make a decision about whether they are recommending walled space, open single-purpose space, or multipurpose space. A suggested agenda for the third meeting is shown in figure 13. The meeting also introduces the gap analysis workform.

This meeting provides the whole committee with an opportunity to review the work of the teams and identify any needs that were not listed. These discussions may raise questions that point to the need for additional data to supplement the workforms the teams have already completed. For example, perhaps once the decor elements for the project have been clarified, the furniture team will return to Workform 9, Have—Furniture and Equipment, to fill in more detailed information about the condition of the furniture they have listed. If the physical plant and technology support team is concerned about colors or patterns matching in the new area, the furniture team may need to provide more details in their descriptions. If this is the case, they would add that new information to the data-gathering workforms.

The next agenda item the committee will take up is making the decision about whether the activity will be offered in walled space, open single-purpose space, or multipurpose space. Workform 7, Project Description—Physical Plant, Space, and Spatial Relationships,

FIGURE 13
Meeting 3: Sample Agenda

Third Committee Meeting

Purpose:	Discuss the information gathering that the committee teams have conducted
	Determine whether the activity will require walled space, single-purpose space, or multipurpose space
	Assign committee members to research options for the gaps in the areas they have researched
Who:	All members of the facility project committee and staff who are currently providing the service or activity under review or some component of the service
Where:	Small conference room
When:	Date, start time, end time (meeting should be scheduled for two hours)
Materials:	Multiple completed copies of any of the following workforms used by your committee: Workform 7, Project Description—Physical Plant, Space, and Spatial Relationships; Workform 8, Need—Furniture and Equipment; Workform 9, Have—Furniture and Equipment; Workform 10, Need—Shelving; Workform 11, Have—Shelving; Workform 12, Need—Physical Plant and Technology; Workform 13, Have—Physical Plant and Technology; Workform 14, Need—Access, Spatial Relationships, and Signage; Workform 15, Have—Access, Spatial Relationships, and Signage; Workform 16, Square Footage—Needed and Current; and Workform 17, Gaps and Options. Provide copies for everyone attending the meeting
Preparation:	Teams bring any of the completed Workforms 8–16 for reference

AGENDA

[Start time]	Review committee findings on workforms 8–16 (60 minutes)
	Clarify if additional information is needed (10 minutes)
	Review rows D and E of Workform 7, Project Description—Physical Plant, Space, and Spatial Relationships
	Determine whether the activity needs walled, single-purpose, or multipurpose space (20 minutes)
	Introduce Workform 17, Gaps and Options and its instructions (15 minutes)
	Assign committee members to determine gaps and research options to fill the gaps in their resource areas by completing Workform 17 for the next meeting (5 minutes)
	Questions (10 minutes)
[End time]	Adjourn

and the parts already completed on Workform 16, Square Footage—Needed and Current, will be useful in this process.

SPACE REQUIREMENTS

Now is a good time to remind yourself and the project committee that this is about *reallocating* space, not building new space. Sections D and E of Workform 7, Project Description—Physical Plant, Space, and Spatial Relationships, provide information about the physical plant requirements of the activity, and part I of Workform 14, Need—Access, Spatial Relationships, and Signage, provides useful information about the access requirements for the activity. Workform 16, Square Footage—Needed and Current, provides an estimate of the amount of square footage required by your project. Now that you know the amount of square footage and the special requirements of the activity your project serves, you can decide if the activity could take place in walled space, single-purpose space, or multipurpose space. Key factors to consider include the amount of space, the security requirements, the access to other resource requirements, and whether noise control is important for the activity.

Walled space. If your activity has special security needs or sound requirements to contain or limit noise so users can focus their attention, then a walled space will be a high priority. These needs would be important for a computer training lab or a local television studio. Unless security or noise considerations are essential for the activity, though, it is unlikely that the activity will require walled space. Because of the expense and disruption to the rest of the library's services, there will be a strong motivation *not* to designate walled space unless one is readily available.

Single-purpose space. If your activity is likely to be used throughout the library's open service hours and requires unique furniture and equipment or facility adaptations, the committee will have a preference for single-purpose space. The Anytown homework center will require group computer stations that would be considered special furniture, which would indicate a single-purpose space. However, since the center will not be used throughout the open hours of the library, perhaps those stations could serve other users in a multipurpose space while the students are in school. The decision to use single-purpose or multipurpose space may be driven as much by the size of your library as by the activity. Smaller facilities are very creative about using their limited space for as many purposes as possible and are often forced to place all activities in multipurpose space. If the building is large, there are always more options. Some libraries have created computer training labs by installing computers in a meeting room, thus turning that meeting room into a multipurpose space. Others have created separate walled-in spaces to house their computer training lab. The decision between going with single-purpose or multipurpose space requires consideration of when the activity will be used by patrons. Can times of use be determined and isolated so the room can be used for other things at other times? For example, a periodical reading room or an area used for public-access computer stations would not be suitable for multiple purposes. Furniture requirements may also drive the decision. Chairs that include a small table for laptop computers will probably be in use most of the open hours for Internet access, and will not be usable for seating in a conversation area to encourage the use of the library as a community commons.

Multipurpose space. If your activity is targeted to a group that will only use the library occasionally, or if it is one that could be in an area used for other purposes or is one that could easily coexist with other activities now in place in the library, then you'll want to designate it multipurpose space. One example is a genealogy room that doubles as a board meeting room. Another example is a community meeting room set up with tables after school for students' group study. Yet another example is that of parenting collections and reading areas placed in the children's services area.

After reviewing the square footage measures collected on Workform 16, the committee should review and discuss the unique requirements of the activity. The amount and type of space may be easily agreed upon based on the data collected, or it may involve a discussion about the amount of compromise the committee agrees will be necessary to implement the new activity. The answers to the questions regarding walled, single-purpose, or multipurpose space on Workform 7, Project Description—Physical Plant, Space, and Spatial Relationships, may make this a straightforward decision. If controlled access to the area or sound control is necessary for the activity, then the committee will recommend walled space. If the activity requires special furniture that cannot be used for other purposes, or involves shelving or equipment that must be dedicated to the new activity, then the committee will recommend single-purpose space. If the activity will only be used in isolated time segments, does not require special access, and uses furniture that can be used for many library activities, the activity will be in multipurpose space. Next, the committee should look at the square footage currently available in the specific type of space they prefer and determine how the needed square footage would affect that space. The conclusions they draw will guide their decision on the amount and type of space. Once the decisions are made in the third committee meeting, the chair records the amount and type of space recommendation on part IV of Workform 16, Square Footage—Needed and Current.

At the end of the meeting, the committee members are charged with completing Workform 17, Gaps and Options. The teams that worked on the paired Need/Have workforms will determine gaps and develop options and record them on Workform 17. They should be advised that the administrators must first approve their decision about the amount and type of space and that the chair will let them know when the committee has been given approval to proceed with the process.

Checking with the Library Administration

Before proceeding with the gap analysis, the committee chair should check with the library's administration to see if the amount of space and type of space the committee is recommending is in line with the administration's expectations. The committee chair should meet with the administrators and, using the total square footage figure and type of space established on Workform 16, Square Footage—Needed and Current, inform them of these requirements.

The administration will basically have one of three responses: approval, caution, or rejection. In the first scenario, the administration will review your expectations for the project, give you their provisional approval, and allow the committee to continue with the process. In the second scenario, the administration will express some concerns about the amount of space or the type of space the committee will be reallocating in the library, but will take a wait-and-see attitude. The committee would then proceed but know there is concern about the scale of the project. If, however, the administration tells you that the project is expected to require too much space in proportion to the goals of the activity, the committee will have to return to the Need workforms in chapter 3 and scale back the project before proceeding. This will mean returning to Workforms 8, 10, 12, and 14 with a critical eye to the basic requirements for the activity and completing a second set of these Need workforms reflecting the scaled-back needs. Obtaining administrative approval, now, of the amount and type of space needed for the project can save the committee a lot of time as it proceeds with the gap analysis.

Key Points to Remember

It is important to include the staff who will provide the new activity in the process of identifying needed facility resources.

Don't get bogged down in arguments about what is required and what is desired. If agreement can't be reached, explore multiple options.

Be creative when identifying future furniture and equipment. The world is changing rapidly, and so are library resources. Recommend flexible furniture and equipment rather than single-purpose items.

Be aware of the Americans with Disabilities Act and local code requirements when discussing access, spatial relationships, and signage.

Be aware of the traffic flow and use patterns of all users when discussing access, spatial relationships, and signage.

It may be difficult to evaluate how access and spatial relationships work in your own library because you are so familiar with them. Ask an outsider to help with your assessment of current conditions.

This process is about reallocating existing space, not about building a new facility. You will be working within the framework of your current facility.

Check in with the library administration to see if the amount and type of space the committee is recommending meets with their approval.

Note

1. Diane Mayo and Jeanne Goodrich, *Staffing for Results: A Guide to Working Smarter* (Chicago: American Library Association, 2002), 39.

Chapter 4

Gap Analysis and Recommendations

MILESTONES

By the time you finish this chapter you will know how to

- identify gaps between needed and existing resources
- develop options for filling the gaps
- identify options for placement of the activity
- research cost estimates for options
- establish criteria and evaluate options
- develop preliminary recommendations for each resource area

In chapter 3 you answered the first two questions in the gap analysis process:

What facility resources will be required to support an activity at the desired levels?

What facility resources do we have that are currently allocated to support the activity?

In this chapter you will use the data you have collected on Workforms 8 through 16 to answer the next two questions in the gap analysis process:

What is the gap between the two?

How can we fill that gap (or, more rarely, reallocate the surplus)?

You will answer the first question by having the committee teams compare the paired workforms they completed on furniture and equipment; shelving; physical plant and technology support; and access, spatial relationships, and signage. This comparison will give you a clear picture of the differences—or gaps—between what you need and what you have. Much of your committee's work will involve creating recommendations to answer the last question in the gap analysis process—how you will fill that gap. Once you have completed the gap process, you will have made a series of decisions leading to recommendations for the report to the administration. If there is no gap, you will simply recommend using existing resources. If a gap is determined, the committee will look for resources that can be reallocated from other uses in the library or decide how to acquire what is needed to fill that gap.

Chapter 4 will introduce Task 6, with five workforms to support the committee's work for this task. See figure 14 to help you determine whether you will use all the workforms for Task 6.

FIGURE 14
When to Use the Workforms That Support Task 6

Workform	When to Use	When Not to Use
Workform 17: Gaps and Options (Steps 6.1 and 6.2)	Complete this workform if you completed any of the following workforms: 8–9,10–11,12–13, or 14–15.	Do not use this workform if you did not complete any of the following workforms: 8–9,10–11,12–13,or 14–15.
Workform 18: Considerations for Placement of the Activity (Step 6.3)	Complete this workform if the activity was not previously offered or if the activity requires more space than is currently available for it in its current location.	Do not use this workform if the administration has directed the committee where to place the activity.
Workform 19: Expense Estimates for Options (Step 6.4)	Complete this workform if cost is a determining factor for an option.	Do not use this workform if you do not need to use cost information to decide which options to recommend.
Workform 20: Preliminary Project Time Estimates (Step 6.4)	Complete this workform if time is a determining factor for an option.	Do not use this workform if time is not a determining factor for an option.
Workform 21: Option Evaluation (Step 6.4)	Complete this workform if the committee created multiple options that need to be prioritized. Use it to record the reasons for your recommendations.	If the committee only developed one option per gap, do not use this workform.

TASK 6: IDENTIFY GAPS AND EVALUATE OPTIONS

Step 6.1
Identify Gaps between Needed and Existing Facility Resources and Space Allocation

You identify resource gaps by comparing what is needed to what exists. You have already collected and organized information about both; now you will use these two sets of information to find the answers to where and how the existing resources are inadequate to meet the needs of the new activity.

This is the analysis phase of the work. The teams that collected the data on each of the facility resources in Workforms 8 through 15 will now serve as the committee's specialists in the areas for which they have collected data. This means they will be determining the gaps for their respective resources. The teams analyze the pair of workforms they completed in Task 5 and record the gaps between what is needed and what is currently available for their resource on a copy of Workform 17, Gaps and Options, in column A. In most cases they will only need to use the columns from the data-gathering workforms in chapter 3 that provide the simple math to determine the gap. Each team will have different types of information to compare, depending on how they described their resource needs. The following sections provide each team with guidance for completing Workform 17.

Furniture and Equipment

The team that completed Workform 8, Need—Furniture and Equipment, and Workform 9, Have—Furniture and Equipment, will complete two copies of Workform 17, Gaps and Options, one for furniture and one for equipment. Workforms 8 and 9 call for the descrip-

---

LEVEL OF EFFORT NOTE
Gaps and Options

The level of effort that the committee must put into determining gaps and developing options to fill the gaps will be based on many things: the charge to the committee, the financial resources that are available for the project, and the current crowding in the library, to name a few. The options you develop will also be greatly simplified by the decision to use walled, single-purpose, or multipurpose space made in the third meeting. If your project is using multipurpose space, it is very likely that you will be adding furniture, equipment, and shelving to an existing area. Either single- or multipurpose spaces in most cases will not involve major facility renovations. Workform 7, Project Description—Physical Plant, Space, and Spatial Relationships, and Workform 16, Square Footage—Needed and Current, will be helpful in deciding the level of effort required in completing the gap analysis. For example, if your library's administration expects to purchase all new furniture, equipment, and shelving for the project, or if all furniture in the library is in a particular style or from one vendor, there will only be one option for filling the furniture gap.

tions of the public use or staff use of both furniture and equipment. On the copies of Workform 17, list *all* furniture gaps and *all* equipment gaps that need to be addressed.

To determine the gap, the furniture and equipment team consults Workform 8, Need—Furniture and Equipment, part I, column B, "Numbers of Items Needed," for each type of item listed and compares these to the numbers on Workform 9, Have—Furniture and Equipment, part I, column B, "Current Number of Items," for the *same items.* The comparison determines the gap. Record the name of the item (and, if applicable, its capacity) and the gap number (or surplus number if you *have* more of that item than you need) in column A of Workform 17. For example, you might record "four-person study tables—gap 2" or "two-person sofa—surplus 1." If Workform 9, part I, column E, "Conditions of Items," indicates that all items are usable, you will use the full number from column B of Workform 9 to calculate if there is a gap. If not all the items are usable, compare Workform 9, part I, columns B and E to determine the number that *are* in acceptable condition to be reallocated; then compare that number with the number of that item needed from Workform 8 to determine the gap or surplus. The needed number of items can easily be compared to the number that you now have. Their condition (Workform 9, part I, column E) is subjective information, but it must be considered to determine any gaps.

The team has developed an estimate of capacity needs for the activity (Workform 8). In the case of chairs for table seating, the number of chairs will equal the capacity. The table capacity will not equal the number of tables. When describing the need for tables, the team requested tables of a certain size as indicated by how many people those tables will seat. A conference room table might need to seat twenty-four people, described on Workform 8 as a 24-person table, while a table intended for tutors working with students might require tables described as two-person tables. It will be important to make sure you are comparing the same size tables to determine any gaps. Record that comparison in column A of Workform 17.

Consider each item of furniture and equipment in this way—one category at a time. If you work with interior designers or architects in planning your project, you may be asked to give them a furnishings list. This will be a listing of all the furniture and equipment that is called for in the committee's recommendations, with the source of each piece of furniture and equipment listed. Directions for the preparation of the furniture and equipment list are included in Task 7: Present Recommendations. It is too early in the process to prepare such a list now, as you have not decided on recommendations, but keep in mind that you may have to develop this list, so be as thorough as possible now with your descriptions.

Equipment gap determinations will involve a numerical comparison between Workform 8, Need—Furniture and Equipment, part II, column B, "Numbers of Items Needed," and Workform 9, Have—Furniture and Equipment, part II, column B, "Current Number of Items." As with the furniture gaps, take into consideration the condition of the equipment shown in Workform 9, part II, column E. The difference between the two constitutes the gap. Record that number on Workform 17 in column A.

Shelving

The team that completed Workform 10, Need—Shelving, and Workform 11, Have—Shelving, will complete a copy of Workform 17 *if* they completed part II, "Significant Collection," of Workform 10. It will be important to maintain the separation of regular and special shelving on separate lines of Workform 17. If there is a need for regular shelving, describe it by using the information in Workform 10, part II, section 1, columns C ("Width of Shelves") and E ("Number of Shelves per Unit") as part of the description. For example, you might write "single-sided, 24-inch-wide shelves, 6/unit—gap = 5 units" when you compare the Have and Need workforms to determine if there is a gap or surplus. In other words, make sure you are comparing the same exact kinds of shelving with each other. For special shelving, describe it in the same detail, so anyone reading Workform 17 can understand that different types of shelving include special shelves. Special shelving might include features like video display inserts or circular spinner displays.

Physical Plant and Technology Support

The team determining the gaps, if any, for physical plant and technology support will not only compare the "Number" columns of Workforms 12 and 13 but also the "Description" columns on those workforms. The "Condition" column on Workform 13 also enters into the equation. For example, the study rooms for Anytown's homework center will require windows to maintain visual supervision of the rooms. Workform 12 indicates the need for two interior fixed windows. On Workform 13 the corresponding sections would be completed if study rooms now exist. The workform might indicate that there is now one window, but that window is an exterior window that opens to the outside. Therefore, there is a gap of two fixed interior windows to be recorded on Workform 17.

A judicious consideration of how much change is necessary can save the library a lot of time and expense. For example, if the objective is to establish a preschool story hour area, suppose Workform 12, Need—Physical Plant and Technology Support, indicates a need to mediate the sound in the area with new acoustic ceiling tiles or brightly colored fabric wall hangings. Workform 13, Have—Physical Plant and Technology Support, indicates no sound mediation is now present in the library. Workform 12 also indicates a need for an area with a vinyl floor surface where children can do messy craft projects, and Workform 13 indicates the area is now all carpeted. The team would then list under decor brightly colored fabric wall hangings and label it as a gap. They would also list the square footage of vinyl flooring specified in Workform 12 in column A of Workform 17, Gaps and Options, and label it as a gap.

Other comparisons of the physical plant and technology support gaps depend upon the type of space approved for the activity. The following sections describe considerations for each type of space.

MULTIPURPOSE SPACE

If your project will be located in a multipurpose space, the physical plant features will reflect the existing area into which the project is placed. It is very likely that if your project is in a multipurpose space, your gaps will only involve electrical outlets, technology access, or modest decor considerations. This will greatly simplify your work. Record the gaps between the needs described on Workform 12, Need—Physical Plant and Technology Support, and what is now in place in the multipurpose areas of the library described on Workform 13, Have—Physical Plant and Technology Support. These comparisons will be numerical in some cases, such as electrical outlets, but will often involve a full description of what is needed, as in the case of decor elements. Include enough detail in describing the gaps on Workform 17, column A, so a reader who has not been part of the data-gathering process can understand the gaps.

SINGLE-PURPOSE SPACE

If your activity requires single-purpose space, you will be using physical plant features from the surrounding area. Record whatever gaps are determined in the comparison of Workform 12 and Workform 13 in column A of Workform 17, Gaps and Options. These gaps will be both numerical, as in cable drops for computer network access, and descriptive, as in full-spectrum lighting or task lighting in the single-purpose area. If the resource requires a description, include enough detail in describing the gap on Workform 17, column A, so a reader who has not been part of the data-gathering process can understand what is needed.

WALLED SPACE

If your project will require walled space, it is more likely that issues of floors, walls, windows, doors, lighting, HVAC, and security may be part of the gap. Record whatever gaps are determined in the comparison of Workform 12 and Workform 13 in column A of Workform 17. Be sure to describe these needs fully so the options developed in the next step will address them appropriately. For example, if the new activity requires walls and a need for visual supervision, as in a teen study room, in the walled area there would be a gap of doors with windows; if, however, the activity requires privacy for the users, as in a tutoring room, there would be a gap of interior doors or window glass that should be etched.

Access and Signage

The team that completed Workform 14, Need—Access, Spatial Relationships, and Signage, and Workform 15, Have—Access, Spatial Relationships, and Signage, will complete a copy of Workform 17, Gaps and Options, listing the access or signage gaps in column A. They will use the spatial relationships information from parts II and III on Workform 14 and Workform 15, later, to determine the location for the new activity. Record on Workform 17 any access gaps determined from a comparison of Workform 14, part I, column D, with the same part in Workform 15. For example, if the committee noted that the activity requires significant staff assistance on Workform 14, record on Workform 17, column A, that the gap is a need for easy access to a service desk.

Until the location is determined, you will not know how many signs are needed, but you now know that a sign designating the area is required and that any existing maps or directories of the library will need to be altered. For example, if the project is establishing a new activity in the library, there will be a need for signs to direct library users to the new service. If you are adding a computer training lab that did not previously exist in the library, plan to add the computer training lab to any existing directories and new signs both for the room or area where you are offering the activity and to direct library users through the library to the area. Workform 14, Need—Access, Spatial Relationships, and Signage, lists the required new signs. Describe the kinds of signs needed in column A of Workform 17, Gaps and Options.

Step 6.2
Identify Options for Filling the Gaps

Identifying options may well be the most creative part of the committee's work as they explore how to fill the gaps and provide the needed resources. You may already know that some of the gaps have just one obvious solution, as is the case with ordering new signs, so there will be no need to try to develop other options in those cases. For the remaining gaps in column A, Workform 17, Gaps and Options, create as many options as possible for filling any gaps. Because each individual item in each resource area may require a different means of appropriation (reallocation, purchase, or a combination of the two), it will take resourcefulness and research to clarify the best way to fill the remaining gaps.

If your committee's charge includes trying to find the least expensive way to implement the activity and, therefore, requires a lot of reallocation of current resources, then the teams will be closely reviewing the items available now and the usage patterns in place in the library. You will also need to use your best problem-solving skills to develop options about where the resources can be found to fill the identified gap. If feasible, outside experts can provide advice about inexpensive ways to acquire resources. For example, interior designers might refer you to upholsterers or help you purchase furniture at their professional discount. If some of the items needed are common household or business items, you could list items of furniture or decor that are needed in the library's newsletter or on the website.

While most administrations would like to implement new activities as inexpensively as possible, they realize that it will cost money, and some resources will have to be purchased. The options you develop should reflect a review of the goals and budget parameters in your charge and on Workform 6, Project Description—General. These documents will help to clarify the expectations of the administration.

The Have workforms used during the data-gathering process provide some information about what resources are currently being used for the activity; now you will also carefully study the way resources are currently being used *throughout* the building or, in some cases, throughout the library system as you try to determine whether furniture, equipment, shelving, and particularly space can be reallocated from their existing use to the new activity.

Everyone should have copies of Workform 17, Gaps and Options, for each resource area. All committee members should be aware of *all* the resource gaps to be filled. The group's extensive knowledge of various parts of the library, one of the key strengths of the committee, will be invaluable as they examine options for filling the gaps.

Developing Options

After completing column A of Workform 17, Gaps and Options, teams will examine the various parts of the library to see if any of the resources needed to fill the remaining gaps for their resource area are currently being underutilized in another part of the library. An example might be an underused two-person sofa in the periodicals reading room, where observation shows that people avoid the sofa because they prefer individual seating when reading periodicals. That same sofa might provide a perfect seat for a parent to read to a child in a new preschool reading area in the children's department.

As you comb the library for items to reallocate, it is important to discuss with those in charge of an area any items you are considering for reallocation to the project. Quite often the people who work in an area or department will have a far better idea of how important a resource is to their operation than someone from another part of the library. Reallocation will go more smoothly if it begins with tactful inquiries. Approach department heads in areas where you have identified a resource, and inform them of the needs for the project. Ask if they think an item could be reallocated without decreasing the service in their department. Explain that you have already collected information about what resources are currently being used for the activity; now you are broadening the scope to possible underused or unneeded resources within the library as a whole. Explain that you are attempting to fill the project needs from within the library's existing resources rather than buying everything new.

As an example, consider the possible scenario of reallocating reference shelving to expand a large-print area. The shelving team determines that they need to fill a gap of ten 12-inch-wide shelving units that are 5 shelves high and 3 feet long for an expanded large-print area. When looking around the library they realize there are a number of empty shelves in the reference area, and these shelves match the criteria for their project. They approach the head of the reference department to ask about the possibility of reallocating some of the reference shelving units. The head of reference explains that the department is about to weed the reference collection in light of the number of resources they now use online. The reference department would like to add more patron-access computers, but this will require creating some open space in the area, so removing the shelving units would be useful for them. The head of reference discusses the reallocation with the reference staff, and they decide that if the reference staff heavily weeds the reference book collection, they can reallocate six of their shelving units to the expanded large-print area. Then the project's shelving team can report that with the cooperation of the reference department, there is an option that they can reallocate 6 shelving units and purchase only 4 of the 10 required for the project.

As another example, the library sets up a new resource area to provide information on health and on local volunteer opportunities to new retirees. The access, spatial relationships, and signage team has determined that the new information center should have one individual hearing-assistance device to accommodate the target user group for this activity. They find that there are currently five individual hearing-assistance devices in the library's large meeting room. The team discuss their need with the meeting room coordinator, who tells them the five hearing-assistance devices are almost never in use at the same time. The coordinator agrees to reallocate one of the hearing-assistance devices to the new activity.

After their investigations, each team lists all the reallocation options they have developed to fill the gaps in their resource area on their copy of Workform 17, Gaps and Options, column B. If committee members have ideas or suggestions about gaps for other resource areas, they share them with the other team.

The following sections provide additional information about option considerations for furniture, equipment, and shelving. Options for gaps disclosed in physical plant, technology support, access, and signage are interdependent and are contingent upon spatial relationships and the *placement* of an activity. Therefore, options for those resources are discussed in Step 6.3: Identify Placement Options.

FURNITURE AND EQUIPMENT OPTIONS

As you develop options for filling furniture gaps, it will be important to consider the current look of your library. Are all pieces of furniture throughout the building in complementary colors and patterns so they can be easily interchanged? On the other hand, perhaps different departments in your library have their own unique furniture that would look inappropriate if moved to another department. Bear in mind that it is also possible to have serviceable soft furniture reupholstered to match the decor in the new area. Consider also that the design of the furniture must match the new activity's service group. For example, if you are creating a conversation area with comfortable seating for seniors, you won't be able to use those brightly colored sling-back chairs from the teen area because, to state the obvious, the preferences and needs of teens and seniors are widely divergent. Regardless of whether they are reallocated or purchased, furnishings will have to fit into the area surrounding the new activity and should be expected to serve for many years.

Reallocated or purchased equipment will also have to be compatible both with the new purpose and with other equipment used for the activity. The most obvious example of this would be reallocated computers that must accommodate the appropriate software for the activity in question and must be compatible with printers and other peripherals needed for the activity. An example would be reallocated computers that could work with the new larger, clearer display flat-screen monitors in a newly established consumer health area, based on the assumption that the area would be used by older readers who would prefer larger viewing screens.

SHELVING OPTIONS

As the shelving team looks for options to fill any gaps, they will seek underutilized shelving throughout the library, keeping in mind not only compatibility with the color scheme in the new area but the different types of shelving needed. For example, just because there is extra shelving in the adult fiction stacks does not mean it can or should be reallocated for an expanded children's picture book section. In this case, both the height and depth of the shelving in adult fiction do not match the shelving needed for picture books. The typical seven-shelves-high shelving often used in the adult fiction stacks will be too high for children to reach the books, and the picture books require 14-inch-deep shelves instead of the 10-inch-deep shelves used to accommodate novels. Consider the items in Workform 11, Have—Shelving, column H, "Percentage of Shelves That Are Empty," and column I, "Does Collection Need Weeding?" and apply them when looking at other areas of the library that do not provide the activity. Through that process you may find areas where, with some adjustments or weeding, shelving could be made available for reallocation.

PHYSICAL PLANT AND TECHNOLOGY SUPPORT AND ACCESS, SPATIAL RELATIONSHIPS, AND SIGNAGE

The teams working on options to fill the physical plant and technology support gaps will find that their options are determined by the infrastructure of the location where the new activity will take place. The access, spatial relationships, and signage team will also find that their options depend on the location of the new activity. Therefore, these two teams must work together to determine their recommendation for a location for the new activity before they proceed to work separately, developing options for the gaps in their respective resource areas.

Step 6.3
Identify Placement Options

The process of identifying options for furniture, equipment, and shelving is fairly straight-forward compared with the development of options for physical plant, technology support, access, spatial relationships, and signage. These latter resources are dependent on the location of the project, which must be decided before viable options can be developed for those resources.

Determining Placement of the Activity

To determine options for placing the activity, the placement will have to meet three requirements: space that meets the spatial relationship needs (Workform 14, Need—Access, Spatial Relationships, and Signage, part II), space that meets the square footage requirements (Workform 16, Square Footage—Needed and Current, part I, column B, "Net Square Footage"), and space that can be used in a way that addresses the gaps (Workform 17, Gaps and Options, column A).

The combined data on these workforms will provide information to guide the development of your options meeting the following requirements:

> spatial relationship needs
>
> special security features
>
> special lighting
>
> load-bearing flooring for dense shelving
>
> HVAC
>
> special wiring
>
> guaranteed visual supervision

First, review the spatial relationship requirements on Workform 14, Need—Access, Spatial Relationships, and Signage, part II, and look for possible areas to find or create available space that meets the adjacency needs. Once you find space that meets the spatial relationship requirements, then look for ways to provide the other resource requirements, such as technology support, in the locations that you have determined meet the adjacency needs.

By beginning with the activity's spatial relationship needs on Workform 14, part II, you can probably eliminate some areas of the library from consideration. In the Anytown example, the homework center should be near reference resources, within sight of the teen librarian, and far from the children's room and adult quiet reading area. Since the children's room can constitute about a third of a small community library, that alone can rule out a lot of territory. Now begin to examine the area around what must be adjacent to the new activity in increasing concentric circles. Using part I, the access needs portion of Workform 14, and the physical plant requirements information on Workform 12, Need—Physical Plant and Technology Support, consider what options might meet the requirements or what areas could reasonably be modified to meet the requirements.

> Is there any open area that is not a pathway?
>
> Are there furnishings or shelving units that are underused and could be removed or relocated to create the square footage required by the project?

Are there different components to the activity that call for different kinds of space? If so, should the square footage for the project be broken into parts?

Keep in mind that physical plant requirements can sometimes drive the placement of the project, too. For example, the addition of self-checkout stations would be driven by proximities to the exits of the building and the availability of staff supervision. If your project involves establishing a computer training lab, then security, lighting, wiring, Internet access, and HVAC might determine placement. If you are expanding a very dense collection, such as mysteries, the load-bearing capabilities of the floor would be especially important in determining the placement.

Technical requirements might also influence the placement of the activity. If your activity requires Internet connectivity, you will want to place it in an area of the building with wireless access or where wires can be pulled into the area. The security of the Internet connection required may also affect these decisions and may require the advice of your technical service people.

Sometimes the access needs of an activity will become the determining element in placing an activity. For example, if the activity will be offered during hours when the whole library is not open to the public, it will be important to locate the activity in an area that can be open to the public while the rest of the library is secured.

Workform 18, Considerations for Placement of the Activity, provides a list of elements of multipurpose spaces in a library. If your committee is recommending single-purpose space or, to a lesser degree, walled space, Workform 18 will also be useful to record spatial relationship considerations for the activity. Comparing the information on spatial relationships from part II of Workform 14, Need—Access, Spatial Relationships, and Signage, to that of part II of Workform 15, Have—Access, Spatial Relationships, and Signage, and column E of Workform 12, Need—Physical Plant and Technology Support, and column E of Workform 13, Have—Physical Plant and Technology Support, will also be useful in determining the location of the new activity. In essence, the physical plant and technology support and access, spatial relationships, and signage teams will be thinking through their gap analyses as they complete Workform 18 and will bring their recommendations for location to the fourth meeting of the committee to discuss and approve. The placement recommendation must be *endorsed* by the full committee in its fourth meeting and *approved* by administrators in the preliminary report to be part of the project.

LEVEL OF EFFORT NOTE
Placement of Activity

The level of effort that the teams must put into determining the placement of the activity and its impact on what options to develop will vary with the square footage requirements of the activity and the conditions that currently exist in your library. If your library is already very crowded and the activity requires a lot of space, you will have a greater challenge than if you are expanding an existing service in a predetermined multipurpose space. If the activity is currently offered and the current space can be expanded, there is no need to complete Workform 18. If the activity is currently being offered in a multipurpose space but the space is not working well, you will want to relocate the activity. If the current space can *not* be expanded or if this is a new activity for the library, the teams will have to find a location for the activity.

If the recommendation is not approved in either of those places, the teams will have to return to Workform 18 to reconsider placement and to Workform 17 to adjust their options. Specific suggestions for determining the placement of the activity for multipurpose, single-purpose, or walled space follow.

LOCATING A MULTIPURPOSE SPACE

As the teams look around the library for a multipurpose space location for the new activity, they will use Workform 18, Considerations for Placement of the Activity, to assess whether areas under consideration possess the physical plant and technology support resources called for on Workform 12, Need—Physical Plant and Technology Support, and meet the spatial relationship needs called for on Workform 14, Need—Access, Spatial Relationships, and Signage, part II. The teams will consider the age of the audience, the amount of sound from the activity that might carry, the types of materials used to support the activity, the types of shelving needed to support the materials, the equipment that may be needed, and any special interior design issues. For example, an activity intended to provide a wide range of services to preschool children from Spanish-speaking homes could share space with the library's other preschool activities. The furniture and shelving would be the right sizes, and the decor would be appropriate for the age group. That same activity could not share space with the teen center, for not only would the furniture and shelving be inappropriate, but teens do not choose to spend their library time with preschoolers and their families.

The teams will assess the present multipurpose areas in the library to determine what space could support the new activity. Considering the services that must be adjacent to the new activity and what it must be distant from will quickly lead the team to specific areas in the library that can then be evaluated using Workform 18, Considerations for Placement of the Activity. Issues of HVAC, windows, lighting, flooring surfaces, and decor will be predetermined in a multipurpose area.

More than one multipurpose space may be suitable to house an activity. For instance, the homework center being planned for the Anytown Library could be housed in an existing teen area. It could also be housed in a part of the general seating area of the library, although that would not be an optimum solution, because the homework center will only be used after school and the general seating must still be available for other users. In a multipurpose area, the team will be most concerned with staff support for the activity and whether noise in the area will affect service delivery.

LOCATING A SINGLE-PURPOSE SPACE

Single-purpose space will be more difficult to carve out of your existing floor plan than multipurpose space. Again, the spatial relationship requirements on Workform 14, Need—Access, Spatial Relationships, and Signage, part II, will quickly lead the teams to specific areas in the library to evaluate. Use Workform 18, Considerations for Placement of the Activity, to determine whether services to support the activity are available nearby. Then the teams will consider the further requirement of being able to isolate the area for the new activity. For example, an option might be to place the furniture, equipment, or shelving as a barrier to create a sense of isolation for the single-purpose space. (See Workform 14, part III, and Workform 15, part III.) The teams may create a placement option that uses decor to indicate to library users the single purpose for which the area will be used. Issues of HVAC, windows, lighting, and flooring surfaces will be predetermined in a single-purpose area, and it would require considerable expense to alter just the single-purpose space.

LOCATING WALLED SPACE

The location of the new activity in walled space will be less expensive and less disruptive to other library services if an existing walled space can be reallocated for the new activity. This reallocation may be such a high priority that if a space just under the net square footage requirements (see Workform 16, Square Footage—Needed and Current) is available, the furnishings and equipment and the shelving teams may be asked if they can scale back the needs identified on Workform 8, Need—Furniture and Equipment, and Workform 10, Need—Shelving, to fit the room that is available. Another option might be to place different parts of the new activity in separate locations; perhaps the collection and shelving might be in an open multipurpose area, while equipment requiring special security would be in walled space behind a door that can be locked.

If the best option is creating a new walled area, be sure to consider the increase in square footage that will be created by building the walls for the area (see Tool Kit A, Calculating Square Footage, "Gross and Net Square Footage"). Using the information on services that must be adjacent, close to, or in sight of the new activity and what it must be away from (Workform 14, Need—Access, Spatial Relationships, and Signage, part II) will quickly lead the team to specific areas in the library that can then be evaluated using Workform 18, Considerations for Placement of the Activity.

Physical Plant and Technology Support Options

After the recommendation for the location of the activity is developed, the physical plant and technology team will consult the gaps listed in column A of Workform 17, Gaps and Options, and will develop options for filling the gaps in the location they are recommending. This may be as simple as counting electrical outlets or as complex as evaluating whether the lighting levels are appropriate for the activity if the gaps involve special lighting needs such as task lighting.

Developing options for technology support can be complex. We usually associate technology support with connectivity for additional computers. Many of the parameters for your options will be found on Workform 12, Need—Physical Plant and Technology Support, and Workform 13, Have—Physical Plant and Technology Support. For any computer installations, you have to take into consideration the need for both physical plant issues like electrical outlets and whether the location provides access to the library's server. If Internet connectivity is called for, the team will also need to check Workform 12, Need—Physical Plant and Technology Support, to determine whether the activity requires a secure Internet connection, the load the new activity will put on existing Internet connections in the area, and just how those computers will be connected to the Internet. One option for network connection cabling can be running cables through many kinds of floor surfaces. Alternately, cables can be dropped from the ceiling along poles, or can run around the periphery of the room. Many libraries install wireless Internet service to address the growing demand of users who bring in their own laptop computers, and this may be worthy of consideration. Is the recommended location within the wireless area? Bear in mind that wireless access is not a panacea; even when users bring in their own equipment, they still require electrical outlet access. Your options should take into consideration decisions about the security of the Internet access. If no one in your library has expertise in this area, your decision-making team might need to bring in a professional with the expertise to advise them.

Access and Signage Options

The access, spatial relationships, and signage team and the physical plant and technology support team have determined the location for the activity. Then the access, spatial relationships, and signage team will begin to develop options for access to the area where it is offered and for access to staff assistance required for the activity. They record the options that were not noted earlier as items that must be purchased on Workform 17, Gaps and Options. If the committee does not approve the recommendation for placement at its fourth meeting, the team will have to find a new location and review the options based on that new location.

Reviewing Options

The fourth meeting of the project committee will provide committee members an opportunity to review all of the gaps and options they have developed on Workform 17, Gaps and Options. Committee members should turn in their completed copies of Workform 17 to the chair a few days before the meeting to allow time to copy them and distribute them to everyone at the meeting. A sample agenda for the meeting is shown in figure 15.

During the meeting, the physical plant and technology support and the access, spatial relationships, and signage teams will present their recommendation for placement of the activity they developed through Workform 18, Considerations for Placement of the Activity. The committee should discuss the recommendation and, if possible, approve it before reviewing the options for filling the gaps. If the committee does not approve the placement recommendation, the meeting can proceed with the review of options. However, the options related to physical plant and technology support and those for access, spatial relationships, and signage will have to be revisited once there is consensus on the location of the activity.

The teams review all gaps and options they identified on Workform 17, and the committee may comment on which ones seem viable. This will involve a lot of careful consideration and discussion. Some resources will have one readily apparent option, and that will simplify the process. It is possible that committee members may ask questions that require individual teams to bring more information to the committee before an option can be evaluated for viability at the next meeting. It is not necessary to limit the options to just one way to fill a resource gap until the committee has a more definite idea of the costs and time inherent in the different options (which will be researched through forthcoming workforms). Many resources will only have one option to fill the gap, but for those resources having multiple options, any option the committee agrees is viable should go forward to the next step.

FIGURE 15
Meeting 4: Sample Agenda

Fourth Committee Meeting

Purpose:	Determine placement of the activity and review Workform 18, Considerations for Placement of the Activity
	Discuss the options that the committee teams have developed for Workform 17, Gaps and Options
	Determine if further information is needed to evaluate the options
	Introduce Workform 19, Expense Estimates for Options, and Workform 20, Preliminary Project Time Estimates
	Assign teams to develop estimates needed for decision making for recommendations for filling gaps
Who:	All members of the facility project committee
Where:	Small conference room
When:	Date, start time, end time (meeting should be scheduled for two hours)
Materials:	Multiple copies of completed Workform 17, Gaps and Options, and Workform 18, Considerations for Placement of the Activity, for everyone who is attending the meeting; blank copies of Workform 19, Expense Estimates for Options, and Workform 20, Preliminary Project Time Estimates
Preparation:	Teams bring their completed Workforms 8–18

AGENDA

[Start time]	Review Workform 18, Considerations for Placement of the Activity
	Discuss and vote on recommendation for placement of activity (20 minutes)
	Review Workform 17, Gaps and Options
	Discuss options and assign teams to collect any further information (70 minutes)
	Introduce Workform 19, Expense Estimates for Options, and Workform 20, Preliminary Project Time Estimates (15 minutes)
	Assign teams to research expense and time estimates and complete Workforms 19 and 20 if applicable for next meeting (5 minutes)
	Questions (10 minutes)
[End time]	Adjourn

Part 7 of the Anytown case study illustrates how the Anytown committee dealt with the placement of the activity and identified options for filling gaps for their homework center. They also determined what further information the teams needed to provide so they could evaluate the viability of options, and they eliminated some options in their fourth meeting.

Anytown Public Library Homework Center

PART 7: Identifying Options

The Anytown homework center committee teams each completed a copy of Workform 17, Gaps and Options. Then the committee was ready for its fourth meeting.

When the committee meeting was convened, the physical plant and technology support and the access, spatial relationships, and signage teams presented their recommendation for the location of the homework center. At the last meeting it was decided that they would split the homework center into a multipurpose space for group computer stations and open study, and two walled study rooms. Options for placement included placing the multipurpose part at the edge of the reference area, in an area divided off from the teen room, or in a wide corridor between reference and the teen room. The quiet study rooms could be located in existing rooms off the reference area, or on the lower level of the library in an area for meeting rooms away from reference. The teams decided that placing the multipurpose study area adjacent to reference services was not viable because even pairs of students working on a project together would disturb the other reference area users, and it would be very difficult to reserve tables in reference for just the students' use. The option of placing the multipurpose area in the teen room met the requirements from Workform 18, Considerations for Placement of the Activity, and Workform 14, Need—Access, Spatial Relationships, and Signage, so this was their recommendation. After discussion, a vote was taken, and the committee unanimously approved their recommendation. Next the committee discussed the team's recommendation for placing the study rooms in the existing rooms adjacent to the reference area, rather than the rooms on the lower level. This location met the requirements from Workform 18, Considerations for Placement of the Activity, and Workform 14, Need—Access, Spatial Relationships, and Signage, by allowing easy access to reference resources for the proposed study rooms. Another vote was taken, and the committee also approved this recommendation.

Then the committee reviewed Workform 17, Gaps and Options. The furniture and equipment team began with their report on looking around the library to see if they could reallocate four 4-person study tables. They said they had considered using the 6-person study tables now in the

WORKFORM 17 **Gaps and Options**

Project Name: Homework Center   *Library or Unit: Anytown*

A. Gaps for Furniture	B. Options for Filling the Gap
1. Four 4-person study tables for multipurpose area	a. Purchase. b. c.
2. Two 6-person tables for study rooms	a. Reallocate two 6-person tables from reference. b. Purchase. c.

4. 37 chairs
    16 chairs for study tables
    9 chairs for group computer stations
    12 chairs for study rooms
	a. Reuse reference table chairs for study rooms.
	b. Purchase chairs for study tables and computer stations.
	c. Reallocate chairs from meeting room for study tables and computer stations.

reference area to fill the gap, but those were larger tables. They could find no tables in the library that would seat four, so they recommended purchasing the four 4-person study tables. However, the team noted that if they found a way to create two walled study rooms, they might be able to use two of the reference area tables to address the gap for two 6-person study room tables. Thus, they had recorded that as an option. When the furniture and equipment team discussed the usage of the reference tables with the reference staff, it was determined that the tables in reference were seldom in use all at once, so those tables could be reallocated. Because the library doesn't have any 3-person group computer stations, they recommended purchasing new group computer stations.

The furniture and equipment team then reported their search for chairs for the homework center's computer stations and tables. They decided that one option would be to use extra stacking chairs from the meeting room at the computer stations. Another option would be to purchase the chairs. The committee members decided the team needed to do further research to determine whether the meeting room chairs were available for reallocation and were an appropriate height before they could determine whether this would be a viable option.

WORKFORM 17 **Gaps and Options**

Project Name: Homework Center   *Library or Unit: Anytown*

A. **Gaps for Equipment**	B. **Options for Filling the Gap**
1. Three computers	a. Purchase—county program, order online, store. b. Reallocate one from teen area. c. Reallocate one from technical services.

The furniture and equipment team went on to report their gap findings and options on the equipment copy of Workform 17. They found that they needed three computers and that one of the Internet access computers now in the teen area could possibly be reallocated to the new homework center. They said that there was also a computer in technical services that might be reallocated because the technical services staff reported that it was seldom used. However, before they could decide whether they could use reallocated computers, they still had to determine whether these computers had all the necessary capabilities needed for the homework center computers, whether they had the memory required, and whether they would work with the printers in the new homework center. Because the Anytown Library doesn't have dedicated information technology staff to determine the existing computers' capabilities, the furniture and equipment team was charged with consulting with the company that provides the library's computer support to determine whether the teen area and technical services computers could be used.

Some committee members ruled out the reallocation of the computer from technical services because it was too old and would not have the USB ports required for connectivity with the color printers required for the homework center. The furniture and equipment team said they hoped that because the computer in the young adult area was recently purchased, it would meet all the requirements. That computer could have all the necessary software loaded on it and was currently connected to the color printer required for the homework center. The team listed options for where to purchase other computers meeting the required specifications. Committee members mentioned options for purchasing that included using the county purchasing program, ordering online, or purchasing through a local store.

Proceeding through Workform 17, the committee reviewed options for all the gaps.

WORKFORM 17 **Gaps and Options**
Project Name: Homework Center   *Library or Unit: Anytown*

A. Gaps for Technology Support	B. Options for Filling the Gap
1. Three computer links to library Internet network	a. Could be connected to library's network by pole drops from ceiling or use wireless network. b. If group computer stations are near pillars, build out pillars and run cabling inside new pillar walls. c. Install wireless network.
2. Network three computers to color printer	a. Use wireless printer connectivity. b. Run wires along path with Internet connectivity, then connect to printer at service desk. c.

Notice that the options listed in the workform do not include any cost estimates. That is because Workform 17 is for trying out ideas—there may be a lot of adding and deleting of options until the final set is decided upon. There is no point in investing time in assessing costs until you are sure of the recommendations you want to present. After the committee has created a list of the options they consider viable, then the job of gathering cost information can begin.

Step 6.4
Evaluate Options

The options the project team assembled on Workform 17, Gaps and Options, represent ways to fill the resource gaps for a new activity without adding new space. The committee now develops criteria so they can decide which options they will recommend. Two universal criteria for evaluating almost all options are cost and delivery time. Many times the period of disruption to the delivery of the library's services will be a deciding factor in determining which options will be used. The committee will also develop criteria to help them decide between multiple options. This will prepare the committee for the next task—Task 7: Present Recommendations.

Estimating Expenses

Cost is a critical consideration affecting the viability of any option. Fiscal control is a prime consideration in every library project. Estimates made at this stage of planning will probably change because costs vary seasonally and often increase during the length of a project, but you should initiate essential fiscal controls now to give funding authorities at least a rough estimate of costs and to ensure that sufficient funds are available to complete the project. The estimates gathered now will help prioritize the options. The following sections on hidden costs, quality, and sources for cost estimates will help you as you complete Workform 19, Expense Estimates for Options. When you have completed the workform, give it to the chair so it can be copied and handed out to the group at your next meeting.

POSSIBLE HIDDEN EXPENSES

Some expenses will be readily apparent as the project committee develops options for specific resources and overall facilities needs for an activity. Others are less apparent. For example, if an option indicates shelving is to be reallocated and moved, hidden costs are associated with this option, such as labor costs for disassembling, moving, and reassembling the shelving. Other costs could include labor to handle the materials as they are removed and then replaced on the moved/new shelves, costs for repainting the shelving, and so on. Storage costs may come into play for the materials while other facility changes are made to allow for the installation of moved or new shelving. On the other hand, you may plan to incur very few bottom-line costs by using library staff to do the materials handling, using agency maintenance staff to move the shelves, and avoiding storage costs by completing the move in just a few days. However, your costs may be extensive if you plan to hire a library-materials moving company to do it all. These two ends of the spectrum of ways to handle shelf moving have very different bottom-line costs. Use existing costs in the regular library budget to estimate additional costs for advertising, utilities, publicity, insurance, labor, and other items on the list in figure 16 that are part of the normal cost of library service. Figure 16 presents expenses to consider as you complete Workform 19, Expense Estimates for Options.

FIGURE 16
List of Possible Hidden Expenses

Furniture and Equipment

Reupholstering/refinishing existing furniture
Packing supplies (boxes, padding, etc.)
Off-site storage
Rental equipment (trucks, ramps, copy machines, etc.)
Damage and replacement costs (for items to be moved, especially equipment)

Shelving

Off-site storage
Rental equipment (trucks, ramps, copy machines, etc.)

Building Features

Expensive or unique light bulbs
Outside experts (architects, contractors, plumbers, movers, etc.)
Labor (to build walls, move materials, etc.)
Advertising to get labor
Supplies for physical plant changes (wood, paint, wiring, etc.)
Moving of phone, electrical, and data lines
Leased space for service delivery while library or part of library is closed
Temporary physical plant changes (interim phone lines, temporary walls, etc.)

Other

Publicity
Insurance (increased coverage because of construction while library is open)
Utilities (increased costs)

QUALITY CONSIDERATIONS

Another consideration affecting cost estimates is quality. Obviously, you want the best products you can get, but everything from toilet seats to floor coverings is available in a range of prices based in part on the quality of the product. Furniture that is built specifically for libraries is expensive because it is made to last and stand up to heavy use. You *could* use household or office furniture, but remember—you get what you pay for. A comfortable chair for a home or office will not last as long as the one designed for public use will. Industrial-quality carpet squares are great for public areas of the library, but they cost more than carpet that comes in a roll. However, because it is easier to replace a single stained or worn carpet square, there may be a long-term replacement or maintenance savings involved. Service desks can be less expensive when purchased in sections from a library furniture vendor instead of being built locally to your specifications, but the ones in a catalog may not match other desks in the library or have the exact configuration you need. Just about everything you buy comes in varying qualities and, therefore, varying costs.

> **LEVEL OF EFFORT NOTE**
> **Quality Decisions**
>
> Quality decisions may be made *for* you if you're working under a requirement that any new items must match existing items, as is often true for furniture and shelving. Sometimes, however, you may be on your own to make this decision. Coming to agreement about quality with the committee and the administration before estimating costs can save a lot of time for the project team.

SOURCES FOR COST ESTIMATES

Cost estimates are just that—estimates. Try not to spend a lot of time coming up with exact costs for specific items because the price can easily change by the time an item is purchased or a contract signed. Workform 19, Expense Estimates for Options, provides a place to record the estimates you collect. Remember that the team will only want to gather information that will affect which options are recommended. The following are some suggested sources of estimates.

Furniture, equipment, and shelving. For information on costs of furniture, equipment, and shelving, you can consult statewide, regional, or library system contracts with established prices for library furnishings. If your project is using experts, they can probably provide cost estimates. Look in vendor catalogs (Brodart, Demco, and Gaylord, for example) to get an idea of the cost ranges for various quality levels. Use *Libris DESIGN* software if you have access to someone who has had the training program. This software allows selection from three levels of pricing for furniture and equipment.

Physical plant and technology support. Information about physical plant and technology support can be obtained by asking the people who do the type of work you want done to give you a ballpark estimate of their fees. If you plan to use a general contractor to manage your physical plant changes, get several estimates.

If you have a library building consultant, he or she can estimate average local construction costs. The costs for a major renovation are customarily estimated in dollars per square foot. Renovation is usually less per square foot than new construction, unless it involves a lot of demolition and replacement of operating systems. However, keep in mind that there may be cost increases if the contractor has to work around the regular functions of a building open to the public.

The cost per square foot will vary depending on where you are located because the construction of public buildings is affected by local conditions. Ask library experts and consultants for an estimate of renovation costs in your area. If your agency's request for proposal, bid, or qualifications process must be followed, you can still get a general idea of costs by asking now even if you are not ready to issue a proposal, bid, or list of qualifications.

Access, signage, and decor. Another area where experts can help you with cost information is that of access, signage, and decor. If your project isn't using experts for signage, window treatments, decorative items, lighting, and other special items, ask several vendors to provide estimates to your specifications. Bear in mind that contractor discounts are available for some of these items if your building contractor or decorator buys them.

Estimating Service and Product Delivery Times

Resource teams may also need to gather some general information so they can consider how long it takes to implement a particular option. Implementation time is sometimes the deciding factor in whether an option is practical. For example, most furniture providers have certain chairs that they always carry in stock in their warehouse and can deliver in a week to ten days. However, if your plan calls for chairs the vendor does not have in stock, it can sometimes take months for them to acquire and deliver the chairs you order, which could cause critical delays in the implementation of your project. Therefore, resource teams should gather delivery information on their options, since an extended delay may cause them to change their recommendations.

Workform 3, Preliminary Task List and Timeline, is an integral part of the charge to the project committee. The time-estimate information the teams develop now is very different from the timeline that accompanied the charge to the committee because the planning committee is projecting how long *various steps* of the option implementation will take. The committee does not know exactly how long project approvals will take and, therefore, when the work of the project will begin. Just as with the budget estimates, many timing elements can change before project implementation begins. Therefore, the team will simply list the steps involved in their options and attach an estimate of how long each step is expected to take. For example, if your project involves purchasing new shelving—and it always takes eight weeks for shelving to arrive after it is ordered—this will be useful information in deciding whether to use that particular shelving. This information will also provide needed data for the implementation of the project. The project implementation committee will develop a schedule so the shelving will be timed to arrive after the floor surface is prepared and before the new materials arrive for the shelves. Use Workform 20, Preliminary Project Time Estimates, to record the information you collect about the time factors involved in different options. These estimates will alert you to options that may need to be reconsidered to accommodate the intended completion date. Turn in your completed workform to the chair so it can be compiled and distributed at the next committee meeting.

Developing Evaluation Criteria and Ranking Options

Evaluation criteria are the standards against which you will compare each option to see which is best, next best, and so on. Local situations and conditions will define the standards you set to provide the activity at the desired level, and every situation has its own unique priorities. The process of ranking options must support the top priority of achieving your stated goal for the project within the library's budget and time allowance, but other priorities can also be important in your library. For example, if library staff have experienced a lot of change in recent years and feel stressed, then options that do not disturb work routines will assume a higher priority on your list. If an option for one project also happens to solve an existing challenge in an adjacent area, you might give that option extra weight because it resolves a number of existing challenges. Some ideas for generally stated standards against which to compare options include the following:

- Option limits disruption of staff work.
- Option is achievable within an acceptable budget.
- Option does not impinge upon other activities.
- Option can be completed within the time frame for the project.

The committee may choose these standards, further refine them, and add other criteria depending on what is important to the committee, users, fellow employees, and library managers. The committee chair should check with administrators regarding the criteria they think will be most important for evaluating options before the fifth meeting, so that management's priorities are represented in the discussion.

At the end of Step 6.4: Evaluate Options the project committee will have evaluated the options so they can make recommendations and explain why they have ranked the options as they have. Decisions about which evaluation criteria, in addition to cost and delivery time, will be used to prioritize the options are made in the committee's fifth meeting. Figure 17 provides a suggested agenda.

In the fifth meeting, committee members will first remove any options that their research for Workform 19, Expense Estimates for Options, and Workform 20, Preliminary Project Time Estimates, showed to be too expensive or too time-consuming for further consideration. Then the committee members brainstorm evaluation criteria and record their ideas on a flip chart. They select the four or five criteria they agree are most important for their library. The committee breaks into resource teams to complete Workform 21, Option Evaluation. Using the criteria the committee has agreed upon and information that was recorded on Workforms 19 and 20, team members rank each option and give reasons for ranking them in that order.

Step 6.5
Develop Committee Recommendations

The final step in Task 6 is a major decision point in the project. The teams compile a list of the recommendations on Workform 21, Option Evaluation. If your teams did not create multiple options and did not complete Workform 21, they may want to use the workform simply to record recommendations and the reasons they are making those recommendations. Each team will report the recommendations they recorded on Workform 21 to the committee to see if the other teams have considerations that might affect their recommendations. At the end of the fifth meeting, the committee has a list of *recommendations* for how to acquire resources to fill the gaps in the project and the reasons why the recommendations are being made. These are the recommendations that will be included in the preliminary report in Task 7. The preliminary report informs the library administration of the committee's decisions and seeks approval of the recommendations.

FIGURE 17
Meeting 5: Sample Agenda

Fifth Committee Meeting

Purpose: Discuss the criteria that teams will use to evaluate the options developed on Workform 17, Gaps and Options; prioritize options

Who: All members of the facility project committee

Where: Small conference room

When: Date, start time, end time (meeting should be scheduled for two hours)

Materials: Flip chart, easel, and markers. Copies of the completed Workform 17, Gaps and Options, showing changes decided upon at meeting 4 for everyone at the meeting. Copies of completed Workform 19, Expense Estimates for Options, and Workform 20, Preliminary Project Time Estimates, for distribution to each committee member. Copies of Workform 21, Option Evaluation, to distribute to the teams

Preparation: Teams bring their completed Workform 12, Need—Physical Plant and Technology Support; Workform 13, Have—Physical Plant and Technology Support; and Workform 16, Square Footage—Needed and Current

AGENDA

[Start time]   Review the list of evaluation criteria suggestions in Step 6.4 (5 minutes)

Review Workform 19, Expense Estimates for Options, and Workform 20, Preliminary Project Time Estimates, to remove options that won't be evaluated (20 minutes)

Distribute Workform 21, Option Evaluation (5 minutes)

Brainstorm criteria appropriate for use to evaluate the options (10 minutes)

Decide on four or five criteria that are most important for recommendations (10 minutes)

Complete Workform 21, Option Evaluation (in resource teams) (15 minutes)

Report team recommendations in each resource area (30 minutes)

Introduce and review the steps in Task 7 (5 minutes)

Distribute and review figure 18, When to Use the Workforms That Support Tasks 7 and 8 (10 minutes)

Questions (10 minutes)

[End time]   Adjourn

It is important to remember that the committee may make recommendations, but it does not have final decision-making authority. This is why it is critical to explain clearly why recommendations were made and to retain information on the other options. The administration will make the final decisions, so it needs the benefit of the committee's research and best thinking.

Key Points to Remember

Identify the gap, or surplus, between what is needed for the project's implementation and what is now in place.

Be creative in developing many options to fill a gap.

Consider the use of resources throughout the library when looking for furniture, equipment, and shelving to reallocate.

Consider what the new activity must be near and what it must be away from when looking for space to reallocate.

Gather pricing and delivery information to help evaluate options.

Only collect data that you will use in evaluating options.

Base priorities on the stated goal of the project and your library's important considerations.

Chapter 5

Prepare Recommendations and Present Reports

MILESTONES

By the time you finish this chapter you will know how to

- estimate a project budget
- present options to library management with recommendations
- complete your final report to the funding authority

Congratulations! Your committee is now ready to prepare a preliminary report informing administrators of your recommendations. This chapter will provide the committee with guidelines and procedures for preparing your report to management in Task 7: Present Recommendations and Task 8: Prepare the Final Report and Get Approvals. Task 7 helps you prepare a preliminary report for your library administrators so they can review all the committee's recommendations and approve them before the final report is prepared. Task 8 will guide you through preparing the final report and submitting it to your library's funding authorities for approval. The tasks in this chapter include two workforms, one for each task. See figure 18 to help you decide if you will use both workforms to complete the tasks.

FIGURE 18
When to Use the Workforms That Support Tasks 7 and 8

Workform	When to Use	When Not to Use
Workform 22: Furniture and Equipment List (Step 7.1)	Complete this workform if your architect, interior designer, or decision makers require a list.	Do not use this form if you are not asked for a furniture list.
Workform 23: Cost Compilations (Step 8.1)	Complete this workform if you need to prepare a budget to get approvals for your project.	If the project does not require a budget or paying for items or labor, do not use this workform.

TASK 7: PRESENT RECOMMENDATIONS

Task 1: Define the Project
Task 2: Plan the Project
Task 3: Prepare the Committee
Task 4: Organize the Data Collection Process
Task 5: Collect Preliminary Data
Task 6: Identify Gaps and Evaluate Options
Task 7: Present Recommendations
    Step 7.1: Prepare the preliminary report
    **Step 7.2: Present the preliminary report
    and seek approvals**
Task 8: Prepare the Final Report and Get Approvals

Task 7 provides guidelines for preparing the information for your preliminary report to library management. You will want to give managers enough information so they can approve the plan—or recommend adjustments to the plan—before you seek final approval from the library's governing body.

The project committee has completed a considerable amount of work and has decided on recommendations for implementing the facility project. The administrators have already approved the square footage and type of space for the project: multipurpose, single-purpose, or walled space. The next challenges are to tell administrators where and how you recommend creating the space for the new activity and to clearly and concisely present the data on which you based your decisions—by providing the readers with enough detail to make your case but without being overwhelming. You must prepare the report so readers can quickly grasp the intent, budget, and timeline of the project. The preliminary report you prepare for management's approval should include workforms and narrative presentations that clearly represent compilations of the data underlying your recommendations: an idea of how long the project will take to be completed, cost estimates for parts of the project that might affect decision making, and an executive summary of the report. The outline shown in figure 19 is a suggested structure for organizing your preliminary report of project recommendations. You present this report to decision makers at Task 7 in the *Managing Facilities for Results* process so they can approve the options they want to implement.

Step 7.1
Prepare the Preliminary Report

Fortunately, the teams have collected and recorded most of the information needed for the preliminary report on the workforms for the planning process. Writing the preliminary

FIGURE 19
Preliminary Report Format

Table of Contents—List sections of the report with their corresponding page numbers

Executive Summary—Quick overview of goals, prioritized options with cost estimates, results of data analysis, and projected timetable for project implementation

Introduction—Brief description of the project, including the rationale behind it, its intended goals and users, and the written charge to the project committee

Part 1: Recommendations—Evaluation criteria for prioritizing options, recommendations and other prioritized options, data-collection process overview

Part 2: Cost and Time Considerations—Estimated costs, furniture and equipment list, and time estimates for the project

Part 3: Workforms—Workforms illustrating the options that the committee considered in making its recommendations

---

LEVEL OF EFFORT NOTE
Preparing the Preliminary Report

The committee chair or someone from the committee delegated by the committee chair will prepare the preliminary report. If additional information, like a detailed list of furniture and equipment, is required, the team that has worked with that resource will gather the additional information and give it to the person delegated to prepare the report.

report should be mainly a matter of organizing the information so it can be easily grasped by someone who has not been through the process with your committee.

Preparing the Executive Summary of the Preliminary Report

Because the committee has amassed a large amount of information about resources needed for the project, it will be important to begin your report with a table of contents to help people find their way to information in the document. The table of contents is followed by a one-page executive summary. Although the executive summary appears at the beginning of the report, it is easier to compile it after you have completed the rest of the report. The executive summary includes a statement of the goals of the activity or service you intend to provide and the population it will serve, an overview of what will be accomplished in the project, and bottom-line figures. This summary serves as an overview of the project and is an efficient way for busy decision makers to get the gist of the recommendations, timeline, and costs. It will highlight important data in a compact format. The following are the questions to answer and elements of the executive summary.

Why are we doing this? Service goals of the project (from committee charge)

How much room will it take? Total square footage affected by the project (from Workform 16, Square Footage—Needed and Current)

What will be displaced? Services currently using space with square footage figures (location decision from the committee's fourth meeting)

What has to be done to the space to create the new service? Proposed changes to space, with square footage figures for the proposed changes (Workform 16, Square Footage—Needed and Current, and Workform 21, Option Evaluation)

How expensive will this be? A list of critical factors that will affect the project, with cost projections for the work being listed; for example, HVAC or lighting adjustments, reorienting of book stacks (Workform 19, Expense Estimates for Options)

What are we buying? A list of furniture, equipment, and shelving requirements with estimated costs (Workform 19, Expense Estimates for Options, and Workform 22, Furniture and Equipment List)

How long will the project take? An estimate of how long you think the project implementation will take (Workform 20, Preliminary Project Time Estimates)

Part 8 of the Anytown case study provides an example of the executive summary for their preliminary report. You can see how this provides a brief overview of the project.

CASE STUDY

Anytown Public Library Homework Center

PART 8: Executive Summary of Preliminary Report

The Anytown Library's homework center committee compiled a preliminary report for the library's administration. After writing the report they prepared an executive summary of it. The Anytown executive summary is shown below.

ANYTOWN PUBLIC LIBRARY HOMEWORK CENTER
Preliminary Report

Executive Summary

The Anytown Public Library established a goal that "Students in Anytown will have the skills and tools they need to succeed in school." The objectives to measure progress toward that goal are

> *Objective 1:* Each year, at least 4,000 students will use the resources of the homework center.

> *Objective 2:* Each year, library staff and volunteers will answer at least 6,000 homework-related reference questions.

To accomplish this level of service, a library staff committee was given a charge to "identify the facility-related changes needed to develop the homework center identified in the library strategic plan and present the recommended changes to the library administrative council by June 30, 2XXX."

The committee recommends creating an area of 450 square feet in the current teen area for 4 group study tables and 3 three-person group study computer stations, and 2 group project rooms in the small rooms adjacent to the reference area. These will be created by consolidating the nonfiction collection onto fewer shelves so one row can be removed and moving four upholstered chairs to another side of the area, so that some of the area can be dedicated to students after school and on weekends.

In the course of a gap analysis conducted by the committee, data was collected and compared on what is needed for the project and what is currently used in the library. The furniture and equipment that cannot be reallocated from within the library and must be purchased to provide what is needed are listed below with estimated costs:

> 3 three-person group computer stations ($1,050)

> 4 four-person study tables ($600)

25 chairs for table and computer station seating ($900)

2 computers ($1,200)

a wireless access point ($100)

installation expenses for the wireless network ($150)

The library will be reallocating 2 study tables, 12 chairs, and 2 small study rooms from the reference area for this project.

The library would like to initiate the service at the beginning of the school year. All furniture and equipment are available for delivery within 6 weeks of placing an order, so it will be possible to begin the new service in September if it is approved in this year's budget cycle. The estimated total cost is $4,000.

Writing the Introduction to the Preliminary Report

Begin by writing the introduction to the report. It should state the activity or service that the library intends to add, since this is the reason for the project. Then include the administrators' original charge to the committee (see Step 1.2: Define the Project's Scope and Intent), the intended goals for the new service, and who the intended users are. Also include some information about who served on the committee and the expertise they brought to the project.

Writing Part 1: Recommendations for the Preliminary Report

The following list shows what to include and how to format part 1, the recommendations.

> Introduction to part 1, which explains what this part of the report covers
>
> Discuss evaluation criteria developed in the fifth committee meeting
>
> Give recommendations, with reasons for their selection
>
> Include other options the committee considered, and why they weren't recommended

INTRODUCTION

The first paragraphs of part 1 give an overview of what will be included in this part of the report. Provide a brief introduction to the way the teams developed their recommendations in order to give readers a context for the recommendations you are presenting. Explain that the process the committee used is founded on data-based decision making. Point out that workforms were completed to gather data about the needs of the activity and the resources currently in place for that activity. Define the gap analysis part of the process as a look at the difference between what is needed and what is now available.

CRITERIA

Because readers of the preliminary report will not have participated in your discussions about establishing evaluation criteria for your options and recommendations, this section of the report will provide them with a better understanding of why you have chosen your recommendations. Explain the process that was used and the evaluation criteria the committee developed, agreed upon, and used to prioritize the options. You can include the list of criteria that was attached to Workform 21, Option Evaluation.

RECOMMENDATIONS

Organize the recommendations by resource area and present them as clearly as possible, along with the reasons the committee recommends them. It is here that you make your case for the recommendations. Be sure to include details about how these recommendations meet your criteria, such as why you think this plan provides the most benefits to the users, how this new service will fit into the library's current service patterns, and why this will be the most effective way to offer the new service or activity. Use bulleted lists, short paragraphs, and titled sections to make this section readable and to ensure that key points stand out.

Clearly presenting the recommendations in a parallel format by resource area throughout the report will make it easy to understand for decision makers who have not been a part of the committee discussions. Be sure to present the recommendations separately from the options that the committee is *not* recommending. Because the workforms that summarize the information you cite here about the recommendations will be included in part 3 of this report, you can cite them in explaining your recommendations.

Develop a narrative format that leads readers through the various elements of your project. For example, you might want to address the requirements of the project in the same order as the workforms the committee used in their research: listing possible contracted professional services (Workform 4, Need for Outside Experts); furniture, equipment, shelving, and physical plant and technology support requirements and any access or signage issues that were addressed (Workform 21, Option Evaluation); and actual space requirements, including the selection of single- or multipurpose space or walled space (Workform 16, Square Footage—Needed and Current).

Give readers a clear picture of how the committee recommendations will appear when implemented. Using comparisons of current space allocations to the space recommendations from Workform 16, Square Footage—Needed and Current, also helps decision makers envision the new area that a service will use in the library. If the space requirement for the new service can be readily compared to a current service area, readers will easily be able to visualize the space required for the recommendation. For example, explain that a project in which the library plans to create a storytelling area in children's services is about half the size of the current picture book area. This comparison will help give readers a good idea of the size of the proposed storytelling area.

At the end of this section, include pertinent observations from the committee's teams. For example, in our case study of the homework center, staff observations about how students are currently seeking help with their homework might help decision makers understand a recommendation to place the center adjacent to the reference area or to place it in the teen services area. Some of these issues may not have been included in Workform 21, Option Evaluation, where the needs of the whole library's services and library staff were under consideration. Include the opinions of staff members who will be implementing the activity. If, for example, you're recommending a teen homework center, the teen services staff and reference staff will probably have opinions based on their knowledge of the user group about the best location for it, and those opinions should also be included here for the administrators' consideration.

OTHER OPTIONS

Presentation of the other options that the committee developed should follow the same order and format that you established for presenting the recommendations. It is important for administrators to see what options you have considered but not accepted and why. This section will contain a lot of information, so it must be very well organized and clearly presented to allow the readers to follow your reasoning.

If you are describing more than one option per category, number the options so they are clearly delineated for readers. Under each resource category, list and number each option that was considered with the reasons for prioritizing particular options lower. Use the information from Workform 21, Option Evaluation, to do this, and reference this workform in part 3 of the report.

Writing Part 2: Cost and Time Considerations

Part 2 of your preliminary report will link the recommendations of the committee with cost and timing information that will affect the approval of the project. This part of your report will use the same sequence of topics as in part 1 to make it easier for readers to link the cost and time data with the recommendations in part 1. Because costs and timelines for the delivery of goods and services can vary greatly, both seasonally and over other time periods, this section will, of necessity, contain general estimates. In addition, you may have to provide a furniture and equipment list with this preliminary report. Interior designers and architects often request such lists to determine where all the furniture and equipment for an area will be allocated.

Point out that the committee is only providing information on issues that might affect decisions about which recommendations in the report are approved for the final plan. Management will probably want at least a broad estimate of how much each recommendation will cost and how long it will take to implement it before they can approve each recommendation.

INTRODUCTION

In the introduction to part 2, provide information from Workform 19, Expense Estimates for Options, and Workform 20, Preliminary Project Time Estimates, about the sources of costs and delivery time information contained in this part. For example, if anything stands out as potentially cost-prohibitive, this is your opportunity to explain why the recommendation stands. If any of the materials will need to be delivered in sequence, you might draw that to the readers' attention. In addition, you should mention here anything that is likely to delay the project so that it can be addressed prior to the implementation stage. The introduction is your opportunity to point out why the committee has made its recommendations, particularly if cost or timing might make another choice appear to be more advantageous.

COST INFORMATION

Remember that for the purposes of the preliminary report, you will only include cost estimates for items that might affect the decision to approve that recommendation. The idea is to clearly present possible obstacles now, in the planning stage, rather than surprising the library administrators with an unexpectedly large expense once the plans have been approved and are being implemented. Include in the report estimated major expenses for the recommendations of the committee. Use the information the teams provided on Workform 19, Expense Estimates for Options, to provide cost information for the most expensive items in the recommendation. If you need to prepare a budget at this preliminary stage, see "The Budget" under Step 8.1: Prepare and Assemble the Final Report. If you have to prepare a budget, be sure to include the items that only had one option along with the items on Workform 19.

THE FURNITURE AND EQUIPMENT LIST

If you will work with an interior designer or architect in implementing your project, ask the furniture and equipment team to provide a list of all the furniture and equipment that is called for in the committee's recommendations. Include the source (whether reallocated or purchased or a combination of both) and cost of each piece of furniture and equipment. Use Workform 22, Furniture and Equipment List, to compile this information. The information for Workform 22 is pulled from Workform 8, Need—Furniture and Equipment, column B; Workform 17, Gaps and Options; the resource list on Workform 19, Expense Estimates for Options; and Workform 21, Option Evaluation.

This list provides the readers with another way to view the resources required for the project. Even though your furniture and equipment list will not have cost information attached to each item on it, such a comprehensive list of all furniture and equipment needed for the activity may be a clearer way for the reader to see the scope of the furniture and equipment that is currently in place, will be reallocated, or must be purchased for the activity.

TIME PROJECTIONS

The implementation time projections will also have an impact on the administration's decision about whether the proposed recommendations will be practical for the library. Workform 20, Preliminary Project Time Estimates, will provide timeline information for the report and should be included in the workforms grouped at the end of the report. Point out to the readers of the report that the committee is only providing estimated times for the implementation of steps for resources, if this might affect decisions about which recommendations in the report are approved for the final plan. The final decisions about what resources are purchased, and therefore how long the project will take, will be determined by the administration, but the report will provide the information they need to guide their decision.

Compiling Part 3: Workforms Supporting the Preliminary Report

Both numerical and nonnumerical data are presented on the workforms in part 3 of the report, and each data type has its own value to decision makers. You will want to include enough of your workforms to demonstrate how you reached your recommendations and describe what other options the committee considered, but not all the data the committee has collected.

Wherever possible, include the workforms that have compiled information from earlier workforms. This will vary depending on which workforms your committee decided were relevant to your project. Some of the workforms that you will probably include will be Workform 4, Need for Outside Experts; Workform 16, Square Footage—Needed and Current; Workform 17, Gaps and Options; Workform 18, Considerations for Placement of the Activity; Workform 19, Expense Estimates for Options; Workform 20, Preliminary Project Time Estimates; Workform 21, Option Evaluation; and Workform 22, Furniture and Equipment List. Not all committees will have used all of these workforms, but include the ones you did complete to provide an overview of how you reached your recommendations.

The person delegated to write the report will write a summary of the nonnumerical data so the readers can quickly grasp the content of the majority of the comments. For example, any comments accompanying the options for furniture for the project will be used to illustrate why a recommendation was made to reallocate current furnishings, rather than to purchase new furniture. For example, if there is an upholstered chair in your current periodicals reading area, you may have considered the options of moving it elsewhere for continued use, reupholstering it to fit the decor in a new quiet reading area, or having the library purchase new furniture that accommodates an adult sitting with a child to share a book in your reconfigured children's services area. It will be helpful for readers of the report to know that you considered all these options before making your recommendation.

Step 7.2
Present the Preliminary Report and Seek Approvals

Distribute copies of the completed preliminary report to everyone on the committee with a message that they should either approve the report as it stands or notify the chair of any corrections to the information by a specific date. Once everyone on the committee has approved the information in the preliminary report and any changes to it, you can distribute the report to the administrative decision makers.

If the committee chair regularly reported the committee's progress throughout the planning process, this report should contain no surprises for administrators. When you submit the report, request a follow-up meeting with decision makers to answer any questions about the recommendations and the data presented in the report. Figure 20 suggests topics for that meeting.

The meeting with administrative decision makers will be an opportunity for them to hear the committee's recommendations and its reasons for making those recommendations. Allow time for decision makers to ask for clarification about any of the data in the preliminary report. They may also have questions about the other options that were considered by the committee and why those options were prioritized lower than the recommendations. If, at the end of this meeting, there remain sets of proposed solutions requiring decisions, propose a date when these decisions can be expected and another date when the committee should submit the final report to the funding authority.

Administrative decision makers may request some further information from the committee or add their own prioritization criteria to be applied to the options the committee has considered. The meeting provides the committee with an opportunity to make their best case for their recommendations, but ultimately the final authority for approval belongs to the administrative decision makers.

FIGURE 20
Meeting 6: Sample Agenda

Sixth Committee Meeting

Purpose:	Answer any questions that administrators have about the preliminary report's recommendations
Who:	Decision-making administrators and facility project committee chair
Where:	Small conference room
When:	Date, start time, end time (meeting should be scheduled for two hours)
Materials:	Extra copies of the preliminary report for attendees; two copies of all workforms
Preparation:	Distribute copies of the preliminary report to all attendees at least a week before the meeting

AGENDA

[Start time]	Welcome and introductions, if needed (5 minutes)
	Review of project goals (5 minutes)
	Review the committee's recommendations and the reasons for recommending them (25 minutes)
	Review other options and why they were prioritized lower (10 minutes)
	Review cost and timeline considerations for recommendations (15 minutes)
	Answer questions about the preliminary report and recommendations (30 minutes)
	Make decision about next steps (10 minutes)
	Questions, clarifications (10 minutes)
	Set next deadline for administrative recommendations for final report (5 minutes)
	Set deadline for the committee to complete final report (5 minutes)
[End time]	Adjourn

Following the administrative review, if the administration has directed the committee to make changes in the report, the team that developed the recommendations for the affected resource will work with the committee chair and anyone else on the committee who has the relevant expertise to develop recommendations that meet the administration's conditions. If the option is one not previously considered in the preliminary report, they will have to gather the data by reusing the appropriate workform for this purpose, if necessary, and present their new option to the decision makers for approval. However, if the recommendation that administrators approved for the final report was decided upon at the report meeting, the committee can proceed with preparation of the final report for the library's funding or governing authorities.

In the following part of the case study, the Anytown administrative decision makers had previously approved the square footage requirement and the recommendation to put the homework center in multipurpose space. However, after reading the preliminary report, they reject the committee's recommended placement of the homework center and prefer the option of placing it elsewhere in the library.

Anytown Public Library Homework Center

PART 9: Anytown Public Library Administrators'
Reaction to Preliminary Report

As part of their preliminary report, the Anytown homework center committee recommended placing the homework center's group computer stations in the teen area and the small group study rooms in rooms adjacent to the reference area. The administration overruled this recommendation. While they appreciated all the data the committee had collected, and they agreed with the committee's reasoning that the teen librarian would ideally be the best person to help the students use the group computer stations, they were more concerned that the teen room was staffed by only one person. Therefore, during the library's service hours, there would often be no staff member in the teen area to assist the students with their homework research and supervise them. The administrators wanted the homework center to be adjacent to the reference area so there would always be a librarian nearby to oversee the students and assist them with their assignments.

All parts of the preliminary report were accepted except the placement of the group computer stations and study tables. Now before they prepare the final report, the Anytown homework center committee is charged to find a way to place the homework center adjacent to the reference area in the library. After discussing with the reference staff the data the committee had collected and the problem of fitting the homework center near the reference area, the reference staff suggest they could create more open space near reference by weeding the reference collection and removing some of the shelving to make room for the group computer stations. Now the committee is ready to prepare their final report, which the administration will give to the funding authority that approves the expenditures for the homework center.

TASK 8: PREPARE THE FINAL REPORT AND GET APPROVALS

Task 1: Define the Project
Task 2: Plan the Project
Task 3: Prepare the Committee
Task 4: Organize the Data Collection Process
Task 5: Collect Preliminary Data
Task 6: Identify Gaps and Evaluate Options
Task 7: Present Recommendations
Task 8: Prepare the Final Report and Get Approvals
    Step 8.1: Prepare and assemble the final report
    Step 8.2: Present the final report to funding authorities

Task 8 focuses on presentations to governing bodies and government funding authorities, but there are many ways that libraries fund new activities. If your library is in the fortunate position of having the funds already in the budget to implement your project, then your final report will only have to gain the staff's support and the director's approval to proceed. In other situations, it may be necessary to reallocate funding from other library projects that are no longer providing effective service to the public in order to find the money in the library's budget to proceed with the new activity. Sometimes the library will seek a sponsor for a new activity that is expected to be popular with library users. For example, one local library funds a series of outdoor summer concerts on the library grounds with sponsorship from local businesses such as a bank. If you are lucky enough to have an active Friends of the Library organization that raises money for library activities, that organization may be willing to fund the improvements required to introduce a new activity. If so, you may have to make your presentation of the project's final plan to the board of the Friends group. No matter from whom you obtain the needed funds, you will need to make a clear and comprehensive presentation in your final plan so readers can quickly grasp the intent, scope, and expense of your project so that you can acquire the financial support you need to proceed to implementation.

Because you will be asking for an approval to commit funds to the project, you will probably have to submit a budget that covers all aspects of the project. Cost categories, in public library accounting, include *operating costs* and *capital costs.* These two basic cost categories can be applied to costs associated with buildings, furniture, and equipment. Facility-related *operating costs* in an annual library budget include expenditure categories such as utilities, cleaning supplies, contracts for services, and small equipment such as printers or personal sound augmentation devices. *Capital costs* are for major (usually one-time) purchases, such as major equipment and renovations or new construction, and are considered separately from the day-to-day expenses. Budgeted funds set aside for capital costs usually move forward from one year to the next if the project spans fiscal years. *Operating costs* are usually for a single year, although in some library financial structures they *can* be rolled forward to the next year.

Budgets for major renovations, or "capital projects," as major renovations are often referred to in budgeting parlance, can include funds for items that would normally be considered part of operating costs if not purchased as part of the renovation. Furniture, computer equipment, shelving, and similar items are usually included in the overall cost of construction in a capital project budget. Whether *capital* or *operating,* funds for the project must be requested in advance and approved for an upcoming budget year by the library governing body.

If you are doing a major renovation that requires building walls, replacing large sections of flooring, or getting a large quantity of new shelving, furniture, or equipment, costs for these items will be built into the capital budget. Your project may not be funded as a capital project if it requires little or no change to the physical plant and will be completed within a single budget year. Related costs would then be requested in the regular annual operating budget. The source of funding and timeline for securing funding may affect the timeline for the project. It will be important for the committee chair to check in with the administration regarding the source of funding and its effect on the project's budget and timeline.

Step 8.1
Prepare and Assemble the Final Report

The committee member who wrote the preliminary report will incorporate the changes and prepare the final report. If the chair wrote the preliminary report, he or she should prepare the final report. It will use much of the same information and has basically the same format as the preliminary report. This time you will only include the final recommendations. Because this report will be read by people outside the library, you will have to present the information as clearly as possible, avoiding any library terms that are not familiar to the general public. Figure 21 shows the elements to include in this final report.

Assembling the Executive Summary to the Final Report

The executive summary will be written last, as a condensation of the whole report. However, the executive summary appears on the opening pages of your final report, and it

FIGURE 21
Final Report Format

Table of Contents—List sections of the report with their corresponding page numbers

Executive Summary—Quick overview of goals and recommendations with bottom-line budget summary and projected timetable for implementation

Introduction—Brief description of the project, including the rationale behind it, its intended goals and users, and the written charge to the project committee

Part 1: Recommendations—Recommendations and brief description of the data collection process used by the committee

Part 2: Budget and Time Considerations—Estimated budget and timeline for the project

Part 3: Workforms—Provide workforms illustrating the committee's decision making

will provide an overview of the facts and figures of your project to those who will vote on funding and implementation. You may use some of the executive summary from the preliminary report if all the recommendations in the preliminary report were accepted. Otherwise, modify the executive summary from the preliminary report with the information representing the new final recommendations from the administrative approval process. Include a bottom-line budget total. (See "The Budget" later in this task.)

Editing the Introduction to the Final Report

The introduction to the final report can be copied from the preliminary report as long as the library administration did not object to anything included in that introduction. Edit it as necessary to reflect any changes to the project per the administrative approval. Replace any library jargon with terms in general use.

Editing Part 1: Recommendations for the Final Report

Edit the introduction from part 1 of the preliminary report to reflect any changes per administrative approval and to ensure that a reader from outside the library will have a context for the recommendations to follow. For example, don't refer to the "circulation desk," but instead call it the "checkout desk." Then edit the remainder of part 1 from the preliminary report to use in the final report. Note that this time, part 1 will contain only the final recommendations the committee and administration have agreed should go forward—it will not include other options. Consequently, in this report there will be less emphasis on the evaluation criteria that were used to prioritize the options and more emphasis on the reasons the recommendations will work well for the implementation of the activity. Once again, organize this part around the workform resource titles and sequence so that references in the report are consistent. Include references to workforms that support the final recommendations.

Editing Part 2: Budget and Time Considerations for the Final Report

Funding and governance authorities are often very interested in how much a project will cost and how much it will disrupt library services. After the executive summary, this section will probably be most important to the group reading the final report, so be sure to present this information as clearly as possible. Clearly link cost and time estimates to the specific resources they affect. Emphasize that the planning committee has only collected estimates for the areas that could possibly affect decisions, and that the implementation team will gather more detailed cost and timing information as they specify the exact items to use. Again, the level of detail that is required in this area for your final report will vary greatly with local requirements. Some funding authorities will want a line-item budget, while others will be content with a general cost per square foot range developed from other similar local projects. Management will provide the committee with guidance on how much information should be included regarding your cost and timing estimates for the project.

INTRODUCTION

In the introduction to part 2, supply information about the sources of budget and time information that will be provided and the reasons you have provided some of the cost information but not a final project budget, if this is the case. Point out that price and time frames for the delivery of goods and services can vary greatly. Thus, this section contains general estimates for the recommendations in the report.

This is your opportunity to explain any items that might stand out as very expensive and to justify their inclusion as recommendations. If you developed a cost per square foot figure for the budget, include that in the introduction to part 2. (See "The Budget" below.)

THE FURNITURE AND EQUIPMENT LIST

If you prepared a furniture and equipment list for the preliminary report, revise it to include all furniture and equipment called for in the final recommendations. While such a list might be of interest, the audience for this report may prefer an overview of the project rather than an examination at this level of detail. If you completed Workform 22, Furniture and Equipment List, it will be easy to create this list. The administration will advise you about whether to include a list of furniture and equipment. Unless directed to do so by the administration, do not develop new information for this report.

THE BUDGET

For the preliminary report, you only researched cost estimates for items that might affect the decision to approve that recommendation. If the administration advised you to revise your recommendations, you may need to gather new cost estimates for the final report. Furthermore, if the administration recommends a more complete budget for the final report, the teams will have to gather additional information to provide the funding or governing authorities with more complete cost information.

To complete Workform 23, Cost Compilations, the same teams that collected data and made recommendations for specific resources will provide an estimate of how much their recommendations will cost. Note that this involves additional research for items for which the only option was purchase, and perhaps for service providers as well. Refer back to the suggestions in chapter 4 for sources of general estimate information, such as professional experts and vendor catalogs. If the committee recommends items from a particular vendor, this information will be easy to locate. Begin completing Workform 23 by listing any professionals, and their estimated fees, that will be contracted to implement the project. Then the teams should list all items or services within their resource area. Workform 4, Need for Outside Experts; Workform 19, Expense Estimates for Options; Workform 21, Option Evaluation; and Workform 22, Furniture and Equipment List, will provide the information needed to develop the full list of resources for the project and some of the cost information. Note that the workform specifies the total cost for each resource listed. If you are buying a number of items (e.g., chairs), be sure you multiply the per-item cost by the number of items needed.

Your budget for the final report will be a line-item budget made up of categories for professional and contractual services; furniture; equipment; shelving; technology support; building components such as windows, flooring surfaces, and walls; signage; and access changes as called for in the recommendations you are presenting. If a project budget is required by your funding authority for the final report, figure 22 provides a suggested format for the estimated budget.

You will see that the budget closely follows Workform 23, Cost Compilations. Those who will read your report are probably used to a traditional budget format; therefore, they may require that the committee transfer the cost information to the budget format.

The costs for new shelving, furniture, equipment, and floor and wall alterations are usually used to develop an estimate, in dollars per square foot, of the area being renovated. This is calculated by dividing the total project cost (including floor coverings, furniture, equipment, shelving, physical plant change, and technology support) by the total square footage of the area being used for the project. For example, if the total cost of your renovation is $140,000 and you are renovating 1,000 square feet, the cost of the renovation would be $140 per square foot. If you have enough cost information to include this figure in the report, do so in this section of the report by comparing it with the regional average. The regional average figure is available from building consultants or building contractors.

If you do not have to supply a formal budget, you can use the same format for cost information that you included in the preliminary report, but make it very clear to even the casual reader that this is not a final budget figure. If the budget includes funding for building renovations to support the new activity, be sure to explain why these renovations will be necessary, since this may not be evident to someone who does not work in the library.

If you are recommending high-quality or expensive furniture, be sure to fully explain why. Use this opportunity to "make your case" to the funding authority for the items you need for the project. Likewise, if the report recommends contracting for professional expertise, explain why that is necessary.

FIGURE 22
Project Budget Format

Project Recommendations	Number of Items	Estimated Cost per Item	Total Estimated Cost
1. Professional and contractual services			
Total for professional services			
2. Furniture			
Total for furniture			
3. Equipment			
Total for equipment			
4. Shelving			
Total for shelving			
5. Wall finishes, floor finishes, decor			
Total for decorating			
6. Special lighting, plumbing, or HVAC			
Total for lighting, plumbing, HVAC			
7. Wiring, cabling, Internet connectivity			
Total for wiring, cabling, Internet connectivity			
8. ADA or general access requirements, new signs, other items			
Total for ADA, other			
Estimated project total cost			

TIME PROJECTIONS

When presenting your time projections, remind readers that timing estimates can change before the project implementation begins; therefore, the report includes an *estimate* of the expected duration of each task supporting a recommendation. In addition to the completed Workform 20, Preliminary Project Time Estimates, state that the library's implementation plan will address the impact that work done as part of the project will have on the library's delivery of services.

Assembling Part 3: Workforms Supporting the Final Report

The final report will include both numerical and nonnumerical data in part 3. Each data type has its own value to decision makers. Once again, include enough completed workforms to demonstrate how you reached your recommendations, but remember that this report does not include the workforms pertaining to other options that the committee considered but did not recommend.

Include the workforms that contain compiled information from the earlier workforms so your data will not overwhelm and confuse readers. In the final report, some of the compilation workforms that you might include are Workform 4, Need for Outside Experts; Workform 16, Square Footage—Needed and Current; Workform 20, Preliminary Project Time Estimates; Workform 21, Option Evaluation; Workform 22, Furniture and Equipment List; and Workform 23, Cost Compilations. These compilations provide readers with an overview of the source of your recommendations.

Step 8.2
Present the Final Report to Funding Authorities

The library administration will decide whom to include in the presentation of the project's final report to the governing body and in presentations to any other funding authorities. Who will make the report presentation—a board member or the library director? Will the committee chair and key members of the committee be invited to participate in presenting the final report for funding approval? These important decisions will be guided by local practice and knowledge of what has worked well for the library when introducing new activities in the past. In some areas, projects are best received by the funding authority when they are presented by the governing body, as fellow taxpayers, with the library staff standing by to serve as content experts and to answer any questions. In other situations, the library director traditionally presents library projects for funding. If you aren't sure how projects are usually presented to your funding authority, ask the chair or president of your board or the appropriate person within your funding authority.

Well in advance of the presentation, distribute copies of the final report to everyone who will be voting on the project. Send the report out with a cover letter that explains how the project came about and how it was developed.

Part 10 of the case study shows how the Anytown Public Library committee decided to present its final report and shows the cover letter that accompanied the report.

Anytown Public Library Homework Center

PART 10: Cover Letter of Anytown's Final Report

When the Anytown committee had prepared their final report, first the committee members reviewed it for accuracy, and then the administration approved it. It was decided that the library's director would present the report to the finance committee for approval, so she would sign the cover letter. Their cover letter follows.

Date
Anytown Public Library
Anytown, USA 00000

Dear Finance Committee Member:

Enclosed is the Anytown Public Library's final report on the proposed homework assistance service that the library plans to offer students of Anytown. This is in support of the library's goal that "Students in Anytown will have the skills and tools they need to succeed in school." The center is designed to serve 4,000 middle and high school students through research assistance, group-study computer stations, quiet study rooms, website support, and programming to improve the students' study skills. This report represents the changes that must be made to the library building to provide the program.

    A committee at the Anytown Library collected data about what they determined was needed to support a homework assistance center and what the library is currently offering students in order to determine the recommendations included in this report. Supporting documentation of their research is included in part 3 of the report.

    If you have any questions about the library's plans, please contact [name], Director of the Anytown Public Library.

Sincerely yours,
[Name]

Anytown Public Library Director

In addition, provide contact information for any pre-presentation questions about the report. The information about how the project came about can be pulled from the goal used to develop the charge for the committee and from Workform 6, Project Description—General. Preparation for the presentation will include decisions about who will present particular elements of the project and, depending on the formality of your organization, might involve preparation of a PowerPoint presentation that features graphic explanations of key elements of the report.

Be organized, calm, and clear in your presentation of the project. Give the background of the project and how the recommendations were developed, as well as the recommendations included in the report. If any questions arise that you cannot answer, tell the questioner that you will do further research and get back with the information. The committee has gathered enough information to substantiate their recommendations. You may need to ask contractors or vendors for more information, but you know what sources to go to from the research you have already documented. Because your report is based on solid data-based decision making, you can proceed with confidence.

What's Next?

You have now successfully completed a plan for facility changes to implement a new activity or service. In some libraries, a different committee with different expertise will be charged with implementation of the plan. Even if your committee is now charged with the implementation of the facility changes, you should receive a new charge reflecting the tasks of implementation. The members of the facility planning team have learned a lot during the planning process—not only about facility elements, but also about successful ways to work together to accomplish goals. Every time a committee successfully completes a committee project, the library administration should encourage that group to share their successes and what they have learned in the process so staff members can continue to build on their success. Celebrate your successes, and use what you have learned when you move on to the next project.

Key Points to Remember

In your final report, use language that is easily understood by people who don't work in libraries.

In all parts of the reports, present the resource information and recommendations in the same sequence.

Distribute reports to decision makers well before any formal meeting, especially one requiring a vote or seeking an approval.

After distributing reports, request a meeting with decision makers to answer any of their questions about the recommendations in the report.

Remove information about options that are not recommended in the final report.

Celebrate your successes.

Tool Kit A

Calculating Square Footage

Reallocating the space in an existing building has in common with planning a new building the need to determine how much space is needed for the various areas of the library and all the equipment, furniture, shelving, and walking-around space in each. In a reallocation project you may not be calculating square footage needs for a whole library building, but you must still know whether what you want to put in an area of the building will fit or not. The charts and lists in this tool kit will help you calculate needed square footage numbers.

Important Information for Using This Tool Kit

Gross and Net Square Footage

The amount of square footage in a building or the area of a building can be stated as a *gross* total or a *net* total.

> *Gross square footage.* "The total area of a building." It includes interior and exterior walls, storage, restrooms, hallways, elevators, stairwells, pillars, and other similar items and spaces.
>
> *Net square footage.* "The space that can be allocated for purposes other than the current purpose." It includes most of the public and staff areas of a library, including space for shelving, seating, service desks, meeting rooms, offices, and so on.

Building planners use a grossing factor—a percentage of the total net square footage—to determine how much of a building's square footage will be used for spaces that cannot be assigned to other uses. The range of grossing factors used in public libraries is fairly wide. It can vary from a low of 20 to 25 percent to a high of 35 percent. The percentage used depends on how large the building is, how open the floor plan is, whether the library has a lot of office space, and similar considerations. In general, larger buildings require a higher percentage.

Many space reallocation projects focus on net square footage. However, if your project will involve significant alterations to the library building, it will be important to keep these definitions and types of square footage in mind as you calculate space needs. You will also want to be aware that the space taken up by walls is included in measurements on architectural drawings.

Furniture, Equipment, and Square Footage Numbers

Square footages for furnishings, equipment, and shelving include the footprint of the item on the floor—how much space each requires—plus the space needed around each item for aisles, seating, and people movement. For example, the square footage needed for a photocopier is given as 50 square feet in the table below. This includes the space the photocopier will sit on, which will vary depending on the size of your copier. If your copier is 5 feet wide by 2½ feet deep, it needs 12.5 square feet (5 × 2½). The remainder of the 50 square feet needed for this item includes space for moving around it, such as a place for people to stand in front of the copier and use it, space behind the person doing the copying so that others can walk around, space on either side for aisles, and space behind the copier for air circulation. While 50 square feet may not be exactly the amount needed for your particular copier, it can serve as a guide as you calculate how much overall space you need.

Square Footage Ranges

Some square footages are given as a range in the following charts in order to allow for two factors:

1. The size of this type of item can vary quite a bit.
2. You may want or need to allow more clear space, rather than just that required, for movement around the item. For example, the Americans with Disabilities Act requires clear pathways of 30 inches within buildings (exclusive of hallways). Furthermore, your state's laws and local requirements may dictate additional requirements.

Square Footage Requirements for Public-Use Furniture and Equipment

Square footage requirements for a variety of furniture types are listed in the following table. Some equipment also makes a footprint on the floor that must be accounted for when calculating square footage needs. The square footages listed include both the item's footprint and the space needed around the item to allow people to move. The measurements in this list are from the *Libris DESIGN* software.[1] The publication *Building Blocks for Planning Functional Library Spaces* also provides a detailed list.[2]

Furniture	Square Footage per Item
Public Seating (per seat)	
At a table for two adults/teens	25
At a table for four adults/teens	25–30
Adult/teen lounge	35–40
Adult/teen carrel	30–40

Furniture	Square Footage per Item
Public Seating (per seat)	
Juvenile table for four	20
Juvenile lounge	25
Rocking chair	20
Bench for two	15
Public Workstations	
Technology workstation for one	40–50 (5 less if freestanding)
Technology workstation for two	50–55
Technology workstation at counter	30–35
OPAC station (stand-alone)	25
Meeting/Presentation Space (per seat)	
Auditorium/meeting room (fixed seats)	10–12
Auditorium/meeting room (stack chairs)	12–15
Stacking chair dolly	15
Stacking table dolly	15
Performance/presentation space (non-theater)	100–200
Conference room table	25–30
Study room table	25–30
Floor seating for children (per child)	10
Coat/hat rack	20
Flip chart with stand	30
Lectern with portable computer space	60
Other	
Atlas stand	30
Audiovisual/technology equipment cart (small)	10
Book return (freestanding)	16
Book truck	15
Change machine	15
Dictionary stand	25
Display case	50
End/lamp table	12
File cabinet, vertical	15
Map file cabinet	35–50
Microform cabinet	16
Photocopier	50
Copier preparation counter	40
Queuing space (per person)	10
Recycling bin	15
Security system gates	75
Self-checkout counter	30
Toy bin	30
Wastebasket	4

Public Area Service Desk and Stations

The calculation of square footage needs for service desks depends on the size of the part of the desk that sits on the floor and how much space you want behind and in front of the desk. Desks can be ordered as modular units with fairly standardized dimensions, or they can be made to order to specific sizes. Service desk design—and therefore the amount of space needed—should be determined with the participation of the staff who will work there. They know how many workstations are needed, what the service lines are like, and what work and storage goes on behind the desk—all factors to consider in allocating the space. Detailed information about service desk design is available in the library literature. Carol R. Brown's *Interior Design for Libraries* offers an excellent discussion.[3]

Staff-Use Furnishings and Office Areas

The amount of space needed for staff can vary greatly depending on the way your library's management has decided to "office" employees. Options range from a locker to store personal items to a corner office with a conference table. Some governing bodies get involved in this decision by establishing maximum office or cubicle sizes for various levels of staff—for example, supervisors get a 100-square-foot separate office, and everyone else gets a 36-square-foot cubicle. If staff spaces are part of your reallocation project, you will want to be aware of any such restrictions as you use the following information.

Offices

An enclosed office space usually houses, at a minimum, a desk, desk chair, one or two guest chairs, and storage space (closet, bookcases, credenza, file cabinet, etc.). It may also include a separate computer workstation, a small-group meeting area with a table and two to four chairs, additional seating such as a couch, and other furnishings as desired by the occupant. Typical office layouts using freestanding furniture and the amount of space needed for each layout are shown in the following list.

Office Layout	Square Footage Needed
Desk and chair, one guest chair or one filing cabinet, credenza/computer workstation	80–90
Desk and chair, two guest chairs, credenza/computer workstation, filing cabinet, bookcase	125–150
Larger desk and chair, two guest chairs, credenza/computer workstation, two additional guest chairs or filing cabinets, bookcase	200–250
Executive desk and chair, two guest chairs, credenza/computer workstation, bookcase, couch with lamp table(s) and two additional chairs (or a table with chairs for four instead of a couch area)	250–300

Cubicles

Cubicles, also called "office systems furniture," "panel furniture," and "landscape furniture," are workstations with built-in work surfaces, storage, and partial walls. They can contain file cabinets, shelving, overhead storage, task lights, keyboard trays, and a built-in wire-management system. They can be stand-alone or connected in a multi-office formation. Figure A-1 shows examples of some cubicle layouts.

The amount of space that each cubicle uses is up to you. Standard layouts are available in a wide variety of sizes, or you can work with a vendor to design a layout and size that meets your specific needs. A few examples follow in figure A-2. These drawings are from the *Libris DESIGN Glossary* under the definition of "Workstation, Office System."[4]

FIGURE A-1

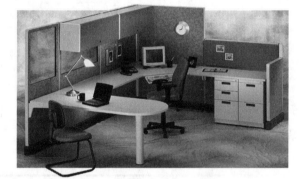

Source: Clone Cubicles, http://www.clonecubicles.com, used with permission.

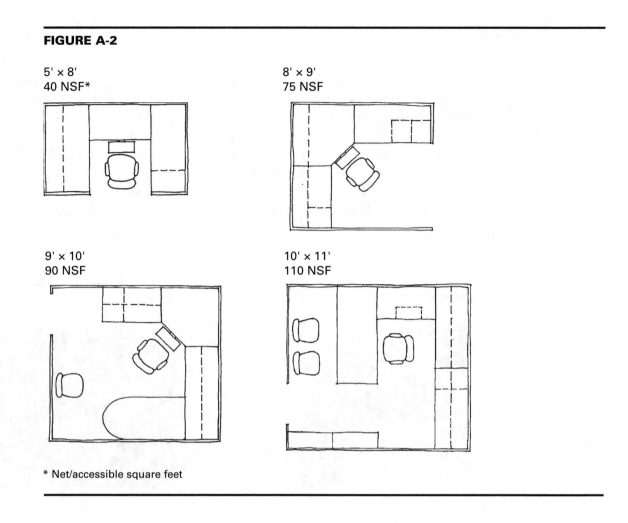

5' × 8'
40 NSF*

8' × 9'
75 NSF

9' × 10'
90 NSF

10' × 11'
110 NSF

* Net/accessible square feet

Staff Lounge

Staff lounges vary in size, but the space needed for equipment and furnishings commonly found in them can help you decide how much overall space you want to dedicate to this area. The following square footages are from *Libris DESIGN.*[5]

Staff Lounge Item	Square Footage Needed
Kitchen unit (with sink, stove top, refrigerator—52 inches wide by 26 inches deep)	25
Two-seat couch	55
Cafe table and four chairs	60
Food preparation area (4 feet wide by 30 feet deep)	30
Locker	5
Garbage container	4–6

Other Furniture and Equipment

The following chart lists square footage requirements for a few pieces of furniture not yet listed that might be used in staff work areas. *Libris DESIGN* uses the following square footage designations.[6]

Other Office Furniture and Equipment Items	Square Footage Needed
Storage cabinet (36 inches wide by 26 inches deep)	15
Visitor chair	15
Task chair	10
File cabinet for flat storage	40
Vertical file cabinet	15
Sink built into countertop	18
60-inch work table	120

Shelving

Two kinds of information are addressed in the sections that follow.

1. How do I find out how much square footage is needed for a specific amount and type of shelving? This is a *space allocation* question.
2. How do I find out how much shelving is needed for a specific amount of library materials? This is a *shelving capacity* question, but it sometimes must be answered before the previous question can be answered.

Space Allocation for Known Amounts of Shelving

Library materials are stored in a variety of ways in public libraries: (a) traditional flat shelves and other media stack shelving and (b) specialty shelving such as bins, spinners, and special media materials shelving. Materials storage for specialty items requires individualized square footage calculations because it varies so much. The variables for calculating the square footages for flat shelving follow.

Double- or single-faced shelves. Flat shelves can be either double-faced (sided) or single-faced. Double-faced shelves have a footprint twice as wide as single-faced shelves.

Shelf depth. Standard shelf base depths are 8 inches (rarely used these days), 10 inches (most common), or 12 inches (often used for reference and Easy books). Shelf depth can be as little as 6 inches (for certain audiovisual media) and as much as 16 inches (for flat newspaper storage or oversize books). If the depth of the base is greater than the depth of the shelves, the base depth measurement is used for square footage calculations.

Unit width. The width of shelving units can vary. Wood shelving can be manufactured to custom widths, although the industry standard width is 36 inches. Cantilever-style steel shelving is almost always 36 inches wide.

Aisle width. The width between rows of shelving can be the minimum ADA requirement of 36 inches; the ADA-preferred width of 42 inches; and it can be more if required by state or local laws. Net square footage for shelving includes not only the amount of space needed for the shelving (the footprint it makes on the floor) but also the space around it used for aisles. Note that half of the square footage taken by each aisle next to a shelving unit or row of units is assigned to that unit or row. If aisles between rows of double-sided shelving are 36 inches, then the amount of aisle attributed to a row of shelving is 18 inches on each side times two aisles for a total of 36 inches added to the depth of double-sided shelving. Just 18 inches is added for single-sided shelving.

Aisles at the ends of rows of stacks must also be accounted for. Since most shelving units in a public library are part of a row and do not stand alone, only the end units in the row have this space. Whether or not the space at the end of rows of shelving is accounted for in the shelving square footage calculations varies depending on who is doing the calculating. Some people don't worry about it at all, figuring it will be made up for in the unallocated space percentage applied to net square footages when calculating gross (or total) square feet needed. Others calculate it based on a floor plan they have in mind which tells them how many row ends need added aisle space.

Variations in dimensions across shelving types. The dimensions of manufacturers' cantilever-style shelving are not exact; they are nominal. By contrast, case-style shelving dimensions are exact or actual. Cantilever shelving, also called "bracket shelving," is metal and is put together from individual components: supports, shelves, base, end panels, and so on. Case-style shelving can be metal or wood and is all of a piece except for the adjustable shelves and optional back. In cantilever-type shelving, the shelves are deeper than the stated size by about ½ inch for double-sided shelving and 1½ inches for single-faced shelving. Decorative end panels can add ½ to 2 inches to the nominal shelving-width dimension. Shelving units are also longer than 36 inches when connected together with reinforcing gussets between frames. These small measurements can make a difference if you are carefully laying out a floor plan and space is tight.

Number of shelving units in a row. You decide how many units of shelving may be in a row, and this decision may vary from one area of the library to another. Many public libraries limit the number of units to five to make it easier for users to find materials, but space constraints may require more units in a row to avoid creating space-eating aisles. Units connected in a row take less space than the same number of units standing alone because there are no aisles. Although there will be very few places in the library where you use a stand-alone unit, some published shelving square-footage calculations are presented per unit.

Shelf height. Shelf height is a variable that does not matter for square footage calculations, but it *is* important if you are trying to find out how much square footage you need for a certain sized collection. The number of linear feet of shelving, and therefore the height of the unit, is used to calculate shelving needs for a known number of items to be shelved.

The bottom line for determining square footage needed for flat shelving is that you either calculate it for yourself, accept the varying calculations published on the topic, or use a combination of the two.

Calculating Shelving Space Allocation

If you calculate your own shelving space allocations, you will want to know the number of aisles and their width, the number of units in each row, and the depth and facing type of shelving in each row or stand-alone unit. The best way to do this is to draw a floor plan showing how the shelving will be laid out, with dimensions and facing types indicated. Then you are ready to do the arithmetic and figure out square footage. If, however, you are moving established shelving in its same pattern to another place, just measure how much space the shelving arrangement currently uses. It's tempting to make this harder than it is. Carol R. Brown's book *Interior Design for Libraries* is a good source for help in understanding shelving arrangements and how to lay them out.

You could also use standardized or published measures. Many publications list square footage needed for library shelving. The following tables give the measures published in three of them: *Libris DESIGN, Building Blocks for Planning Functional Library Space,* and the *Wisconsin Library Building Project Handbook.*[7]

Libris DESIGN is interactive building program software developed for the California State Library. It uses an averaged square footage per unit for calculating all shelving square footage needs. Its measures are based on a study of many medium- and large-sized public library shelving floor plans. Because there are so many shelving types and aisle selections (California requires 44-inch aisles in some instances), developers "opted to do everything based on 12"/24"-deep units, and then if you purchase 10"/20" units, you get an extra 4 inches in the aisle. It is unwise to plan on a 20" unit for space calculations unless you are certain that the end panel will also be only 20" wide, because if you calculate with less aisle space and the end panel infringes on the aisle clearance, then you are in noncompliance with the ADA. These numbers are ballpark. They don't work for a very small installation, like one or two sections in an enclosed room, and for a very large installation, they might seem very spacious. We find that about 90 percent of the time for public libraries they are right on the mark."[8]

Floor Space in Square Feet for One Shelving Unit on a 36-Inch Aisle per *Libris DESIGN*

Single-faced (12 inches)	12
Double-faced (24 inches)	18

Building Blocks for Planning Functional Library Space is an update of a 1995 publication developed by the Library Administration and Management Association, a division of the American Library Association. It offers a menu of furniture, equipment, and functions with space allotments for each. It is intended for use in calculating assignable square footages and was used as a resource in the development of *Libris DESIGN.*

The *Wisconsin Library Building Project Handbook* offers not only a range of square footage requirements for various base and aisle widths, but also the advice that "for most shelving environments, a good average is ten square feet per shelving unit."[9] This average is for a standard single-faced shelving unit.

Floor Space in Square Feet for One 36-Inch-Wide Single-Faced Shelving Unit (double the square footage for double-faced)

Unit Base Width	Aisle Width	Building Blocks for Planning Functional Library Space (Floor Space in Square Feet)	Wisconsin Library Building Project Handbook (Floor Space in Square Feet)
10"	36"	8.75	7.70 to 8.75
	42"	9.70	8.53 to 9.69
	48"	10.65	9.35 to 10.63
12"	36"	9.40	8.25 to 9.38
	42"	10.30	9.08 to 10.31
	48"	11.25	9.90 to 11.25
15"	36"	10.30	9.08 to 10.31
	42"	11.25	9.90 to 11.25
	48"	12.20	10.73 to 12.19
18"	36"	11.25	
	42"	12.20	
	48"	13.15	

Specialty shelving sizes can be found in vendor catalogs. The following are some very general rules of thumb for determining square footage for these storage and display units.

Spinners—44.4 square feet for a single unit

Magazine display—use square footage for the base size from the table above (although some of this shelving is 24 inches deep), single-faced

Display shelving—use 36-inch base for double-faced, 18-inch for single-faced

Bins and other specialty storage—varies with size of item; add additional space on all four sides (15 inches of additional space if 30 inches of clear space is needed and 18 inches of additional space if 36 inches is needed) plus the measurements of the floor area occupied by the item

Compact shelving—vendors will provide square footage requirements based on the amount of shelving purchased

Shelving Capacity

The following information on determining how much shelving is needed for specific numbers of items in a collection assumes that you have already subtracted the average percentage of the collection that is checked out. Since checked-out items do not need to be shelved—and you can count on a percentage of the collection being out at all times—no shelving is planned for that percentage. Capacity, or the number of items that can be stored on *flat* shelving units, is based on a formula.

Formula	Example
Items per linear foot of shelf	8 items
× number of feet per shelf	× 3 feet
	= 24
× number of shelves per unit	× 5 shelves per single-faced unit
= number of items	= 120 items per unit of this type

The number of items per shelf depends on how full you keep your shelving and the type of material being shelved. More picture books fit on a shelf than do reference books, for example. Shelf capacity is considered optimum at about 70 percent to 75 percent full; the numbers used for capacity per shelf usually produce 25 percent empty space. The extra space is used for reshelving returned items, shelving new items, and other purposes for efficient collection management. *Libris DESIGN* uses the volumes per linear foot of shelf measures as shown in the following table.[10]

Material Type	Volumes per Linear Feet of Shelving
Audiovisual	
Audiocassette	19
Audio compact disc, CD-ROM, DVD	30
Audiobook cassette	10
Videocassette	10
Children's/Juvenile/Teen Books	
Children's circulating	20
Children's reference	8
Juvenile circulating	13–16
Juvenile paperbacks	16
Teen (young adult)	12
Adult Books—Reference	
Encyclopedias	12
Legal	7
Other	6
Adult Books—Fiction	
Fiction	8
Spanish language	17
Adult Books—Nonfiction	
Nonfiction	10
Spanish language	8
Paperbacks	16

Average Number of Shelves per Unit

The following table provides information about the average number of shelves in standard shelving units. Like many of the other tables in this tool kit, the data come from *Libris DESIGN*.[11]

Height of Unit	Average Number of Shelves (this includes the bottom shelf of the unit)
45-inch Steel Shelving Unit	
Children's picture books	3
Encyclopedias	4
Indexes	2
Ready reference	3
66-inch Steel Shelving Unit	
Juvenile	5
Young adult materials	5
90-inch Steel Shelving Unit	
Adult fiction	7
Adult nonfiction	7
Adult biography	7

Notes

1. California State Library, *Libris DESIGN: Computer Software for Library Facility Planning,* Version 6.0 (2006), http://www.librisdesign.org.

2. Library Administration and Management Association, Building and Equipment Section, Function Space Requirements Committee, *Building Blocks for Planning Functional Library Spaces* (Lanham, MD: Scarecrow, 2001).

3. Carol R. Brown, *Interior Design for Libraries: Drawing on Function and Appeal* (Chicago: American Library Association, 2002).

4. California State Library, *Libris DESIGN Glossary,* http://www.librisdesign.org/help/glossary.html.

5. Ibid.

6. Ibid.

7. California State Library, *Libris DESIGN;* Library Administration and Management Association, *Building Blocks;* Anders Dahlgren, *Wisconsin Library Building Project Handbook* (Madison: Wisconsin Department of Public Instruction, 1997).

8. E-mail from Linda Demmers, *Libris DESIGN* project manager, February 26, 2005.

9. Dahlgren, *Wisconsin Library,* 56.

10. California State Library, *Libris DESIGN.*

11. Ibid.

Assessing Your Library's Physical Message

Issues

Routine assessment of the condition of your building and the message your building projects to users are part of facilities management. The vision and the mission, the image the library staff has of itself, are demonstrated in the routine care for the library facility. The public library's image is part of the community's image. The physical message of your library is as important as the programs and services provided. The way your library looks, feels, and smells affects people who come to the library even before they begin to access the resources you provide for them. If the message of your building is one of neglect, a stale appearance, and a lack of attention to cleanliness, users may turn away long before you can show them the services you would like to provide.

Looking at the facility with fresh or "new eyes" from time to time is important. If you have unsuccessfully struggled with a problem like cracked foundations, or peeling paint that must be refinished every four years, you may find yourself overlooking those problems that are apparent to someone entering the library for the first time who only sees the unattractive feature but doesn't understand why it exists. For this reason it is well worth the time invested to ask someone not connected with your library's organization to conduct a walk-about assessment. The lists below can help someone conduct an impartial assessment of your building.

Assessing the Exterior

Before users can enter a library, they must find out where it is and when it is open. How easily can new users determine where your building and main entrance are located? Congratulations if your library has attained the users' ideal of 24/7 service hours; but if it is only open during designated hours, how easily can a user determine whether your building is open for business and when it will be open? Can they conveniently get this information from their car? Other questions to ask when reviewing the building's exterior are the following.

Signage

- Is there a sign for the library clearly visible from the street?
- Is the sign in good repair?
- Can the hours be read from the street?

Landscaping

- Is the exterior of the library attractive and inviting?
- Do the lawns need mowing?
- Is the landscaping trimmed back away from the road and walkways to enable good sight lines around the building, and does the landscaping contribute to a welcoming appearance of the library?
- Do the library grounds and building exterior meet or exceed community standards?

Parking

- Are driveways and parking areas well lit, and are walkways to entrances safely out of the flow of traffic around the library?
- Are there a sufficient number of parking spaces for the users of your library to have easy access, and are they well marked?
- Is the pavement cracked or broken?

Building Exterior

- Does the foundation have any visible cracks or water seepage?
- Are the doorways clearly marked, in good working order, and unobstructed by signs, book returns, and landscaping?
- Are all entrances to the library ADA-compliant, with appropriately pitched ramps and appropriate hardware on all doors so they can be opened from a wheelchair with a minimum amount of resistance? (See Tool Kit C, Americans with Disabilities Act Requirements.)

Assessing the Interior

Visitors to your library will be most successful in using its resources if they can easily find their way through the building. Good design involves an orientation point within ten to twenty feet of the entrance where a first-time user can figure out the basic layout of services. More than signage, people depend on visual cues to direct them through the building. Has anyone on your staff ever complained that no one reads your signs? That is most people's first response. Visual cues are actually more significant than signage in directing people through a new or unfamiliar space. These cues include path carpeting, walls painted in unique colors for the various departments and services in the library, placement of shelving and furnishings, and different lighting or styles of furnishings; these can all send a message to users about the purpose of an area of the library before they locate and interpret the signage. This is not to imply that you should not also make every effort to provide clear directional signage throughout the building.

Lighting can affect the feel of the library, and many contend that lighting also affects the mood and health of those who spend long hours there. Many libraries in areas of the country where winter means short, dark days for many months of the year invest in full-spectrum lighting for high-intensity-use areas like information services and circulation/user services.

Some questions to ask when reviewing your library's interior are the following.

Directionals

- Is the entryway clean, well lit, and inviting?
- When new users enter the building, can they easily find their way to an information or public assistance desk?
- Do visual cues lead users through the building so they can find the services sought (i.e., path carpeting, walls painted in unique colors for the various departments and services, placement of shelving and furnishings, and different lighting or different styles of furnishings)?
- Is there adequate and consistent signage guiding users to services?

Lighting

- Does your library make the best use it can of natural light?
- Are your window treatments clean, in working order, and consistent throughout individual areas of the library?
- Are there adequate light levels, so index labels on books on the bottom rows of shelving can be easily read and identified?

Walls

- Is sound controlled in high-use areas (such as the children's programming area), and have measures like extra carpeting, fabric wall panels, or acoustical tiles been installed to prevent noise from bouncing around on the hard surfaces of the library?
- Are the walls in good repair and fresh and clean?
- Are windows or glass partitions clean and in good repair?
- Are decorations like wall hangings, plants, or local art cleaned regularly and well kept?

Ceilings

- Are the ceilings in good repair?
- Are ceilings painted light and well lit to reflect back the most light possible?
- Is there dirt around the air flow vents?

Floors

- Do the library's floors feel solid?
- Do the floor treatments contribute to the appearance of a well-maintained building?
- Are rugs securely fastened down?

Facilities Policy and Maintenance Plan

Policy

Libraries should have and keep current a policy about building maintenance. A list of questions that must be addressed in developing this policy is provided in Appendix A of *Creating Policies for Results,* a companion volume in the Planning for Results series.[1] Preventive maintenance can prevent costly and inconvenient facility breakdowns. This is accomplished by scheduled inspections conducted at regular intervals and by the systematic scheduling of cleaning, lubrication, repair, and replacement of parts of building systems. Cost-effectiveness is the justification for maintaining a preventive maintenance schedule. The maintenance staff or someone in library administration will want to keep accurate records of maintenance tasks so the schedule reflects realistic needs for the systems in your building. It is also helpful to keep an up-to-date list of those who regularly service the systems in your library like the plumber, electrician, those who maintain the HVAC, elevators, and snow removal (depending on where you are in the country). A single list of names, numbers, and last maintenance task and date will serve the facilities coordinator well as a handy reference.

Maintenance Plan

A maintenance plan should describe the maintenance duties of staff on all levels and will contain general guidelines or standards. The purpose of the maintenance plan is to clearly lay out what is expected, how frequently, and by whom. Staff members responsible for programming may not be expected to vacuum their rooms after use, but if food or glue land on the carpet they may be expected to clean it up as soon as possible. This role clarification can increase the life of the carpet by preventing food or debris from being ground in and becoming more difficult to clean.

Most libraries don't have an abundance of maintenance time available to them, so it is wise to establish a list of prioritized maintenance tasks to assist the maintenance crew in setting priorities and moving through these weekly, monthly, and annual inspections. The following table is an example of a sample preventive maintenance schedule. All staff should be aware of the basic schedule the maintenance staff follows. Then they can alert the maintenance workers if their programming interferes with that regular schedule, or if there is a problem that may need addressing before the next scheduled round of maintenance. It is also important that permissions and notifications for special events like shampooing all the rugs are clearly defined to ensure that maintenance events don't conflict with major library events for patrons. If programmers have planned a library open house for National Library Week, that will not be the ideal weekend to shampoo rugs. The maintenance staff may be unaware of National Library Week when they schedule the work.

Sample Preventive Maintenance Schedule

	Responsibility	Priority
WEEKLY		
Emergency generator	Maintenance	Top priority
Septic pumps	Maintenance	High priority
Heating/hot water	Maintenance	Top priority
Program room kitchen	Maintenance	High priority
Staff room kitchen	Maintenance	Low priority
Alarm system	Security	High priority
Electrical outlets	Maintenance	High priority
MONTHLY		
Emergency lights	Security	Top priority
Fire extinguishers	Maintenance	High priority
JANUARY		
Elevator inspection	State inspector	Top priority
FEBRUARY		
Fire alarms	Outside vendor	Top priority
MARCH		
Air-handling units	HVAC provider	High priority
Parking lot line painting	Maintenance	Low priority
APRIL		
Boiler inspection	HVAC provider	High priority
Air conditioner	HVAC provider	High priority
MAY		
Smoke detectors	Security	Top priority
JUNE		
Fire inspection	Fire department	Top priority

Housekeeping expectations should also be clear, whether they are done by maintenance staff or others. The following table demonstrates a clear way to present expectations regarding frequency and standards for cleaning. Such a checklist may be helpful in communicating between shifts which tasks are done and what still needs to be done.

Housekeeping Checklist

Library Areas/Tasks	Daily	Done	Weekly	Done	Comments/Supplies Needed
RESTROOMS					
Toilets/urinals cleaned, disinfected					
Basins cleaned, disinfected					
Changing tables cleaned, disinfected					
Countertops cleaned, disinfected					
Dispensers restocked					
Mirrors cleaned					
Floors wet mopped					
Walls and partitions cleaned					
FLOORS					
Carpeting vacuumed					
Entryway, wet mopped					
MECHANICAL ROOMS					
Floors swept					
Floors damp mopped					
GENERAL BUILDING					
Wastebaskets emptied					
Furniture dusted					
Windowsills dusted					
Drinking fountains cleaned					
Front door glass cleaned					
Elevators cleaned					

Assessing ADA Compliance

Public libraries have a commitment to serve all parts of the population in their communities. The combination of the aging population in most communities and the passage of the 1990 Americans with Disabilities Act has forced libraries to become much more aware of the access to their buildings. Tool Kit C, Americans with Disabilities Act Requirements, in this volume includes many of the issues that affect libraries in this regard. For further information, visit http://www.access-board.gov/ada-aba/.

Note

1. Sandra Nelson and June Garcia, *Creating Policies for Results: From Chaos to Clarity* (Chicago: American Library Association, 2003), 143.

Tool Kit C

Americans with Disabilities Act Requirements

New public library facilities or major renovations of facilities must conform to the requirements of the Americans with Disabilities Act, which became federal law in 1990. Reviews of existing space and plans for reallocation of space should also consider these requirements. The *ADA and ABA Accessibility Guidelines for Buildings and Facilities,* developed by the U.S. Access Board in 2004, is an update to the original regulations and provides regulations under the ADA and the Architectural Barriers Act, another federal law.[1] The *Accessibility Guidelines* document contains requirements for accessibility to facilities and to elements within facilities by individuals with disabilities and is an important tool for planning the use of space. All areas of newly designed and newly constructed buildings and facilities and altered or leased portions of existing buildings and facilities must comply with the requirements. In addition, most states and some municipalities have laws regarding access to and within public places; you should be aware of the laws that affect your locale.

The technical requirements in the *Accessibility Guidelines* are based on adult dimensions; the document also includes requirements based on children's dimensions, specifically for water fountains, water closets, toilet compartments, lavatories and sinks, dining surfaces, and work surfaces. Children's needs were not addressed in the original regulations. Now that they are, library space planners must be aware of the regulations and should make every effort to meet the standards.

This document does not specifically mention libraries. The requirements for the width of aisles between rows of shelving and accessible reach for magazine display shelving and card catalogs, which were detailed in the first publication of regulations after passage of the ADA, are covered by more generally stated requirements in the *Accessibility Guidelines.*

The material below is copied directly from chapter 3 of the *ADA and ABA Accessibility Guidelines for Buildings and Facilities.* The rest of this tool kit has some of the information you need to know about the ADA requirements. Be sure to consult the full guidelines document at http://www.access-board.gov/ada-aba/ to be fully informed.

Selected Information about Access within a Building

F206.2.2 Within a Site. At least one accessible route shall connect accessible buildings, accessible facilities, *accessible elements, and accessible spaces* that are on the same site. [italics added]

F206.2.3 Multi-Story Buildings and Facilities. At least one accessible route shall connect each story and mezzanine in multi-story buildings and facilities.

Selected Information from Chapter 3: Building Blocks

302 FLOOR OR GROUND SURFACES

302.1 General. Floor and ground surfaces shall be stable, firm, and slip resistant and shall comply with 302.

302.2 Carpet. Carpet or carpet tile shall be securely attached and shall have a firm cushion, pad, or backing or no cushion or pad. Carpet or carpet tile shall have a level loop, textured loop, level cut pile, or level cut/uncut pile texture. Pile height shall be ½ inch (13 mm) maximum. Exposed edges of carpet shall be fastened to floor surfaces and shall have trim on the entire length of the exposed edge. Carpet edge trim shall comply with 303.

> *Advisory 302.2 Carpet.* Carpets and permanently affixed mats can significantly increase the amount of force (roll resistance) needed to propel a wheelchair over a surface. The firmer the carpeting and backing, the lower the roll resistance. A pile thickness up to ½ inch (13 mm) (measured to the backing, cushion, or pad) is allowed, although a lower pile provides easier wheelchair maneuvering. If a backing, cushion or pad is used, it must be firm. Preferably, carpet pad should not be used because the soft padding increases roll resistance.

303 CHANGES IN LEVEL

303.1 General. Where changes in level are permitted in floor or ground surfaces, they shall comply with 303.

Vertical Change in Level

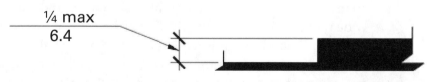

303.3 Beveled. Changes in level between ¼ inch (6.4 mm) high minimum and ½ inch (13 mm) high maximum shall be beveled with a slope not steeper than 1:2.

Beveled Change in Level

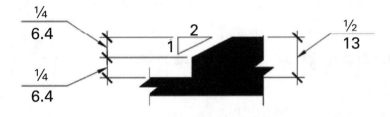

303.4 Ramps. Changes in level greater than ½ inch (13 mm) high shall be ramped, and shall comply with 405 or 406.

304 TURNING SPACE

304.1 General. Turning space shall comply with 304.

304.2 Floor or Ground Surfaces. Floor or ground surfaces of a turning space shall comply with 302. Changes in level are not permitted.

EXCEPTION: Slopes not steeper than 1:48 shall be permitted.

304.3 Size. Turning space shall comply with 304.3.1 or 304.3.2.

304.3.1 Circular Space. The turning space shall be a space of 60 inches (1525 mm) diameter minimum. The space shall be permitted to include knee and toe clearance complying with 306.

304.3.2 T-Shaped Space. The turning space shall be a T-shaped space within a 60 inch (1525 mm) square minimum with arms and base 36 inches (915 mm) wide minimum. Each arm of the T shall be clear of obstructions 12 inches (305 mm) minimum in each direction and the base shall be clear of obstructions 24 inches (610 mm) minimum. The space shall be permitted to include knee and toe clearance complying with 306 only at the end of either the base or one arm.

T-Shaped Turning Space

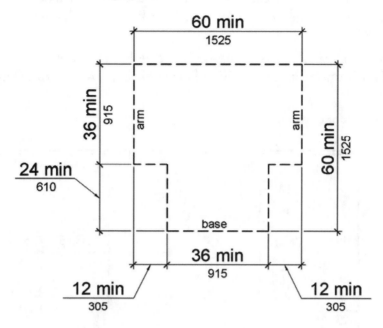

304.4 Door Swing. Doors shall be permitted to swing into turning spaces.

305 CLEAR FLOOR OR GROUND SPACE

305.1 General. Clear floor or ground space shall comply with 305.

305.2 Floor or Ground Surfaces. Floor or ground surfaces of a clear floor or ground space shall comply with 302. Changes in level are not permitted.

305.3 Size. The clear floor or ground space shall be 30 inches (760 mm) minimum by 48 inches (1220 mm) minimum.

Clear Floor or Ground Space

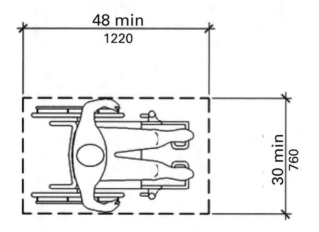

305.4 Knee and Toe Clearance. Unless otherwise specified, clear floor or ground space shall be permitted to include knee and toe clearance complying with 306.

305.5 Position. Unless otherwise specified, clear floor or ground space shall be positioned for either forward or parallel approach to an element.

Position of Clear Floor or Ground Space

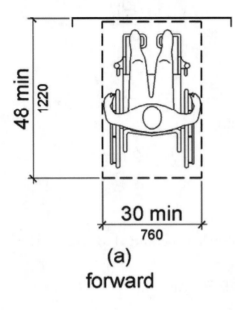

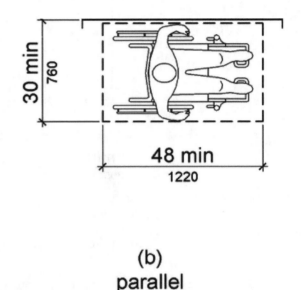

(a)
forward

(b)
parallel

Maneuvering Clearance in an Alcove, Forward Approach

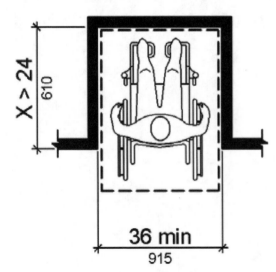

305.6 Approach. One full unobstructed side of the clear floor or ground space shall adjoin an accessible route or adjoin another clear floor or ground space.

305.7 Maneuvering Clearance. Where a clear floor or ground space is located in an alcove or otherwise confined on all or part of three sides, additional maneuvering clearance shall be provided in accordance with 305.7.1 and 305.7.2

305.7.1 Forward Approach. Alcoves shall be 36 inches (915 mm) wide minimum where the depth exceeds 24 inches (610 mm).

305.7.2 Parallel Approach. Alcoves shall be 60 inches (1525 mm) wide minimum where the depth exceeds 15 inches (380 mm).

Maneuvering Clearance in an Alcove, Parallel Approach

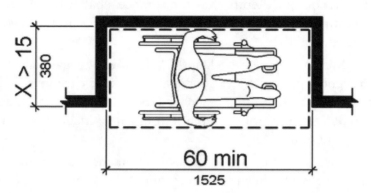

306 KNEE AND TOE CLEARANCE

306.1 General. Where space beneath an element is included as part of clear floor or ground space or turning space, the space shall comply with 306. Additional space shall not be prohibited beneath an element but shall not be considered as part of the clear floor or ground space or turning space.

> *Advisory 306.1 General.* Clearances are measured in relation to the usable clear floor space, not necessarily to the vertical support for an element. When determining clearance under an object for required turning or maneuvering space, care should be taken to ensure the space is clear of any obstructions.

306.2 TOE CLEARANCE

306.2.1 General. Space under an element between the finish floor or ground and 9 inches (230 mm) above the finish floor or ground shall be considered toe clearance and shall comply with 306.2.

306.2.2 Maximum Depth. Toe clearance shall extend 25 inches (635 mm) maximum under an element.

Toe Clearance

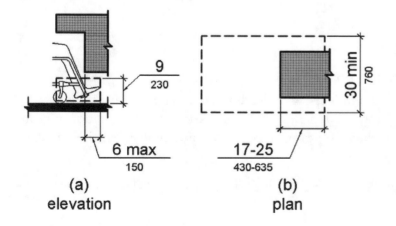

(a) elevation

(b) plan

306.2.3 Minimum Required Depth. Where toe clearance is required at an element as part of a clear floor space, the toe clearance shall extend 17 inches (430 mm) minimum under the element.

306.2.4 Additional Clearance. Space extending greater than 6 inches (150 mm) beyond the available knee clearance at 9 inches (230 mm) above the finish floor or ground shall not be considered toe clearance.

306.2.5 Width. Toe clearance shall be 30 inches (760 mm) wide minimum.

306.3 KNEE CLEARANCE

306.3.1 General. Space under an element between 9 inches (230 mm) and 27 inches (685 mm) above the finish floor or ground shall be considered knee clearance and shall comply with 306.3.

306.3.2 Maximum Depth. Knee clearance shall extend 25 inches (635 mm) maximum under an element at 9 inches (230 mm) above the finish floor or ground.

306.3.3 Minimum Required Depth. Where knee clearance is required under an element as part of a clear floor space, the knee clearance shall be 11 inches (280 mm) deep minimum at 9 inches (230 mm) above the finish floor or ground, and 8 inches (205 mm) deep minimum at 27 inches (685 mm) above the finish floor or ground.

306.3.4 Clearance Reduction. Between 9 inches (230 mm) and 27 inches (685 mm) above the finish floor or ground, the knee clearance shall be permitted to reduce at a rate of 1 inch (25 mm) in depth for each 6 inches (150 mm) in height.

306.3.5 Width. Knee clearance shall be 30 inches (760 mm) wide minimum.

Knee Clearance

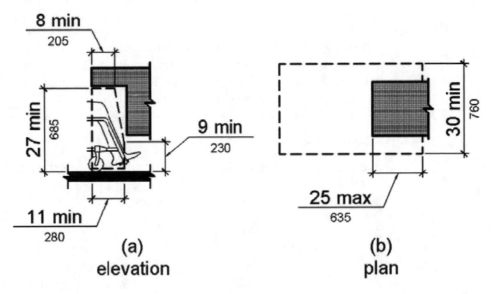

307 PROTRUDING OBJECTS

307.1 General. Protruding objects shall comply with 307.

307.2 Protrusion Limits. Objects with leading edges more than 27 inches (685 mm) and not more than 80 inches (2030 mm) above the finish floor or ground shall protrude 4 inches (100 mm) maximum horizontally into the circulation path.

EXCEPTION: Handrails shall be permitted to protrude 4½ inches (115 mm) maximum.

Limits of Protruding Objects

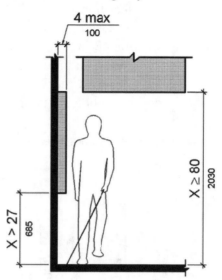

307.5 Required Clear Width. Protruding objects shall not reduce the clear width required for accessible routes.

308 REACH RANGES

308.1 General. Reach ranges shall comply with 308.

Unobstructed Forward Reach

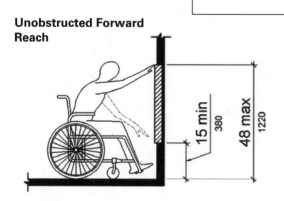

308.2 Forward Reach.

308.2.1 Unobstructed. Where a forward reach is unobstructed, the high forward reach shall be 48 inches (1220 mm) maximum and the low forward reach shall be 15 inches (380 mm) minimum above the finish floor or ground.

308.2.2 Obstructed High Reach. Where a high forward reach is over an obstruction, the clear floor space shall extend beneath the element for a distance not less than the required reach depth over the obstruction. The high forward reach shall be 48 inches (1220 mm) maximum where the reach depth is 20 inches (510 mm) maximum. Where the reach depth exceeds 20 inches (510 mm), the high forward reach shall be 44 inches (1120 mm) maximum and the reach depth shall be 25 inches (635 mm) maximum.

Obstructed High Forward Reach

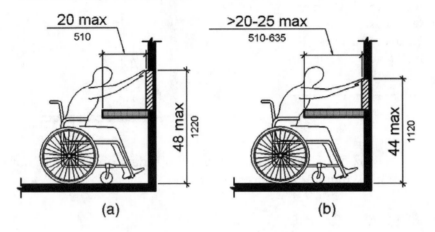

308.3 Side Reach.

308.3.1 Unobstructed. Where a clear floor or ground space allows a parallel approach to an element and the side reach is unobstructed, the high side reach shall be 48 inches (1220 mm) maximum and the low side reach shall be 15 inches (380 mm) minimum above the finish floor or ground.

EXCEPTIONS: 1. An obstruction shall be permitted between the clear floor or ground space and the element where the depth of the obstruction is 10 inches (255 mm) maximum. 2. Operable parts of fuel dispensers shall be permitted to be 54 inches (1370 mm) maximum measured from the surface of the vehicular way where fuel dispensers are installed on existing curbs.

Unobstructed Side Reach

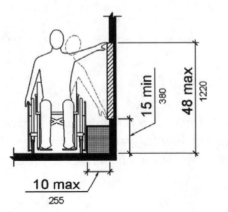

308.3.2 Obstructed High Reach. Where a clear floor or ground space allows a parallel approach to an element and the high side reach is over an obstruction, the height of the obstruction shall be 34 inches (865 mm) maximum and the depth of the obstruction shall be 24 inches (610 mm) maximum. The high side reach shall be 48 inches (1220 mm) maximum for a reach depth of 10 inches (255 mm) maximum. Where the reach depth exceeds 10 inches (255 mm), the high side reach shall be 46 inches (1170 mm) maximum for a reach depth of 24 inches (610 mm) maximum.

Obstructed High Side Reach

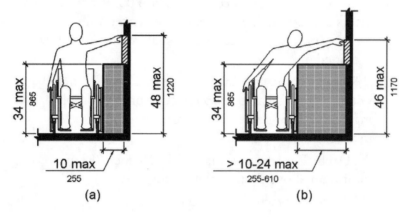

Selected Information about Walking Surfaces

403 WALKING SURFACES

403.1 General. Walking surfaces that are a part of an accessible route shall comply with 403.

403.2 Floor or Ground Surface. Floor or ground surfaces shall comply with 302.

403.3 Slope. The running slope of walking surfaces shall not be steeper than 1:20. The cross slope of walking surfaces shall not be steeper than 1:48.

403.4 Changes in Level. Changes in level shall comply with 303.

403.5 Clearances. Walking surfaces shall provide clearances complying with 403.5.

Clear Width of an Accessible Route

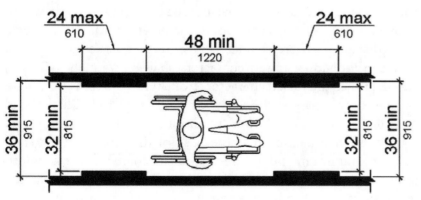

EXCEPTION: Within employee work areas, clearances on common use circulation paths shall be permitted to be decreased by work area equipment provided that the decrease is essential to the function of the work being performed.

403.5.1 Clear Width. Except as provided in 403.5.2 and 403.5.3, the clear width of walking surfaces shall be 36 inches (915 mm) minimum.

EXCEPTION: The clear width shall be permitted to be reduced to 32 inches (815 mm) minimum for a length of 24 inches (610 mm) maximum provided that reduced width segments are separated by segments that are 48 inches (1220 mm) long minimum and 36 inches (915 mm) wide minimum.

Selected Information from Chapter 7: Communication Elements and Features

703.1 General. Signs shall comply with 703. Where both visual and tactile characters are required, either one sign with both visual and tactile characters, or two separate signs, one with visual, and one with tactile characters, shall be provided.

703.2 Raised Characters. Raised characters shall comply with 703.2 and shall be duplicated in braille complying with 703.3. Raised characters shall be installed in accordance with 703.4.

> *Advisory 703.2 Raised Characters.* Signs that are designed to be read by touch should not have sharp or abrasive edges.

703.2.1 Depth. Raised characters shall be $\frac{1}{32}$ inch (0.8 mm) minimum above their background.

703.2.2 Case. Characters shall be uppercase.

703.2.3 Style. Characters shall be sans serif. Characters shall not be italic, oblique, script, highly decorative, or of other unusual forms.

703.2.4 Character Proportions. Characters shall be selected from fonts where the width of the uppercase letter "O" is 55 percent minimum and 110 percent maximum of the height of the uppercase letter "I".

703.2.5 Character Height. Character height measured vertically from the baseline of the character shall be $\frac{5}{8}$ inch (16 mm) minimum and 2 inches (51 mm) maximum based on the height of the uppercase letter "I".

EXCEPTION: Where separate raised and visual characters with the same information are provided, raised character height shall be permitted to be $\frac{1}{2}$ inch (13 mm) minimum.

703.2.6 Stroke Thickness. Stroke thickness of the uppercase letter "I" shall be 15 percent maximum of the height of the character.

Height of Raised Characters

703.2.7 Character Spacing. Character spacing shall be measured between the two closest points of adjacent raised characters within a message, excluding word spaces. Where characters have rectangular cross sections, spacing between individual raised characters shall be $\frac{1}{8}$ inch (3.2 mm) minimum and 4 times the raised character stroke width maximum. Where characters have other cross sections, spacing between individual raised characters shall be $\frac{1}{16}$ inch (1.6 mm) minimum and 4 times the raised character stroke width maximum at the base of the cross sections, and $\frac{1}{8}$ inch (3.2 mm) minimum and 4 times the raised character stroke width maximum at the top of the cross sections. Characters shall be separated from raised borders and decorative elements $\frac{3}{8}$ inch (9.5 mm) minimum.

703.2.8 Line Spacing. Spacing between the baselines of separate lines of raised characters within a message shall be 135 percent minimum and 170 percent maximum of the raised character height.

703.3 Braille. Braille shall be contracted (Grade 2) and shall comply with 703.3 and 703.4.

703.3.1 Dimensions and Capitalization. Braille dots shall have a domed or rounded shape and shall comply with Table 703.3.1. The indication of an uppercase letter or letters shall only be used before the first word of sentences, proper nouns and names, individual letters of the alphabet, initials, and acronyms.

703.3.2 Position. Braille shall be positioned below the corresponding text. If text is multi-lined, braille shall be placed below the entire text. Braille shall be separated ³/₈ inch (9.5 mm) minimum from any other tactile characters and ³/₈ inch (9.5 mm) minimum from raised borders and decorative elements.

703.4 Installation Height and Location. Signs with tactile characters shall comply with 703.4.

703.4.1 Height Above Finish Floor or Ground. Tactile characters on signs shall be located 48 inches (1220 mm) minimum above the finish floor or ground surface, measured from the baseline of the lowest tactile character and 60 inches (1525 mm) maximum above the finish floor or ground surface, measured from the baseline of the highest tactile character.

Height of Tactile Characters above Finish Floor or Ground

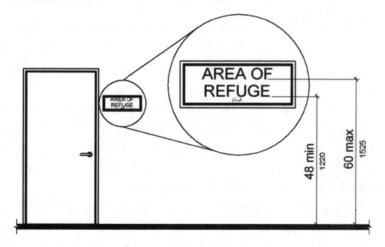

703.4.2 Location. Where a tactile sign is provided at a door, the sign shall be located alongside the door at the latch side. Where a tactile sign is provided at double doors with one active leaf, the sign shall be located on the inactive leaf. Where a tactile sign is provided at double doors with two active leafs, the sign shall be located to the right of the right hand door. Where there is no wall space at the latch side of a single door or at the right side of double doors, signs shall be located on the nearest adjacent wall. Signs containing tactile characters shall be located so that a clear floor space of 18 inches (455 mm)

minimum by 18 inches (455 mm) minimum, centered on the tactile characters, is provided beyond the arc of any door swing between the closed position and 45 degree open position.

EXCEPTION: Signs with tactile characters shall be permitted on the push side of doors with closers and without hold-open devices.

Location of Tactile Signs at Doors

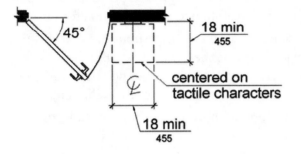

703.5 Visual Characters. Visual characters shall comply with 703.5.

EXCEPTION: Where visual characters comply with 703.2 and are accompanied by braille complying with 703.3, they shall not be required to comply with 703.5.2 through 703.5.9.

703.5.1 Finish and Contrast. Characters and their background shall have a non-glare finish. Characters shall contrast with their background with either light characters on a dark background or dark characters on a light background.

> *Advisory 703.5.1 Finish and Contrast.* Signs are more legible for persons with low vision when characters contrast as much as possible with their background. Additional factors affecting the ease with which the text can be distinguished from its background include shadows cast by lighting sources, surface glare, and the uniformity of the text and its background colors and textures.

703.5.2 Case. Characters shall be uppercase or lowercase or a combination of both.

703.5.3 Style. Characters shall be conventional in form. Characters shall not be italic, oblique, script, highly decorative, or of other unusual forms.

703.5.4 Character Proportions. Characters shall be selected from fonts where the width of the uppercase letter "O" is 55 percent minimum and 110 percent maximum of the height of the uppercase letter "I".

703.5.5 Character Height. Minimum character height shall comply with Table 703.5.5. Viewing distance shall be measured as the horizontal distance between the character and an obstruction preventing further approach towards the sign. Character height shall be based on the uppercase letter "I".

703.5.5 Visual Character Height

Height to Finish Floor or Ground from Baseline of Character	Horizontal Viewing Distance	Minimum Character Height
40 inches (1015 mm) to less than or equal to 70 inches (1780 mm)	less than 72 inches (1830 mm)	$5/8$ inch (16 mm)
	72 inches (1830 mm) and greater	$5/8$ inch (16 mm), plus $1/8$ inch (3.2 mm) per foot (305 mm) of viewing distance above 72 inches (1830 mm)
Greater than 70 inches (1780 mm) to less than or equal to 120 inches (3050 mm)	less than 180 inches (4570 mm)	2 inches (51 mm)
	180 inches (4570 mm) and greater	2 inches (51 mm), plus $1/8$ inch (3.2 mm) per foot (305 mm) of viewing distance above 180 inches (4570 mm)
greater than 120 inches (3050 mm)	less than 21 feet (6400 mm)	3 inches (75 mm)
	21 feet (6400 mm) and greater	3 inches (75 mm), plus $1/8$ inch (3.2 mm) per foot (305 mm) of viewing distance above 21 feet (6400 mm)

703.5.6 Height From Finish Floor or Ground. Visual characters shall be 40 inches (1015 mm) minimum above the finish floor or ground.

EXCEPTION: Visual characters indicating elevator car controls shall not be required to comply with 703.5.6.

703.5.7 Stroke Thickness. Stroke thickness of the uppercase letter "I" shall be 10 percent minimum and 30 percent maximum of the height of the character.

703.5.8 Character Spacing. Character spacing shall be measured between the two closest points of adjacent characters, excluding word spaces. Spacing between individual characters shall be 10 percent minimum and 35 percent maximum of character height.

703.5.9 Line Spacing. Spacing between the baselines of separate lines of characters within a message shall be 135 percent minimum and 170 percent maximum of the character height.

703.6 Pictograms. Pictograms shall comply with 703.6.

703.6.1 Pictogram Field. Pictograms shall have a field height of 6 inches (150 mm) minimum. Characters and braille shall not be located in the pictogram field.

Pictogram Field

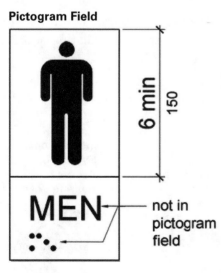

6 min
150

MEN — not in pictogram field

703.6.2 Finish and Contrast. Pictograms and their field shall have a non-glare finish. Pictograms shall contrast with their field with either a light pictogram on a dark field or a dark pictogram on a light field.

Advisory 703.6.2 Finish and Contrast. Signs are more legible for persons with low vision when characters contrast as much as possible with their background. Additional factors affecting the ease with which the text can be distinguished from its background include shadows cast by lighting sources, surface glare, and the uniformity of the text and background colors and textures.

703.6.3 Text Descriptors. Pictograms shall have text descriptors located directly below the pictogram field. Text descriptors shall comply with 703.2, 703.3 and 703.4.

703.7 Symbols of Accessibility. Symbols of accessibility shall comply with 703.7.

703.7.1 Finish and Contrast. Symbols of accessibility and their background shall have a non-glare finish. Symbols of accessibility shall contrast with their background with either a light symbol on a dark background or a dark symbol on a light background.

Advisory 703.7.1 Finish and Contrast. Signs are more legible for persons with low vision when characters contrast as much as possible with their background. Additional factors affecting the ease with which the text can be distinguished from its background include shadows cast by lighting sources, surface glare, and the uniformity of the text and background colors and textures.

703.7.2 Symbols.

703.7.2.1 International Symbol of Accessibility. The International Symbol of Accessibility shall comply with Figure 703.7.2.1.

703.7.2.2 International Symbol of TTY. The International Symbol of TTY shall comply with Figure 703.7.2.2.

703.7.2.3 Volume Control Telephones. Telephones with a volume control shall be identified by a pictogram of a telephone handset with radiating sound waves on a square field such as shown in Figure 703.7.2.3.

703.7.2.4 Assistive Listening Systems. Assistive listening systems shall be identified by the International Symbol of Access for Hearing Loss complying with Figure 703.7.2.4.

International Symbol of Accessibility

International Symbol of TTY

Volume Control Telephone

International Symbol of Access for Hearing Loss

Service Counters

904.4.2 Forward Approach [to a service counter]. A portion of the counter surface that is 30 inches (760 mm) long minimum and 36 inches (915 mm) high maximum shall be provided. Knee and toe space complying with 306 shall be provided under the counter. A clear floor or ground space complying with 305 shall be positioned for a forward approach to the counter.

Note

1. U.S. Access Board, *ADA and ABA Accessibility Guidelines for Buildings and Facilities* (*Federal Register,* July 23, 2004).

Workforms

Instructions

Purpose

Use this workform to review the activities that support a goal to determine if they will require facility resources.

Note about Electronic Version

Use the Microsoft Word version of this workform (available at http://elearnlibraries.com) to add or delete rows and expand the size of rows.

Sources of Data for Workform 1

Sources of data include the library's strategic plan, a grant project, or a service identified by some other means.

Factors to Consider When Completing Workform 1

1. This workform is normally completed by one or more members of the library's management team.

2. This workform assumes you have formal plans with goals, objectives, and activities or that you are working from a grant project that has goals and objectives. If you are not, you don't need to use this workform.

3. Complete a copy of this workform for *each* goal in your planning document or grant. If there are no written goals, use some other method for grouping similar activities, such as a category of service.

How to Complete the Columns and Rows on Workform 1

Write in a goal, grant name, or service.

Write the name of the library or unit.

A. List the activities for the goal, grant, or service (from your planning document or other source).

B. Check this column if there are no implications for facility resources related to the activity. If you check this column, you will not complete columns C–G for this activity.

C. Check this column if the current facility support for the activity is adequate. If you check this column, you will not complete the other columns for this activity.

D. Check this column if the activity will require new or modified public spaces.

E. Check this column if the activity will require new or modified staff space or storage space,

F. Check this column if the activity will require new or modified furnishings, equipment, or shelving that will need floor space.

G. Check this column if the activity will require facility support for new or expanded technology.

Finally, complete the information at the bottom of the workform.

Factors to Consider When Reviewing Workform 1

1. Have you listed all of the activities under the goal, grant, or service, even those that have no apparent facility implications?

2. Have you involved subject experts in the review if necessary?

3. Have you explored all of the possible facility implications of each activity?

4. Is the same activity listed under two or more goals? If so, are the facility implications the same in both places, and do the workforms reflect that similarity?

Goal, Grant, or Service: _____   Library or Unit: _____

Facility Requirements of the Activities That Support the Goal, Grant, or Service

A. Activity	B. No Facility Requirements	C. Current Facilities Adequate	D. Requires Additional or Modified Public Space	E. Requires Additional or Modified Staff or Storage Space	F. Requires Additional or Modified Furnishings, Equipment, or Shelving	G. Requires Support for New or Expanded Technology

Completed by _____   Date completed _____

Source of data _____

Instructions

Purpose

Use this workform to write a brief project description, record decisions about the priority of each project, and identify projects that have been selected for the current year.

Note about Electronic Version

Use the Microsoft Word version of this workform (available at http://elearnlibraries.com) to add or delete rows and expand the size of rows.

Sources of Data for Workform 2

The data for columns A and B come from Workform 1: Facility Projects.

Factors to Consider When Completing Workform 2

1. This workform is normally completed by one or more members of the library management team.

2. Be sure to move all of the activities that require facility resources from all completed copies of Workform 1: Facility Projects to this workform.

3. You can use the priority rankings suggested in chapter 1 to determine the priority, or you can develop your own priority rankings.

How to Complete the Columns and Rows on Workform 2

Write in the fiscal year in which the work is to take place. For multiyear projects, estimate the number of years needed.

Write the name of the library or unit.

A. List the goal and activity number of each activity that will require facility resources from all copies of Workform 1: Facility Projects.

B. Briefly describe the facility project that will be required to implement the activity. Include a list of the facility resources identified on Workform 1: Facility Projects.

C. Determine the priority of the project, and record it here, with 1 = critical, 2 = important, and 3 = desirable but not necessary now.

D. Provide specific information about why a given priority was assigned to each project.

E. Decide if each project will be completed during the current year, and place an X in the "yes" or "no" column.

Finally, complete the information at the bottom of the workform.

Factors to Consider When Reviewing Workform 2

1. Is there adequate staff time and energy to do all of the facility projects identified for the current year?

2. Is it possible or desirable for a project committee to work on the facility portion of more than one activity?

3. Some facility projects take more than a year to complete. Could this year just be the planning year, with implementation to follow in the next year or later?

Projects for Fiscal Year: _____   Library or Unit: _____

A. Goal/Activity Number	B. Project Description	C. Priority	D. Why	E. Selected	
				Yes	*No*

Completed by _____   Date completed _____

Source of data _____

WORKFORM 3 Preliminary Task List and Timeline

Instructions

Purpose

Managers use this workform to provide direction to a project manager or the facility reallocation committee about the major tasks and time frames for a facilities review and space-reallocation project.

Note about Electronic Version

Use the Microsoft Word version of this workform (available at http://elearnlibraries.com) to add or delete rows and expand the size of rows.

Sources of Data for Workform 3

The tasks in column A are selected from the lists of tasks and steps shown in figure 2, Tasks and Steps in the *Managing Facilities for Results* Process, in the introduction to this book.

Factors to Consider When Completing Workform 3

1. This workform is normally completed by one or more members of the library's management team.

2. The project timeline should include time for all the components of the project. If a committee will be responsible for all of the steps of a facility-reallocation project from planning through implementation, then be sure the time allocated is adequate to do the work.

3. The project timeline can be affected by any number of factors. Think about possible delays, and be realistic about how long it will take to complete the project.

How to Complete the Columns and Rows on Workform 3

Write the name of the project (Homework Help Center Facility Resources Project, for example).

Write the name of the library or unit.

A. Using the list of project tasks and steps in figure 2 in the introduction, list the major activities to be carried out by the project committee.

B. Decide when work on the task or step should begin, and write the month and year in the column.

C. Decide when work on the task or step should be completed and write the month and year in the column.

Finally, complete the information at the bottom of the workform.

Factors to Consider When Reviewing Workform 3

1. Did you consider holidays, the summer reading program, and other regular events when you planned the schedule?

2. Have you allowed enough time for the people responsible for the project to complete tasks and steps *and* still do their jobs?

3. Are all of the tasks and steps you identified really needed to complete the project?

WORKFORM 3 **Preliminary Task List and Timeline**

Project Name: _____

Library or Unit: _____

A. Tasks to Be Completed	B. Starting Date (month and year)	C. Ending Date (month and year)

Completed by _____ Date completed _____

Source of data _____

Instructions

WORKFORM 4 Need for Outside Experts

Purpose

Use this workform to record information and decisions about experts that will be used for a facility review and space-reallocation project. The information will be used in the charge to the project committee.

Note about Electronic Version

Use the Microsoft Word version of this workform (available at http://elearnlibraries.com) to add or delete rows and expand the size of rows.

Sources of Data for Workform 4

Information for completing columns A and B is available in Step 2.2 in chapter 1 and from your past experience. The data needed to complete column C is available from the library or city/county budget office. The data for columns D1 and D2 come from past experience, consultation with experts, and the library's budget.

Factors to Consider When Completing Workform 4

1. This workform is initially completed by members of the library's management team during the preliminary planning for the project. It also may be used later in the project by the project manager or committee.

2. Be cautious about ruling out expert help because you think you can't afford it.

How to Complete the Columns and Rows on Workform 4

Write the name of the project (Homework Help Center Facilities Resources Project, for example).

Write the name of the library or unit.

A. Using the list of outside consultants and experts in chapter 1, write in the types of experts you think might be needed.

B. List the reasons for using each type of expert listed in column A. Identify what each type of expert will be responsible for, if you decide to use an expert of that type.

C. Describe the process to be used to procure the expert. Examples include a formal bid process, selecting from a list of city-approved experts, and preparing a request for pro bono work.

D. Estimate the cost for using each type of expert in column D1, and indicate how much money is available to support hiring an expert in column D2. This should be a gross estimate provided from your own knowledge and previous experience or communication with experts to do the type of work listed in column B. The cost may be expressed as a maximum amount of money you are willing to commit to the expert rather than an estimate.

Finally, complete the information at the bottom of the workform.

Factors to Consider When Reviewing Workform 4

1. Have you considered all sources of expertise, including other departments of the city or county, system or state library staff, and staff from other libraries?

2. Is it possible to train someone on the library staff to provide the needed expertise? Is it cost-effective to do so?

3. Does your agency have specific requirements about when requests for proposal/bid/qualifications are required, whether phone bids will suffice, or whether any competitive process is needed at all?

4. Does your purchasing department have specified selection processes?

5. Have you checked with your purchasing department to determine whether a purchase order, a letter of agreement, or a contract is used to commit to paying the expert and to indicate what is to be paid?

WORKFORM 4 Need for Outside Experts

Project Name: _____

Library or Unit: _____

A. Type of Expertise Needed	B. Expert's Responsibilities	C. Selection and Procurement Methods	D. Cost	
			1. Cost Estimate	2. Funds Available

Completed by _____ Date completed _____

Source of data _____

Instructions

WORKFORM 5 Facility Resources—Data Elements

Purpose

Use this workform to guide the discussion of facility-related data elements and to provide a place for committee members to take notes during the discussion.

Note about Electronic Version

Use the Microsoft Word version of this workform (available at http://elearnlibraries.com) to add or delete rows and expand the size of rows.

Sources of Data for Workform 5

Definitions will come from figure 8, Facility Resources—Data Elements; examples may come from the list of common elements in figure 7, Facility Resources—Common Elements; possible sources of data may come from a list of the data elements the library currently collects.

Factors to Consider When Completing Workform 5

1. Distribute a copy of the workform to each committee member during the first meeting of the project committee.

2. Remember that this workform is *not* intended to be used to develop an exhaustive list of examples and sources of the facility resources that apply to the activity under review. It is simply a tool to help provide a structure for discussion and an easy way for members to take notes.

How to Complete the Columns and Rows on Workform 5

Write the name of the project.

Write the name of the library or unit.

A1–A6. The definition for each of these data elements can be found in figure 8 in chapter 2. Review the definitions with the committee members and discuss any questions or issues. Encourage committee members to record the definition of each data element in this column.

B1–B6. Committee members should list examples of each data element. They can work individually or in groups, but the whole committee should discuss all of the examples to be sure that everyone agrees that the examples are appropriate.

C1–C6. Committee members should list possible sources of each example of data they identified in column B. They can work individually or in groups, but the whole committee should discuss each of the suggested sources to be sure that everyone agrees that they are appropriate.

Finally, complete the information at the bottom of the workform.

Factors to Consider When Reviewing Workform 5

The committee chair may want to ask one or two committee members to develop a composite of all the completed copies of the workform to be distributed to the committee. This would ensure that everyone is working from the same definitions and can refer to the same examples if they need guidance.

Project Name: _____

Library or Unit: _____

Data Element	A. Definition	B. Examples of Data	C. Possible Sources of Data
1. Capacity			
2. Use			
3. Condition and age			
4. Access			
5. Impact of technology			
6. Spatial relationships			

Completed by _____ Date completed _____

Source of data _____

WORKFORM 6 Project Description—General

Instructions

Purpose

Use this workform to record the committee's expanded description of the project.

Note about Electronic Version

Use the Microsoft Word version of this workform (available at http://elearnlibraries.com) to add or delete rows and expand the size of rows.

Sources of Data for Workform 6

Sources of data include the library's strategic plan or a grant project, if the activity is a part of a grant.

Factors to Consider When Completing Workform 6

1. This workform will provide the starting point for the identification of the facility resources that will be needed and for the resources that are currently allocated to support the activity. It will provide a framework for the data collection needed to complete the gap analysis process.

2. The information that you enter on this workform will probably be fairly general. For example, you may know that you will need new seating but not be ready to describe the needed seating in detail. Provide as much information as possible. This type of description will be developed in more detail in chapter 3.

3. It will be important to consult the people who will be implementing the activity when answering the questions on this workform.

4. The members of the project committee can only make recommendations. They do not have the authority to make final decisions.

5. The completed workform should be presented to the library's management team before moving ahead with Tasks 5 and 6.

6. Note that the questions focus on what is needed or required; that is, they focus on what is considered absolutely essential.

How to Complete the Columns and Rows on Workform 6

Write the name of the project.
Write the name of the library or unit.

A. Describe the age or grade level of the audience.

B. List any special conditions to be considered when designing spaces for the audience described in B. For example, if the audience for the activity is seniors, you could indicate that the audience might include people with physical limitations, including reduced mobility or poor eyesight.

C. List the number of people to be served at any one time. This is the number that will be needed to determine the capacity of the facility resources that will be required to support the project.

D, E. Mark the appropriate column to answer questions 1–7.

F1–F7. Complete this column for all questions for which you answered *Yes* in column D. Provide as much detail as possible. For example, if the project will require new staff (1), indicate the number of staff and their classifications. If new materials will be purchased for the project (4), or materials will be deleted (5), indicate how many materials will be purchased or deleted and the format, age level, and classification of the materials. For F4, also indicate if this is a one-time purchase or an ongoing annual purchase.

Finally, complete the information at the bottom of the workform.

Factors to Consider When Reviewing Workform 6

1. Have you provided enough information on each of your recommendations in column F to ensure that the administrators who review your recommendations understand the reasons for those recommendations?

2. Are your recommendations based on what is *required* (not on what would be nice to have but is not essential) for the project?

WORKFORM 6 Project Description—General

Project Name: _____

Library or Unit: _____

A. Age (grade level) of the people to be served: _____

B. Special conditions to be considered about people to be served: _____

C. Number of people to be served: _____

	D. Yes	E. No	F. If Yes, Describe Here
1. Will new or reassigned staff be needed?			
2. Will furnishings be required to support the activity?			
3. Will equipment be required to support the activity?			
4. Will materials be added to the collections?			
5. Will materials be deleted from the collections?			
6. Will public access to technology be required?			
7. Will staff access to technology by required?			

Completed by _____   Date completed _____

Source of data _____

163

WORKFORM 7 Project Description—Physical Plant, Space, and Spatial Relationships

Instructions

Purpose

Use this workform to describe the physical plant and space requirements of the activity.

Note about Electronic Version

Use the Microsoft Word version of this workform (available at http://elearnlibraries.com) to add or delete rows and expand the size of rows.

Sources of Data for Workform 7

Sources of information include Workform 6, Project Description—General, and Step 4.1: Define the Project in Detail, in chapter 2.

Factors to Consider When Completing Workform 7

1. This workform will provide the starting point for the identification of the facility resources that will be needed and for the resources that are currently allocated to support the activity. It will provide a framework for the data collection needed to complete the gap analysis process.

2. It will be important to consult the people who will be implementing the activity when answering the questions on this workform.

3. The members of the project committee can only make recommendations. They do not have the authority to make final decisions.

4. The completed workform should be presented to the library's management team along with the completed Workform 6, Project Description—General, before moving ahead with Task 5: Collect Preliminary Data.

5. Note that many of the questions are about what is *needed* or considered absolutely essential.

How to Complete the Columns and Rows on Workform 7

Write the name of the project.

Write the name of the library or unit.

A, B. Mark the appropriate column to answer each of the questions in D1–D4, E1–E3, and F1–F4.

C. Use this space to write a brief rationale for the answers you gave in columns A or B.

D5. Answer *Yes* here if you have answered *Yes* to any of the questions in D1–D4.

E4. Answer *Yes* here if you have answered *Yes* to E1 or E2. Your answer to E3 may or may not require single-purpose space.

Finally, complete the information at the bottom of the workform.

Factors to Consider When Reviewing Workform 7

1. Have you provided enough information on each of your recommendations in column C to ensure that the administrators who review your recommendations understand the reasons for those recommendations?

2. Are your recommendations based on what is *required* (not on what would be nice to have but is not essential) for the project?

3. Are there other physical plant or space issues that need to be addressed before the members of the committee can move on to the data collection process?

Project Name: _____

Library or Unit: _____

	A. Yes	B. No	C. Why
D. Walled Space			
1. Do you need to restrict access to the space?			
2. Do you need to control how many people can be in the space at the same time?			
3. Does the space need to be soundproof, either to keep sound in or to keep sound out?			
4. Is the space needed when the library is not open?			
5. Will the activity need to be presented in a walled space?			
E. Single-Purpose or Multipurpose Space			
1. Will the furniture, equipment, or shelving needed to support the activity make it hard to use the space for other purposes?			
2. Is the anticipated layout of the space so specialized that it will be hard to use the space for other purposes?			
3. Will the activity be available during the entire time the library is open?			
4. Will the activity need to be presented in a single-purpose space?			
F. Spatial Relationships			
1. Does the activity need to be *in the line of sight* of a service desk?			
2. Does the activity need to be presented in space that is *adjacent* to other parts of the library?			
3. Does the activity need to be presented in space that is *close* to other parts of the library?			
4. Does the activity need to be presented in space that is *away from* other parts of the library?			

Completed by _____ Date completed _____

Source of data _____

Instructions

Purpose

Use this workform to identify the types and capacity of the furniture and equipment that the public and the staff will need to support the activity and to estimate the amount of square footage that each will require.

Note about Electronic Version

Use the Microsoft Word version of this workform (available at http://elearnlibraries.com) to add or delete rows and expand the size of rows.

Sources of Data for Workform 8

Sources may include figure 7, Facility Resources—Common Elements, in chapter 2; Workform 6, Project Description—General; discussions with staff who will be providing the activity; information from other libraries that currently offer the service; furniture and equipment vendor catalogs and websites; and Tool Kit A, Calculating Square Footage.

Factors to Consider When Completing Workform 8

1. Record *needs*—not what would be desirable but is unnecessary.

2. Work with staff that will be responsible for carrying out the activity to find out more about furniture and equipment requirements.

3. Do not enter data in the shaded boxes.

How to Complete the Columns and Rows on Workform 8

Write the name of the project.
Write the name of the library or unit.

PART I: FURNITURE

1–11. List and describe the types of items needed for public use (1–6) and for staff use (7–11) in this column. Be as specific as you can.

A. Record the maximum number of people who are expected to use each of the furnishings listed in 1–11 at the same time.

B. Record the number of each of the items listed in 1–11 that will be required to provide the needed capacity recorded in column A. For example, if the estimated project capacity is 20, you would need a total of 20 chairs of one or a combination of various types.

C. Record the approximate square footage required for each item listed in 1–11. You can find information on square footage in Tool Kit A, Calculating Square Footage.

D. Calculate the total square footage required for each item listed in 1–11 by multiplying the number of items (recorded in column B) by the square footage for each (recorded in column C).

12. Add the total furniture square footage required for items 1–11 (recorded in number D), and enter the total here.

PART II: EQUIPMENT

1–4. List and describe the types of equipment that the public (1–2) and staff (3–4) will need to use this service.

A. Record the maximum number of people who are expected to use the equipment at the same time, listed in 1–4.

B. Record the number of each of the items listed in 1–4 that will be required to provide the needed capacity recorded in column A.

C. Record the approximate square footage required for each item listed in 1 and 3. (There will be no square footage required for items listed in 2 and 4.) You can find information on square footage in Tool Kit A, Calculating Square Footage.

D. Calculate the total square footage required for items listed in 1 and 3 by multiplying the number of items (recorded in column B) by the square footage for each (recorded in column C).

5. Add the total equipment square footage required for items 1 and 3 (recorded in column D), and enter the total here.

6. Add the total square footage for furniture (Part I, line 12) and the total square footage for equipment (Part II, line 5), and record the grand total here.

Finally, complete the information at the bottom of the workform.

Factors to Consider When Reviewing Workform 8

1. Will any of the equipment items listed in Part II require furniture? If so, has that furniture been included in Part I?

2. Are all of the items of furniture and equipment that are listed *required* to provide the service?

3. Have you explored the various types of furniture and equipment that are available?

4. Have you paid particular attention to trends in library furnishings and equipment?

5. Have you considered whether self-service equipment might be appropriate for this project?

WORKFORM 8 Need—Furniture and Equipment

Project Name: _____

Library or Unit: _____

PART I: FURNITURE

Furniture for Public Use	A. Capacity Needed	B. Number of Items Needed	C. Square Footage per Item	D. Total Square Footage for Items
1. Seating				
2. Tables				
3. Meeting/conference/study room furniture				
4. Technology workstations				
5. Fixed furnishings				
6. Other				

(Cont.)

WORKFORM 8 **Need—Furniture and Equipment** (Cont.)

PART I: FURNITURE (Cont.)

	A. Capacity Needed	B. Number of Items Needed	C. Square Footage per Item	D. Total Square Footage for Items
Furniture for Staff Use				
7. Staff desks or work counters				
8. Staff chairs				
9. Technology workstations				
10. Fixed furnishings				
11. Other				
12. *Total* square footage for furniture				

(Cont.)

PART II: EQUIPMENT

	A. Capacity Needed	B. Number of Items Needed	C. Square Footage per Item	D. Total Square Footage for Items
Equipment for Public Use				
1. Freestanding equipment				
2. Equipment that doesn't occupy floor space				
Equipment for Staff Use				
3. Freestanding equipment				
4. Equipment that doesn't occupy floor space				
5. *Total* spare footage for equipment				
6. *Grand total* square footage for furniture and equipment				

Completed by _____   Date completed _____

Source of data _____

WORKFORM 9 Have—Furniture and Equipment

Instructions

Purpose

Use this workform to describe the furniture and equipment items that are currently allocated for public and staff use to support the activity and to estimate the amount of square footage that each requires.

Note about Electronic Version

Use the Microsoft Word version of this workform (available at http://elearnlibraries.com) to add or delete rows and expand the size of rows.

Sources of Data for Workform 9

Sources will include building inventories and observation; figure 9, Suggested Indicators to Measure Age and Condition; Workform 5, Facility Resources—Data Elements; Tool Kit A, Calculating Square Footage; and discussions with staff who are providing the activity.

Factors to Consider When Completing Workform 9

1. Only record information about existing furniture and equipment that is used to support the activity under review. Do not record information about existing furniture and equipment that could be reallocated to support the activity. You will be looking at those issues in chapter 4.

2. Work with staff who are responsible for carrying out the activity to find out more about the current furniture and equipment.

3. Do not enter data in the shaded boxes.

How to Complete the Columns and Rows on Workform 9

Write the name of the project.

Write the name of the library or unit.

PART I: FURNITURE

1–11. List and describe the types of items that currently support the activity and are available for public use (1–6) and for staff use (7–11) in this column. Be as specific as you can.

A. Record the maximum number of people who can use each of the furnishings listed in 1–11 at the same time.

B. Record the number of each of the items listed in 1–11 that are currently used to support the activity.

C. Record the approximate square footage of each item listed in 1–11. You can find information on square footage in Tool Kit A, Calculating Square Footage.

D. Calculate the total square footage for each item listed in 1–11 by multiplying the number of items (recorded in column B) by the square footage for each (recorded in column C).

E. Indicate the condition of each item listed in 1–11, using the scale in figure 9, Suggested Indicators to Measure Age and Condition. For example, if four lounge chairs are evaluated and two are in good condition, but two are in unacceptable condition, record that two are usable but two are unacceptable, so only two can count as "have." If the committee members modified the list of indicators, use the modified version, attaching the list of indicators you used.

F. Write *Single* in this column for each item in 1–11 that is used solely to support the activity and *Multi* in this column for each item that is used for other purposes as well.

12. Add the total furniture square footage for items 1–11 (recorded in column D), and enter the total here.

PART II: EQUIPMENT

1–4. List and describe the types of equipment that currently support the activity and are available to the public (1–2) and staff (3–4).

A. Record the maximum number of people who can use the equipment listed in 1–4 at the same time.

B. Record the current number of each of the items listed in 1–4.

C. Record the approximate square footage of each item listed in 1 and 3. (There is no square footage required for items listed in 2 and 4.) You can find information on square footage in Tool Kit A, Calculating Square Footage.

D. Calculate the total square footage listed in 1 and 3 by multiplying the number of items (recorded in column B) by the square footage for each (recorded in column C).

E. Indicate the condition of each item listed in 1–4, using the scale in figure 9, Suggested Indicators to Measure Age and Condition. For example, if there are three public access computers but only two can utilize wireless cards—and if the project involves wireless access—you will only count two computers as "have." If the committee members modified the list of indicators, use the modified version. Attach a copy of the criteria to the completed workform.

(Cont.)

WORKFORM 9 **Have—Furniture and Equipment** *Instructions* (Cont.)

F. Write *Single* in this column for each item in 1–4 that is used solely to support the activity, and *Multi* in this column for each item that is used for other purposes as well.

5. Add the total equipment square footage for items 1 and 3 (recorded in column D), and enter the total here.

6. Add the total square footage for furniture (Part I, row 12) and the total square footage for equipment (Part II, row 5), and record the grand total here.

Finally, complete the information at the bottom of the workform.

Factors to Consider When Reviewing Workform 9

1. Do any of the equipment items listed in Part II sit on furniture? If so, has that furniture been included in Part I?

2. Are all of the items of furniture and equipment that are listed actually used to provide the service?

3. Have you listed every piece of furniture and equipment that is used to support the service, both in the public areas of the library and in the staff areas of the library?

4. Have you used the same criteria to evaluate the condition of all of the items and attached a copy of those criteria to the workform?

WORKFORM 9 **Have—Furniture and Equipment**

Project Name: _____

Library or Unit: _____

PART I: FURNITURE

	A. Current Capacity	B. Current Number of Items	C. Square Footage per Item	D. Total Square Footage for Items	E. Condition of the Items	F. Single-Purpose or Multipurpose Use
Furniture for Public Use						
1. Seating						
2. Tables						
3. Meeting/conference/study room furniture						
4. Technology workstations						
5. Fixed furnishings						
6. Other						

(Cont.)

PART I: FURNITURE (Cont.)

	A. Current Capacity	B. Current Number of Items	C. Square Footage per Item	D. Total Square Footage for Items	E. Condition of the Items	F. Single-Purpose or Multipurpose Use
Furniture for Staff Use						
7. Staff desks or work counters						
8. Staff chairs						
9. Technology workstations						
10. Fixed furnishings						
11. Other						
12. *Total* square footage for furniture						

(Cont.)

PART II: EQUIPMENT

	A. Current Capacity	B. Current Number of Items	C. Square Footage per Item	D. Total Square Footage for Items	E. Condition of the Items	F. Single-Purpose or Multipurpose
Equipment for Public Use						
1. Freestanding equipment						
2. Equipment that doesn't occupy floor space						
Equipment for Staff Use						
3. Freestanding equipment						
4. Equipment that doesn't occupy floor space						
5. *Total* square footage of current equipment						
6. *Grand total* square footage of current furniture and equipment						

Completed by _____   Date completed _____

Source of data _____

Instructions

Purpose

Use this workform to determine the number of regular and special shelving units needed for materials that support the activity and to estimate the total square footage required for that shelving.

Note about Electronic Version

Use the Microsoft Excel version of this workform (available at http://elearnlibraries.com) to add columns and automatically compute totals.

Sources of Data for Workform 10

Sources of data include Workform 6, Project Description—General; existing inventories; Tool Kit A, Calculating Square Footage; measurements from the library's current shelving areas; manufacturers' catalogs; and Case Study Part 6 in chapter 3.

Factors to Consider When Completing Workform 10

1. Complete Part I of this workform if you will be adding a relatively small number of new items to the collection and you think that the items can be shelved on existing shelving. Complete Part II of this workform if you will be adding a large number of items to the collection and will need to add additional shelving. The number of items that are considered *small* or *large* will vary by library.

2. Use the information in Tool Kit A as a basis for the estimates needed to complete this workform whenever possible.

3. Do not let the amount of data collected on the workform scare you. It is all very straightforward and easy to collect or calculate.

4. Complete this workform in cooperation with the staff that will be implementing the program of services associated with the activity.

How to Complete the Columns and Rows on Workform 10

Write the name of the project.
Write the name of the library or unit.

PART I: MINIMAL COLLECTION

1. Enter the format and classification of the items to be added to the collection. For example, you might enter "print, nonfiction," or "media, juvenile."

   A. Enter the number of items to be added to the collection to support the activity. See chapter 3 and Case Study Part 6 for more information.

   B. Enter the total number of items in the current collection that are of each of the classifications and formats recorded in column A.

   C. Calculate the percentage of the collection that will be represented by the new items and record here.

   (1) Add the total number of new items (recorded in column A) and the number of similar items (recorded in column B).

   (2) Divide the number of items to be added to the collection (recorded in column A) by the total number of items (the sum of columns A and B).

   (3) Convert the result to a percentage by multiplying by 100. For example, if you are adding 100 new items to an existing collection of 4,900 items, you would add the two numbers to get a total of 5,000 and then divide 100 by 5,000. You would multiply the result (.02) by 100 and find that the new items would represent 2 percent of the collection.

   D. Look at the shelves that are currently being used to house the type of items listed in column 1. Estimate the average percentage of the shelves that are empty and record it here.

   E. Place a check mark in the appropriate box.

2. Review the data in columns A through E and decide if the new items can be shelved on existing shelving.

(Cont.)

F. Check here if the existing shelving will be adequate.

G. Check here if the new shelving will be needed, and complete Part II of this workform.

PART II: SIGNIFICANT COLLECTION

Regular Shelving

1. List the types of regular shelving that will be required to support the activity in this column. For example, you might list single-sided case shelving for books; double-sided cantilevered shelving for books; single-sided case shelving for media, and so on.

A. Enter the number of items to be added to the collection to support the activity. See chapter 3 and Case Study Part 6 for examples.

B. Calculate the total linear feet of shelving that will be needed to house the items to be added to the collection (to the desired capacity on the shelves) and enter the result.

   (1) Use Tool Kit A, Calculating Square Footage, to determine the average number of items that can be shelved per linear foot. If the information in Tool Kit A does not apply, refer to Step 5.2 for information on making your own estimates.

   (2) Divide the number of items to be shelved (recorded in column A) by the average number of items per linear foot to determine the number of linear feet of shelving needed.

C. Enter the width of the shelves to be used. Typically, this will be the same width as your current shelves holding similar items.

D. Calculate the number of shelves needed, and enter the result. To do this, divide the number recorded in column B by the number recorded in column C.

E. Enter the shelves that will be *used* per unit. If your library leaves the top or bottom shelves empty, do not include those shelves in this total.

F. Calculate the number of units that will be needed, and enter the number. To do this, multiply the shelves needed (recorded in column D) by the number of shelves per unit (recorded in column E).

G. Use the information in Tool Kit A, Calculating Square Footage, to estimate the square footage required for each unit of shelving.

H. Multiply the square feet per unit (column G) by the number of units needed (column F), and enter the result.

2. Total column F and column H, and enter the results in this row.

Special Shelving

3. List the types of special shelving that will be needed in this column. Examples include display shelving, paperback spinners, media shelving, and so on.

A. Enter the number of items to be added to the collection to support the activity. See chapter 3 and Case Study Part 6 for more information.

B. Enter the number of items that can be shelved in a single unit of the type of shelving listed in column 3. You may get this information by looking at similar shelving already in use in your library, or you may need to refer to manufacturers' catalogs.

C. Divide the total number of items to be shelved (column A) by the number of items that can be shelved in each unit (column B) to determine the number of units required.

D. Enter the square footage for each unit using information from Tool Kit A or from manufacturers' catalogs.

E. Multiply the square feet per unit (column D) by the number of units needed (column C).

4. Total column C and column E, and enter the results in this row.

5. Add the results recorded in Regular Shelving H2 and Special Shelving E4, and record the total here.

Finally, complete the information at the bottom of the workform.

Factors to Consider When Reviewing Workform 10

1. Did you consider shelving for all of the types of materials that might be purchased to support this activity?

2. Did you plan for enough empty space on the shelves to accommodate the expected growth of the collection?

3. Did you base your shelving design (number and width of shelves, width of aisle) on the library's current practice?

Project Name: _____

Library or Unit: _____

PART I: MINIMAL COLLECTION

1. Format and Classification of New Items	A. Number of New Items to Be Shelved	B. Number of Items of This Format and Classification in Collection	C. Percent of the Collection Consisting of New Items to Be Added	D. Percentage of Shelves That Are Empty	E. Does Collection Need Weeding?	
					Yes	*No*

2. Can the new items be shelved in current shelving?

F. Yes _____

G. No _____ Complete Part II of Workform 10

(Cont.)

PART II: SIGNIFICANT COLLECTION

	Needed Number of Shelving Units					**Needed Square Footage for Shelving**	
	A. Number of New Items to Be Shelved	**B.** Linear Feet of Shelves Needed	**C.** Width of Shelves	**D.** Number of Shelves Needed	**E.** Number of Shelves per Unit	**F.** Number of Units Needed	**G.** Square Footage per Unit	**H.** Total Square Footage
1. Regular Shelving								
2. *Total* regular shelving units and square footage								

	Needed Number of Shelving Units			**Needed Square Footage for Shelving**	
	A. Number of Items to Be Shelved	**B.** Number of Items per Unit	**C.** Number of Units	**D.** Square Footage per Unit	**E.** Total Square Footage
3. Special Shelving					
4. *Total* special shelving units and square footage					
5. *Total* square footage for shelving					

Completed by _____   Date completed _____

Source of data _____

Instructions

Purpose

Use this workform to describe the number of regular and special shelving units currently being used for materials that support the activity and to estimate the total square footage currently allocated for that shelving.

Note about Electronic Version

Use the Microsoft Excel version of this workform (available at http://elearnlibraries.com) to add columns and automatically compute totals.

Sources of Data for Workform 11

Sources of data include reports from the library's automated circulation system, and observation.

Factors to Consider When Completing Workform 11

1. Use the information in Tool Kit A, Calculating Square Footage, as a basis for the estimates needed to complete this workform whenever possible.

2. Complete this workform in cooperation with the staff that will be implementing the program of services associated with the activity.

How to Complete the Columns and Rows on Workform 11

Write the name of the project.

Write the name of library or unit.

Regular Shelving

1. List the types of regular shelving that are currently being used to support the activity in this column. For example, you might list single-sided case shelving for books; double-sided cantilevered shelving for books; single-sided case shelving for media, and so on.

   A. Enter the number of items in the existing collection that support this activity. You should be able to get this information from the people who manage the library's automated circulation system.

   B. Count the number of shelves currently used for the materials that support the activity, and record the total here.

   C. Enter the width of the shelves.

   D. Enter the number of shelves in each unit of shelving that is holding materials that support the activity.

   E. Enter the number of units of shelving holding materials that support the activity.

   F. Use the information in Tool Kit A, Calculating Square Footage, to estimate the square footage required for each unit of shelving.

   G. Multiply the square feet per unit (column F) by the number of units (column E), and record the answer here.

   H. Look at the shelves that are currently being used to house the items, and estimate the average percentage of the shelves that are empty. Record the percentage here.

   I. Put an X in the appropriate box.

2. Total each column, E and G, and enter the results in this row.

Special Shelving

3. List the types of special shelving that will be needed in this column. Examples include display shelving, paperback spinners, media shelving, and so on.

   A. Enter the number of items in the existing collection that support this activity. You should be able to get this information from the people who manage the library's automated circulation system.

   B. Enter the average number of items shelved in each unit.

   C. Enter the number of units of each type of specialty shelving holding materials that support the activity.

   D. Use the information in Tool Kit A, Calculating Square Footage, to estimate the square footage required for each unit of shelving.

   E. Multiply the square feet per unit (column D) by the number of units (column C), and record the answer here.

   F. Estimate the average percentage of the units that are empty, and record it here.

   G. Put an X in the appropriate box.

4. Total each column, C and E, and enter the results in this row.

5. Total the numbers in Regular Shelving 2G and Special Shelving 4E, and record the number here.

Finally, complete the information at the bottom of the workform.

(Cont.)

Factors to Consider When Reviewing Workform 11

1. Did you consider shelving for all of the types of materials that are being used to support this activity?

2. Did you consult with the staff who will work with the collection before answering the questions about the need to weed the collection?

3. Did you look at the turnover rate and slow-moving-items reports to help inform your answers to the questions about the need to weed the collection?

Project Name: _____

Library or Unit: _____

1. Regular shelving

	A. Number of Items in Collection	B. Number of Shelves Holding Materials	C. Width of Shelves	D. Number of Shelves per Unit	E. Number of Units	F. Square Footage per Unit	G. Total Square Footage	H. Percentage of Shelves That Are Empty	I. Does Collection Need Weeding? Yes	No
1. Regular shelving										
2. *Total* regular shelving units and square footage										

3. Special shelving

	A. Number of Items in Collection	B. Number of Items per Unit	C. Number of Units	D. Square Footage per Unit	E. Total Square Footage	F. Percentage of Units That Are Empty	G. Does Collection Need Weeding? Yes	No
3. Special shelving								
4. *Total* special shelving units and square footage								
5. *Total* shelving square footage								

Completed by _____ Date completed _____

Source of data _____

WORKFORM 12   **Need—Physical Plant and Technology Support**

Instructions

Purpose

Use this workform to identify physical plant and technology support that will be needed to support the activity under review.

Note about Electronic Version

Use the Microsoft Word version of this workform (available at http://elearnlibraries.com) to add or delete rows to meet your needs for listing items.

Sources of Data for Workform 12

Sources of data for this workform include figure 7, Facility Resources—Common Elements; the completed and approved copy of Workform 7, Project Description—Physical Plant, Space, and Spatial Relationships; discussions with library staff who will be providing the activity; and discussions with staff from other libraries that provide the activity. You may also need to refer to some of the outside experts listed on Workform 4, Need for Outside Experts, while completing this workform.

Factors to Consider When Completing Workform 12

1. Based on the project description, record *needs*—not what would be desirable but is unnecessary—to fulfill the project at desired levels.

2. Expert help may be needed to complete some of the information on this workform.

3. Work with staff that will be responsible for carrying out the project to find out more about physical plant and space requirements.

4. Do not enter data in shaded areas of the workform.

How to Complete the Columns and Rows on Workform 12

Write the name of the project.

Write the name of the library or unit.

A. This column lists the common elements found in library spaces. Add additional elements as needed in row 13.

B. Place an *X* in this column if the item will not be needed to support the activity.

C. Place an *X* in this column if the item will be needed to support the activity.

D. Enter the number of items that will be needed for each item that has an *X* in column C.

E. Describe each item that has an *X* in column C. Provide as much detail as possible.

F. Provide a brief explanation for your recommendations for each item on this list. Include reasons for items that will be needed and for those that won't be needed.

Finally, complete the information at the bottom of the workform.

Factors to Consider When Reviewing Workform 12

1. Did you carefully review the activity to identify any unique physical plant needs? Did you include all of the unique physical plant needs on the workform?

2. Have you provided clear descriptions of the physical plant items that are required?

3. Are your recommendations based on *need*, not *want?*

4. If you used outside experts, did you attach a summary of their comments or a copy of their reports?

Project Name: _____

Library or Unit: _____

A. Item	B. Not Needed	C. Needed	D. Number	E. Description	F. Rationale
1. Floors					
2. Walls					
3. Doors					
4. Windows					
5. Electrical outlets					
6. HVAC					
7. Lighting					
8. Plumbing					
9. Security					
10. Wiring/cabling for computers					
11. Wireless Internet access					
12. Decor					
13. Other					

Completed by _____ Date completed _____

Source of data _____

WORKFORM 13   Have—Physical Plant and Technology Support

Instructions

Purpose

Use this workform to identify physical plant and technology support currently allocated to support the activity under review.

Note about Electronic Version

Use the Microsoft Word version of this workform (available at http://elearnlibraries.com) to add or delete rows to meet your needs for listing items.

Sources of Data for Workform 13

Sources of data for this workform include discussions with staff who provide the activity and observations; the completed and approved Workform 7, Project Description—Physical Plant, Space, and Spatial Relationships; figure 7, Facility Resources—Common Elements; and figure 9, Suggested Indicators to Measure Age and Condition, from chapter 2. You may also need to refer to some of the outside experts listed on Workform 4, Need for Outside Experts, while completing this workform.

Factors to Consider When Completing Workform 13

1. Expert help may be needed to complete some of the information on this workform.

2. Work with staff that will be responsible for carrying out the project to find out more about physical plant and space requirements.

3. Do not enter data in shaded areas of the workform.

How to Complete the Columns and Rows on Workform 13

Write the name of the project.

Write the name of the library or unit.

A. This column lists the common elements found in library spaces. If the space housing the activity has additional elements, add them under row 13.

B. Enter the number of each item used to support the activity in this column. If the item does not exist in the space or is not used to support the activity, enter a *0* in the column.

C. Describe each item that has a number in column B except those that have a *0*. Provide as much detail as possible.

D. Indicate the condition of each item using the scale in figure 9, Suggested Indicators to Measure Age and Condition. If the committee members modified the list of indicators, use the modified version. Exclude items that have a *0* in column B. Attach the list of indicators you used. If you use outside experts, attach a summary of their comments or a copy of their reports.

E. Write *Single* in this column for each item that is used solely to support the activity, and *Multi* in this column for each item that is used for other purposes as well. Exclude items that have a *0* in column B.

F. Calculate the square footage of the space now used for the activity, and enter the result here. Measure the length and width of the space and multiply the two figures. For example, a room that is 10 by 15 feet is 150 square feet.

Finally, complete the information at the bottom of the workform.

Factors to Consider When Reviewing Workform 13

1. Did you include all of the unique aspects of the physical plant on the workform?

2. Have you provided clear descriptions of the physical plant items that are being used?

3. Did you attach figure 9, Suggested Indicators to Measure Age and Condition, or your modified list of criteria?

4. If you used outside experts, did you attach a summary of their comments or a copy of their reports?

WORKFORM 13 **Have—Physical Plant and Technology Support**

Project Name: _____

Library or Unit: _____

A. Item	B. Number	C. Description	D. Condition	E. Single-Purpose or Multipurpose Use
1. Floors				
2. Walls				
3. Doors				
4. Windows				
5. Electrical outlets				
6. HVAC				
7. Lighting				
8. Plumbing				
9. Security				
10. Wiring/cabling for computers				
11. Wireless access to the Internet				
12. Decor				
13. Other				

F. Approximate Square Footage Used _____

Completed by _____ Date completed _____

Source of data _____

WORKFORM 14 Need—Access, Spatial Relationships, and Signage

Instructions

Purpose

Use this workform to identify access, spatial relationships, and signage needs for the activity or service.

Note about Electronic Version

Use the Microsoft Word version of this workform (available at http://elearnlibraries.com) to add or delete rows to meet your needs for listing items.

Sources of Data for Workform 14

Sources of data for this workform include Tool Kit C, Americans with Disabilities Act Requirements; information from chapter 2 on spatial relationships; the completed and approved copies of Workform 6, Project Description—General; Workform 7, Project Description—Physical Plant, Space, and Spatial Relationships; discussions with library staff that will be providing the activity; and discussions with staff from other libraries that provide the activity.

Factors to Consider When Completing Workform 14

1. Work with staff who will be responsible for carrying out the project to find out more about the access, spatial relationships, and signage requirements, if any.

2. Access does not refer solely to issues relating to the Americans with Disabilities Act.

How to Complete the Columns and Rows on Workform 14

Write the name of the project.

Write the name of the library or unit.

PART I: ACCESS TO ACTIVITY OR SERVICE

A. This column lists four access questions to consider and space to add additional questions here if your activity or service has unique access needs.

B. Place an *X* in this box if the answer to the question in column A is *Yes*, and complete column D.

C. Place an *X* in this box if the answer to the question in column A is *No*, and do not complete column D.

D1–D4. Place an *X* by each type of access that will be needed for each question that has an *X* in column B.

D5. List the type of access needed to address the issue raised in question A5.

PART II: SPATIAL RELATIONSHIPS—AREAS OF THE LIBRARY

A. This column lists the four main spatial relationships.

B1. List the areas of the library that should be adjacent to the area in which the activity is housed.

B2. List the areas of the library that should be close to the area in which the activity is housed.

B3. List the areas of the library that should be in line of sight of the area in which the activity is housed.

B4. List the areas of the library that should be away from the area in which the activity is housed.

C. Explain the recommendations in B1–B4.

PART III: SPATIAL RELATIONSHIPS—WITHIN THE AREA HOUSING THE SERVICE

A1–A4. List the subareas, furnishings, equipment, and other items that may require special spatial relationships.

B. List the subareas, furnishings, equipment, or other items that should be adjacent to the items listed in column A.

C. List the subareas, furnishings, equipment, or other items that should be close to the items listed in column A.

D. List the subareas, furnishings, equipment, or other items that should be in line of sight of the items listed in column A.

E. List the subareas, furnishings, equipment, or other items that should be away from the items listed in column A.

F. Explain the recommendations in columns B–E.

(Cont.)

PART IV: SIGNAGE

A. This column lists the four types of signs.

B. Place an *X* in the appropriate box. Complete columns C–F for all rows in which you place an *X* in the *Yes* box.

C. Enter the language or languages that should be used on the signs.

D. Describe where the signs should be placed.

E. Estimate the number of signs that will be needed.

F. Briefly describe the design or format of the needed signs. For example, "matching all other library signs" or "using the colors and logo from the teen center."

Finally, complete the information at the bottom of the workform.

Factors to Consider When Reviewing Workform 14

1. Are your recommendations based on *need*, not on *want?*

2. Are there any other access issues to be considered?

3. Have you identified all of the subareas, furniture, and equipment that may require special spatial relationships?

4. Are the rationales that you wrote clear enough so that people who were not involved in your decisions will understand your reasoning?

WORKFORM 14 **Need—Access, Spatial Relationships, and Signage**

Project Name: _____   Library or Unit: _____

PART I: ACCESS TO ACTIVITY OR SERVICE

A. Questions to Consider	B. Yes	C. No	D. Access Needed
1. Will the activity be offered when the library is closed?			___ Exterior/parking lot ___ Restrooms ___ Kitchen ___ Security ___ Other
2. Will the activity be offered to groups of people at the same time?			___ Elevator ___ Stairwells ___ Path to location ___ Other
3. Is the activity or service one that will be used if people can see it but not one that people are likely to search for?			___ Front door ___ Circulation desk ___ Other
4. Is the activity one in which users will need significant staff assistance?			___ Path to service point ___ Other
5. Other questions to consider			___ ___ ___

(Cont.)

WORKFORM 14 **Need—Access, Spatial Relationships, and Signage** (Cont.)

PART II: SPATIAL RELATIONSHIPS—AREAS OF THE LIBRARY

A. Relationship	B. Unit/Area of the Library	C. Rationale
1. Adjacent		
2. Close		
3. In line of sight		
4. Away from		

(Cont.)

PART III: SPATIAL RELATIONSHIPS—WITHIN THE AREA HOUSING THE SERVICE

A. Item	B. Adjacent to	C. Close to	D. In Line of Sight	E. Away from	F. Rationale
1. Subarea					
2. Furniture					
3. Equipment					
4. Other					

(Cont.)

WORKFORM 14 **Need—Access, Spatial Relationships, and Signage** (Cont.)

PART IV: SIGNAGE

A. Type	B. Needed		C. Language	D. Placement	E. Quantity	F. Format and Design
	Yes	No				
1. Directory						
2. Directional						
3. Identification						
4. Information/instruction						

Completed by _____   Date completed _____

Source of data _____

WORKFORM 15 Have—Access, Spatial Relationships, and Signage

Instructions

Purpose

Use this workform to describe the current spatial relationships of the area that houses the activity.

Note about Electronic Version

Use the Microsoft Word version of this workform (available at http://elearnlibraries.com) to add or delete rows to meet your needs for listing items.

Sources of Data for Workform 15

Sources of data for this workform include discussions with library staff who provide the activity; observation; and figure 9, Suggested Indicators to Measure Age and Condition.

Factors to Consider When Completing Workform 15

1. Work with staff who will be responsible for carrying out the project to find out more about current access, spatial relationships, and signage, if any.

2. Consider drawing a Venn diagram (see chapter 2) to help identify special relationships.

How to Complete the Columns and Rows on Workform 15

Write the name of the project.

Write the name of the library or unit.

PART I: ACCESS TO ACTIVITY OR SERVICE

A. This column lists four access questions to consider and space to add additional questions, if needed.

B. Place an X in this box if the answer to question in column A is *Yes*, and complete column D.

C. Place an X in this box if the answer to question in column A is *No*, and do not complete column D.

D1–D4. Place an X by each type of access that is used for each question that has an X in Column B.

D5. List the type of access that addresses the issue raised in question A5.

PART II: SPATIAL RELATIONSHIPS—AREAS OF THE LIBRARY

A. This column lists the four main spatial relationships.

B1. List the areas of the library that are adjacent to the area in which the activity is housed.

B2. List the areas of the library that are close to the area in which the activity is housed.

B3. List the areas of the library that are in line of sight of the area in which the activity is housed.

B4. List the areas of the library that are away from the area in which the activity is housed.

PART III: SPATIAL RELATIONSHIPS—WITHIN THE AREA HOUSING THE SERVICE

A. List the subareas, furnishings, equipment, and other items in the existing area that require special spatial relationships.

B. List the subareas, furnishings, equipment, or other items that are adjacent to the items listed in column A.

C. List the subareas, furnishings, equipment, or other items that are close to the items listed in column A.

D. List the subareas, furnishings, equipment, or other items that are in line of sight of the items listed in column A.

E. List the subareas, furnishings, equipment, or other items that are away from the items listed in column A.

PART IV: SIGNAGE

A. This column lists the four types of signs.

B. Place an X in the appropriate box. Complete columns C–F for all rows in which you place an X in the *Yes* box.

C. Enter the language or languages of the current signs.

D. Describe where the signs are placed.

E. Enter the number of signs of each type.

F. Briefly describe the design or format of the current signs. For example, "matches all other library signs" or "uses the colors and logo from the teen center."

(Cont.)

G. Indicate the condition of each type of sign using the scale in figure 9, Suggested Indicators to Measure Age and Condition. If the committee members modified the list of indicators, use the modified version. Attach the list of indicators you used.

Finally, complete the information at the bottom of the workform.

Factors to Consider When Reviewing Workform 15

1. Did you observe how users access the area that currently houses the service?

2. Did you identify all of the current spatial relationships?

3. Have you identified all of the subareas, furniture, and equipment that require special spatial relationships?

4. Have you attached a copy of your age and condition indicators?

WORKFORM 15 Have—Access, Spatial Relationships, and Signage

Project Name: _____ Library or Unit: _____

PART I: ACCESS TO ACTIVITY OR SERVICE

A. Questions to Consider	B. Yes	C. No	D. Current Access
1. Is the activity offered when the library is closed?			_____ Exterior/parking lot _____ Restrooms _____ Kitchen _____ Security _____ Other
2. Is the activity typically offered to groups of people at the same time?			_____ Elevator _____ Stairwells _____ Path to location _____ Other
3. Is the activity or service one that is used if people can see it but not one that people are likely to search for?			_____ Front door _____ Circulation desk _____ Other
4. Is the activity one in which users need significant staff assistance?			_____ Path to service point _____ Other
5. Other questions to consider			_____ _____

(Cont.)

WORKFORM 15 **Have—Access, Spatial Relationships, and Signage** (Cont.)

PART II. SPATIAL RELATIONSHIPS—AREAS OF THE LIBRARY

A. Relationship	B. Unit/Area of the Library			
1. Adjacent				
2. Close				
3. In line of sight				
4. Away from				

(Cont.)

PART III: SPATIAL RELATIONSHIPS—WITHIN THE AREA HOUSING THE SERVICE

A. Item	B. Adjacent to	C. Close to	D. In Line of Sight	E. Away from
1. Subarea				
2. Furniture				
3. Equipment				
4. Other				

(Cont.)

WORKFORM 15 **Have—Access, Spatial Relationships, and Signage** (Cont.)

PART IV: CURRENT SIGNAGE

A. Type	B. Current		C. Language	D. Placement	E. Quantity	F. Format and Design	G. Condition
	Yes	*No*					
1. Directory							
2. Directional							
3. Identification							
4. Information/ instruction							

Completed by _____ Date completed _____

Source of data _____

Instructions

Purpose

The physical plant and technology support team use this workform to summarize the square footage needed to support the activity and to record the square footage currently supporting the activity, if any. The workform also provides space to record the committee's conclusions about the amount and type of space needed for the activity.

Note about Electronic Version

Use the Microsoft Word version of this workform (available at http://elearnlibraries.com) to add or delete rows to meet your needs for listing items.

Sources of Data for Workform 16

Sources of data for this workform are Workform 7, Project Description—Physical Plant, Space, and Spatial Relationships; Workform 8, Need—Furniture and Equipment; Workform 9, Have—Furniture and Equipment; Workform 10, Need—Shelving; Workform 11, Have—Shelving; and Workform 13, Have—Physical Plant and Technology Support.

Part IV will record the amount of square footage and the decision made in the third meeting about the type of space required for the activity.

Factors to Consider When Completing Workform 16

1. This is a summary of previously gathered data. You will gather some of the information from the furniture and equipment and shelving teams.

2. Part IV will be completed at the third meeting of the committee.

How to Complete the Columns and Rows on Workform 16

Write the name of the project.

Write the name of the library or unit.

PART I: NEEDED NET SQUARE FOOTAGE—FURNITURE, EQUIPMENT, AND SHELVING

B1. Record the total square footage for needed furniture and equipment from Part II, row 6 of Workform 8, Need—Furniture and Equipment.

B2. Record the total square footage needed for shelving from Part II, column E5 of Workform 10, Need—Shelving.

C. Add B1 and B2, and record the total here.

PART II: CURRENT FURNITURE, EQUIPMENT, AND SHELVING SQUARE FOOTAGE

B1. Record the total square footage for current furniture and equipment from Part II, row 6 of Workform 9, Have—Furniture and Equipment.

B2. Record the total square footage for current shelving from Part II, column E5 of Workform 11, Have—Shelving.

C. Add B1 and B2, and record the total here.

PART III: CURRENT SPACE

B. Record the information from line F of Workform 13, Have—Physical Plant and Technology Support, on the appropriate line. If the activity is offered in more than one type of space, record the square footage being used for each type of space.

C. If you completed more than one line of Part A, record the total square footage here.

PART IV: CONCLUSION—AMOUNT AND TYPE OF SPACE

Use this space to record decisions agreed upon in the third meeting regarding the amount and type of space.

Finally, complete the information at the bottom of the workform.

Factors to Consider When Reviewing Workform 16

1. Have you accurately transcribed the data from the corresponding workforms?

2. Have you recorded the decisions made in the committee's third meeting in Part IV?

WORKFORM 16 Square Footage—Needed and Current

Project Name: _____

Library or Unit: _____

PART I: NEEDED NET SQUARE FOOTAGE—FURNITURE, EQUIPMENT, AND SHELVING

A. Item	B. Net square footage
1. Furniture and equipment	
2. Shelving	
C. Total	

PART II: CURRENT FURNITURE, EQUIPMENT, AND SHELVING SQUARE FOOTAGE

A. Item	B. Net square footage
1. Furniture and equipment	
2 Shelving	
C. Total	

PART III: CURRENT SPACE

A. Space	B. Net square footage
1. Walled	
2. Single-purpose	
3. Multipurpose	
C. Total	

PART IV: CONCLUSION—AMOUNT AND TYPE OF SPACE

Completed by _____

Date completed _____

Source of data _____

Instructions

Purpose

Use this workform to record gaps and, in the next step, options that the committee develops to fill the gap that must be met to implement the project.

Note about Electronic Version

Use the Microsoft Word version of this workform (available at http://elearnlibraries.com) to add or delete rows and expand the size of rows.

Sources of Data for Workform 17

Sources of data for this workform include Workform 4, Need for Outside Experts; Workform 8, Need—Furniture and Equipment; Workform 9, Have—Furniture and Equipment; Workform 10, Need—Shelving; Workform 11, Have—Shelving; Workform 12, Need—Physical Plant and Technology Support; Workform 13, Have—Physical Plant and Technology Support; Workform 14, Need—Access, Spatial Relationships, and Signage; and Workform 15, Have—Access, Spatial Relationships, and Signage.

Factors to Consider When Completing Workform 17

1. Each resource team will complete a copy of Workform 17 for their resource area or areas.

2. This workform will provide a place to record the gaps between facility resources that will be needed and the resources that are currently allocated to support the activity, and any options that first the teams and then the entire committee propose to fill the gaps.

3. It will be important to consult with the people who will be implementing the activity when completing this workform.

WORKFORM 17 Gaps and Options

4. This is the place to record the committee's best brainstorming for options to fill the gaps.

5. The options that are developed will be evaluated later in the process.

How to Complete the Columns and Rows on Workform 17

Write the name of the project.

Write the name of the library or unit.

Enter the name of the resource group, for example, furniture, equipment, shelving, and so on.

A. To make a clear column heading, repeat the name of the resource group entered above. Below that, list the gaps by comparing the paired Need and Have workforms the team completed. Provide as much detail as possible. The information may be numerical, as in "four two-person tables," or it may be a descriptive statement, such as "interior, fixed windows."

B. In the next step, record the options that teams develop for each gap. Be sure each option is linked to the specific gap it is intended to fill. Some gaps may have only one option.

Finally, complete the information at the bottom of the workform.

Factors to Consider When Reviewing Workform 17

1. Have you provided enough information on each gap you identified in column A to ensure that someone who reviews your ideas will understand them?

2. Have you included *all* viable options?

Project Name: _____ Library or Unit: _____

A. Gaps for	B. Options for Filling the Gap
1.	a.
	b.
	c.
2.	a.
	b.
	c.
3.	a.
	b.
	c.
4.	a.
	b.
	c.
5.	a.
	b.
	c.

Completed by _____ Date completed _____

Source of data _____

WORKFORM 18 Considerations for Placement of the Activity

Instructions

Purpose

Use this workform to identify needed elements in multipurpose areas that could be used to support the activity under review. If the activity will require a walled or single-purpose space, use the workform to determine spatial relationships that would be appropriate.

Note about Electronic Version

Use the Microsoft Word version of this workform (available at http://elearnlibraries.com) to add or delete rows to meet your needs for listing items.

Sources of Data for Workform 18

Sources of data for this workform include figure 7, Facility Resources—Common Elements; the completed and approved copy of Workform 7, Project Description—Physical Plant, Space, and Spatial Relationships; Workform 12, Need—Physical Plant and Technology Support; Workform 14, Need—Access, Spatial Relationships, and Signage (Part II); and Workform 15, Have—Access, Spatial Relationships, and Signage.

Factors to Consider When Completing Workform 18

1. Workform 18 is used to evaluate whether a multipurpose space is suitable for the activity by determining if it has the elements needed for the activity; or to describe appropriate adjacencies for walled or single-purpose space.

2. Use only Part II of Workform 14, Need—Access, Spatial Relationships, and Signage, to evaluate the suitability of the area under consideration.

3. Follow the directions given for the type of space that has been approved for the activity.

How to Complete the Columns and Rows on Workform 18

Write the name of the project.
Write the name of the library or unit.

A. This column lists a number of elements found in multipurpose spaces in the library. Add additional elements to consider under row 9.

For a Multipurpose Space

B. Briefly describe the element under consideration. For example, in row 1, you might describe the Young Adult area as having teen-friendly, brightly colored, casual furniture.

C. Place an *X* in this column if you think that this element of the space is suitable for the activity.

D. Place an *X* in this column if you think that this element of the space is *not* suitable for the activity.

E. Briefly describe the rationale for your decisions in columns C and D.

For a Walled or Single-Purpose Space

B. Briefly describe the element under consideration. For example, in row 1, you might describe a children's craft room as having child-sized tables and chairs.

C. Place an *X* in this column if this element could be housed adjacent to or close to the space under consideration.

D. Place an *X* in this column if you think that this element should be away from the activity.

E. Briefly describe the rationale for your decisions in columns C and D.

Finally, complete the information at the bottom of the workform.

Factors to Consider When Reviewing Workform 18

1. Did you consider all of the physical plant and spatial relationship needs of the activity?

2. Have you provided clear descriptions of the physical plant items that are located in the area?

3. Are the rationales that you wrote clear enough so that people who were not involved in your decisions will understand your reasoning?

WORKFORM 18 **Considerations for Placement of the Activity**

Project Name: _____

Library or Unit: _____

A. Resources to Share	B. Description	C. Suitable	D. Not Suitable	E. Rationale
1. Furniture				
2. Shelving area				
3. Computer lab				
4. Meeting room				
5. Public seating areas				
6. Administrative/staff areas				
7. Storage areas				
8. Service desks				
9. Other				

Completed by _____ Date completed _____

Source of data _____

Instructions

Purpose

Use this workform to record cost estimates that the committee collects to evaluate and compare options to fill the gaps that must be met to implement the project.

Note about Electronic Version

Use the Microsoft Word version of this workform (available at http://elearnlibraries.com) to add or delete rows and expand the size of rows.

Sources of Data for Workform 19

Sources of data for this workform include outside experts, vendor catalogs, Workform 17, Gaps and Options, and other sources mentioned in chapter 4.

Factors to Consider When Completing Workform 19

1. Each resource team will complete a copy of this workform for their resource area.

2. The information that you enter on this workform is just an estimate. For example, you will now be specific about the kind of new seating being considered for recommendation for the project, but will only be able to provide a range of prices from library furniture vendor catalogs. Provide as much information as possible about the source of your estimate.

3. At this point, the committee may still be entertaining more than one option for filling a gap. If the options call for very different levels of furnishings, outside assistance, or construction, for example, complete an estimate for each option.

4. The estimates that are developed when completing this workform will provide a framework for decisions the committee will be making about how to prioritize the options.

WORKFORM 19 Expense Estimates for Options

How to Complete the Columns and Rows on Workform 19

Write the name of the project.

Write the name of the library or unit.

Enter the name of the resource group, for example, furniture, equipment, shelving, and so on.

A. List one option that will involve costs on each line. Use Workform 17, Gaps and Options, as your source of options. Include costs for any contracted services or ancillary costs that require estimates.

B. List the corresponding estimated cost.

C. List the corresponding source of information.

Finally, complete the information at the bottom of the workform.

Factors to Consider When Reviewing Workform 19

1. Have you collected estimate information only if the committee needs to use it to determine which option will be recommended?

2. Have you provided enough information about the source of your estimate to give administrators an idea of how accurate these figures might be?

Project Name: _____

Library or Unit: _____

Resource Addressed: _____

A. Options	B. Estimated Cost	C. Source
1.		
2.		
3.		
4.		
5.		
6.		
7.		
8.		
9.		
10.		
11.		
12.		
13.		
14.		

Completed by _____ Date completed _____

Source of data _____

Instructions

WORKFORM 20 **Preliminary Project Time Estimates**

Purpose

Committee teams use this workform to record information about the projected time frames for the steps involved in purchasing or allocating the resources for the project. Use this workform only to record information on options that might delay the project.

Note about Electronic Version

Use the Microsoft Word version of this workform (available at http://elearnlibraries.com) to add or delete rows and expand the size of rows.

Sources of Data for Workform 20

Consult Workform 4, Need for Outside Experts; Workform 17, Gaps and Options; and figure 16, List of Possible Hidden Expenses, to develop a list of activities to assign time estimates to options and steps.

Factors to Consider When Completing Workform 20

1. This workform should be completed by the teams that completed the gap analysis and recommendations for that resource.

2. The estimate should include times for all the major steps to put the option in place, particularly those that may cause delays that would affect which recommendations are approved.

3. Time estimates can be affected by where materials are warehoused and by seasonal fluctuations in the availability of personnel. Consider possible delays, and be realistic about how long it will take to complete each task.

How to Complete the Columns and Rows on Workform 20

Write the name of the project.

Write the name of the library or unit.

Enter the name of the resource group, for example, furniture, equipment, shelving, and so on.

A. On each numbered line, list the options from Workform 17, Gaps and Options, for your resource that may delay the project.

   List the steps required to put that option in place. For example, if the option is 6 five-shelf, three-foot units of shelving, the steps would be ordering the shelving, assembling the shelving, and moving collection materials onto the shelving.

B. Provide the contractor or vendor's estimate of the time required to complete each step. Again, ask for a rough estimate, but a completion time of six months or more might trigger another option choice or alert managers that this may be a driver for the project's implementation timeline.

C. State the source for the time estimate that was listed in column B. This could be a furniture, equipment, or shelving vendor or a contracted expert such as an electrician.

Finally, complete the information at the bottom of the workform.

Factors to Consider When Reviewing Workform 20

1. Are the estimates realistic enough to alert managers to possible problems?

2. Have you considered supply factors that might affect the time estimates?

WORKFORM 20 **Preliminary Project Time Estimates**

Project Name: _____

Library or Unit: _____

Resource Addressed: _____

A. Options and Steps	B. Estimated Time to Complete	C. Source
1.		
2.		
3.		
4.		

Completed by _____ Date completed _____

Source of data _____

Instructions

Purpose

Use this workform to prioritize options developed to fill the gaps that must be met to implement the project.

Note about Electronic Version

Use the Microsoft Word version of this workform (available at http://elearnlibraries.com) to add or delete rows and expand the size of rows.

Sources of Data for Workform 21

Sources of data for this workform include Workform 17, Gaps and Options; Workform 19, Expense Estimates for Options; Workform 20, Preliminary Project Time Estimates; and the evaluation criteria developed by the committee.

Factors to Consider When Completing Workform 21

1. This workform will provide a place to record the recommendations that the committee has decided will most effectively fill the gap between the facility resources that will be needed and the resources that are currently allocated to support the activity. Your evaluations will be used to prioritize how options are listed in the committee's report.

2. Only complete this workform for the resource areas that still have multiple options.

3. The information that you enter on this workform will be determined by the factors the committee decides are most important for your library. For example, if you have a heavily used service area affected by the project, minimum disruption to existing services might be a very important factor in evaluating the options.

WORKFORM 21 **Option Evaluation**

How to Complete the Columns and Rows on Workform 21

Write the name of the project.

Write the name of the library or unit.

Enter the name of the resource group, for example, furniture, equipment, shelving, and so on.

A. Repeat the name of the resource group entered above. Below that, list each gap that has multiple options identified in Workform 17, Gaps and Options (column A), within the numbered areas, one per number.

B. In column B, list the options for allocating the resources in order of preference based on your discussions of the evaluation criteria the committee agreed upon, for example: 1. Locate small study rooms adjacent to reference area. 2. Locate small study rooms on lower level.

C. Record the reasons the team has recommended the top option and the reasons others were prioritized lower, for example: 1. Study rooms near reference area are closer to reference resources and assistance for research. 2. Study rooms on lower level are further from supervision, reference resources, and staff assistance.

Attach a copy of the criteria to the workform. Complete the information at the bottom of the workform.

Factors to Consider When Reviewing Workform 21

1. Have conditions in your library determined the priority you gave various factors in the evaluation process?

2. Have you included a list of the criteria?

Project Name: _____

Library or Unit: _____

Resource Addressed: _____

A. Gaps for	B. Options in Priority Order	C. Reasons for Recommending or Putting Lower on the List
1.	1.	1.
	2.	2.
	3.	3.
2.	1.	1.
	2.	2.
	3.	3.
3.	1.	1.
	2.	2.
	3.	3.
4.	1.	1.
	2.	2.
	3.	3.

Completed by _____ Date completed _____

Source of data _____

Instructions

WORKFORM 22 **Furniture and Equipment List**

Purpose

The furniture and equipment team uses this workform to compile the information about all the furniture and equipment that will be needed for the project and how it will be allocated.

Note about Electronic Version

Use the Microsoft Word version of this workform (available at http://elearnlibraries.com) to add or delete rows and expand the size of rows.

Sources of Data for Workform 22

Sources of data for this workform include Workform 8, Need—Furniture and Equipment; Workform 17, Gaps and Options; Workform 19, Expense Estimates for Options; Workform 21, Option Evaluation; and information obtained from vendors and outside experts.

Factors to Consider When Completing Workform 22

1. This workform should be completed by the furniture and equipment team.

2. You may complete columns B or C or both (if the gap is filled by both reallocation and purchases).

3. Costs may be incurred by reallocation of an item, for example, reupholstering.

How to Complete the Columns and Rows on Workform 22

Write the name of project.

Write the name of the library or unit.

PART I AND PART II

1–2. List and describe all the furniture and equipment needed for the project. Use Workform 8, Need—Furniture and Equipment, for this information.

A. Using Workform 8, Need—Furniture and Equipment, list the number of furniture and equipment items recommended for the project.

B. Using Workform 17, Gaps and Options, state the projected reallocation source for the resource listed in column A.

C. Using Workform 17, Gaps and Options, and any information the team has gathered from vendors and outside experts, state the projected purchase source for the resource listed in column A.

D. Using information from Workform 19, Expense Estimates for Options, and any information the team has gathered from vendors and outside experts, state the total cost of the furniture (Part I) or equipment (Part II) listed in column A, if there is a cost involved.

Finally, complete the information at the bottom of the workform.

Factors to Consider When Reviewing Workform 22

1. Did you explore the various types of available furniture and equipment?

2. Have you considered recent trends in library furniture and equipment?

Project Name: _____

Library or Unit: _____

	A. Number of Items	B. Source of Reallocation	C. Source of Purchase	D. Total Cost
PART I. FURNITURE				
1. Furniture for public use				
2. Furniture for staff use				
3. *Total expense* for furniture				

(Cont.)

WORKFORM 22 **Furniture and Equipment List** (Cont.)

	A. Number of Items	B. Source of Reallocation	C. Source of Purchase	D. Total Cost
PART II. EQUIPMENT				
1. Equipment for public use				
2. Equipment for staff use				
3. *Total expense* for equipment				

Completed by _____ Date completed _____

Source of data _____

Instructions

Purpose

Use this workform to list the cost estimates necessary for funding approvals.

Note about Electronic Version

Use the Microsoft Word version of this workform (available at http://elearnlibraries.com) to add or delete rows and expand the size of rows.

Sources of Data for Workform 23

Sources of data for this workform may include Workform 4, Need for Outside Experts; Workform 17, Gaps and Options; Workform 19, Expense Estimates for Options; and Workform 22, Furniture and Equipment List (if done).

Factors to Consider When Completing Workform 23

1. Complete the rows of this workform that are applicable for the project.

2. Total the expense for each resource area after all estimate information is provided for all items needed.

How to Complete the Columns and Rows on Workform 23

Write the name of project

Write the name of the library or unit.

1–13. (odd-numbered rows)

Record all items that have costs associated with them, whether purchase or service costs. If you completed Workform 22, Furniture and Equipment List, use that information for rows 3 and 5.

A. Record the number of items for each resource.

B. If the item or labor will be purchased, state the vendor or supplier. Some of the estimate information should be available from Workform 19, Expense Estimates for Options.

C. Record the estimated cost for the total number of items or services from the vendor or supplier you have listed. If you are reallocating the item, the expense might be for refurbishing.

2–14. (even-numbered rows)

Add the cost of items within each resource category for a resource total. For example, add the cost of wall paint and floor carpeting for total construction.

Row 15.

Add the totals of rows 2, 4, 6, 8, 10, 12, and 14 for the estimated project grand total.

Finally, complete the information at the bottom of the workform.

Factors to Consider When Reviewing Workform 23

1. Have you collected estimate information for each recommendation that has associated costs?

2. Have you checked your addition for totals and the grand total?

WORKFORM 23 **Cost Compilations**

Project Name: _____   Library or Unit: _____

	A. Number of Items	B. Source of Purchase	C. Estimated Total Cost
1. Professional contracted services			
2. *Total expense* for professional services			
3. Furniture			
4. *Total expense* for furniture			
5. Equipment			
6. *Total expense* for equipment			

(Cont.)

	A. Number of Items	B. Source of Purchase	C. Estimated Total Cost
7. Shelving			
8. *Total expense* for shelving			
9. Construction, wall or floor finishes			
10. *Total expense* for construction			
11. Systems—lighting, plumbing, HVAC			
12. *Total expense* for systems			
13. Special access, signs, other			
14. *Total expense* for special access, other			
15. *Grand total*			

Completed by _____   Date completed _____

Source of data _____

Index

Cheryl Bryan is a consultant, trainer, speaker, and writer who specializes in guiding librarians through service changes to support today's needs and expectations. She has presented training programs and consulted with libraries about long-range planning and building programs for more than a decade. Bryan has worked in large and small public libraries for over thirty years, most recently as the assistant administrator for consulting and continuing education for the SouthEastern Massachusetts Library System. She has served as president of the New England Library Association, as chairman of the InterLibrary Cooperation and Networking Section of the Association of Specialized and Cooperative Library Agencies (a division of the American Library Association), and as a member of many other local and national committees working to improve library service.